writing about the
ARTS AND HUMANITIES

Third Edition

David B. Paxman
Dianna M. Black

Brigham Young University

PEARSON

Custom
Publishing

Cover Photo: *Angel, Rome,* by Mary Kocol.

Printed in the United States of America

20 19 18 17 16 15 14 13 12 11

ISBN 0-536-73891-2

BA 997436

JC/DE

Please visit our web site at *www.pearsoncustom.com*

PEARSON CUSTOM PUBLISHING
75 Arlington Street, Suite 300, Boston, MA 02116
A Pearson Education Company

Copyright Acknowledgments

Contributors

This book has been a collaborative effort and would not have been possible without the help of many colleagues.

We acknowledge **Nancy Rushforth**, who helped define the course, collect materials, and design and try out assignments. We also thank

Mary Lynn Cutler for parts of the interpretation assignment

C. Jay Fox for permission to use his PASS-F assignment format (Purpose, Audience, Scope, Schedule, Format)

Susan Miller for the formal analysis assignment and some of the workshop sheets

Vern Swanson for information on selection criteria at the Springville Art Museum

We also acknowledge the contributions of Roger Baker, Ana Preto-Bay, Kristi Bell, Lynn Christie, Nancy Gunn, Eric Freeze, John S. Harris, Kevin Klein, GaeLyn Henderson, Pam Johstoneaux, Mary Pollington, Robbyn Scribner, and Nicole Wistisen.

We thank the many students who gave us permission to use their works for teaching purposes.

Note to Instructors

This book is best used in conjunction with a rhetoric text or handbook that gives instruction on essay strategies, style, and mechanics.

Table of Contents

Introduction

Knowledge of the arts and humanities and effective writing about them go hand in hand. Without knowledge and insight, writing skill is empty technique. Without writing skill, knowledge often remains fuzzy, unformulated, and private. Believing in the hand-in-hand relation, we have four main goals for the course:

- Help you improve your basic writing skills, which we define as writing convincingly, clearly, and coherently, and doing so with correct grammar, sentence structure, spelling, and punctuation.

- Give you practice in the types of writing you will most likely produce if you work in the arts and humanities after graduation.

- Help you improve your ability to adapt basic writing skills to different audiences and purposes.

- Help you discover new perspectives on, and knowledge within, the arts you study.

For our purposes, the term *arts* refers to the production and performance of art: painting, sculpture, music, dance, theater, photography, graphics, design, literature, film and other media. The term *humanities* refers to the interpretation, evaluation, criticism, and study of the arts. It includes languages and history.

People who make careers in the arts and humanities discover that writing is a vital ingredient of success. Producing and performing artists need to write well to promote their projects, gain commissions, and give commentary on their work. They have more influence if they can express their views clearly and convincingly. Students of the humanities need to write well because their disciplines, whether art history, literature, or languages, exist to promote understanding of the arts and their relations to other human endeavors. That understanding is gained and shared primarily through words.

Our purposes derive from observing the present and future "writing life" of arts and humanities students. Here is what we have learned:

- Good writing will help you succeed both in college and in your career.

- Most arts and humanities students do not work in their fields of study but find careers in other fields, such as business and government. Writing instruction should, therefore, help in other careers.

- Those of you who find in careers in the arts and humanities will do a lot of practical writing—proposals, memos, letters, and brochures—all of which have a vital impact on your own success and that of the organizations—museums, theaters, studios, and galleries—for which you work.

- The writing that college teachers require differs from the writing that artists do after college. Our task is to help you succeed in both arenas. A concert report, critical analysis, or journal entry occurs more in college than in careers after graduation. Essays and research writing occur in both. To these we add on-the-job types of writing to help you make the transition from college to work. Basic writing skills are important to both and transfer easily to different audiences, purposes, and occasions.

PART **1**

Writing at Work

Many arts students don't see why they should learn to write practical reports and memos of the sort that business people write, reasoning that success as a film director, graphic designer, painter or playwright will follow excellence in the art and not skill in mundane memos. Humanities students, by contrast, may envision themselves publishing essays and treatises in which they share their insights with fellow art historians, eager students, and a reverent public.

The world doesn't fulfill either set of expectations. To be fair, it is certain that your success will depend partly on your artistic vision, skill, or insightful interpretations. However, even those students who achieve success in the arts and humanities write to secure commissions, have projects approved, and promote their work. Furthermore, for every arts graduate who finds work producing and performing, ten find work in business, industry, and government. The same applies to the humanities.

This situation isn't unique to the arts and humanities. Except for those who become high school or college teachers, only a small fraction of students in political science, sociology, history, psychology, foreign languages, linguistics, philosophy, biology, zoology, physical education, and economics actually make careers in their undergraduate major.

Even those art history students who find full-time work in museums or state arts councils spend little time writing essays, articles, and reviews. In fact, very few people support themselves by writing about the arts. Most who do so are academics who have time and salaries to pursue their interests, regardless of whether their writing earns income.

So whether you work in the arts or not, much of the most important writing you will do will be required by your job. This type of writing keeps businesses, institutions, and government agencies functioning to fulfill their objectives. Work-related writing is vitally important because it helps these organizations

- Secure and maintain funding
- Plan the organization's activities and implement its plans
- Take care of the needs of the organization for space, equipment, publicity, and personnel
- Promote the organization's work to its sponsors and public
- Inform the public by way of brochures, guides, program notes, and labels

This section will help train you to write as a member of an organization who needs to communicate, on behalf of an organization, both within an organization and without. It will help you learn effective ways to state your purposes, present complex information clearly, adapt to different audiences, and organize information so that different readers can quickly find what they need.

Writing Letters of Application and Résumés

Your ultimate goal is to prepare for the fulfilling life and career you have dreamed of. Your goal in writing letters of application and résumés is, of course, to obtain interviews that will start that dream in motion. Kenneth W. Houp, Thomas E. Pearsall, and Elizabeth Tebeaux (among other experts) report that "a good letter of application, sometimes called a *cover letter*, and resume will not guarantee that you get [the position you want], but bad ones will probably guarantee that you do not" (382). And even very good ones need to catch the eye and secure the interest of the reader. Another researcher, Arthur H. Bell, believes that

> No single piece of paper is as important to your job search as your résumé. This summary of who you are, what you have done, and what you can do will be the primary evidence by which you are judged at first levels of review in company personnel offices. (360)

In discussing the "total look" of a document, Bell maintains that "the reader should form positive impressions of you *even before reading a single word on the résumé*" (360). Randall A. Wells concurs: "Even the design of a printed text can have a nonverbal persuasive appeal. A business letter will make a better impression on heavy paper, under an attractive letterhead, and in a conventional format" (153).

If, then, you are serious about your dream, you need to think seriously about what you wish to include in each letter and résumé you send (and you must modify your information for each application) and about how you want the final copies to look.

You may wish to approach this assignment from an angle that allows you to "view" yourself more objectively. From time to time, many of you have received *sales letters* offering products and services that could provide some benefit to you. If you look at yourself as a "product" or as a "service" that could benefit a company or business, what specific ideas would you emphasize as you write? Keep in mind that effective products and services are designed and offered with a certain consumer in mind. Consider, too, what your underlying concerns in creating the document would be. In writing of sales letters in general, Wells outlines the goals that such a letter tries to accomplish:

- *Get attention.* Other things are competing for the reader's time.
- *Arouse interest.*
- *Ask for action.* The letter does more than to convince the reader that something is desirable: It requests concrete action. (195)

If you consult "Helpful Hints for Writing Your Letter" in this section, you will see that the elements of your letter of application fit into the structure just above.

Writing your letter and résumé has recently become more complex. Only a few years ago, all résumés were submitted as hard copy in traditional format; today, you will probably have to learn how to create not only the traditional but also the scannable and on-line types, which differ in structure and graphics, fonts, highlighting, and verb and noun choices.

For this assignment, described below, most instructors will require that you create a traditional hard copy résumé. If not, your instructor will advise you.

LETTER AND RÉSUMÉ ASSIGNMENT

Purpose

To get an interview for a position or program open to someone with your qualifications. This may include any position you hope to fill after your graduation or any position on or off campus you may want to apply for now. If you plan to do post-graduate work, you may apply for a graduate program in your field or for a medical, dental, or other professional school. Think of your letter and résumé as the intermediaries between what you have to offer (your qualifications) and the job you wish to apply for. Your goal in sending the letter and résumé is to secure an interview.

Audience

The appropriate representative of the company to which you apply. You must, therefore, do some research. If possible, find out the *name* of the personnel director, human resource manager, chair of the acceptance committee, recruitment officer, or other representative you will deal with. Once you have a name, be sure to find out whether that person is male or female — this may keep you from making a serious blunder. Is it Toni or Tony? Is Pat a woman or a man? If Pat is female, does she prefer Mrs., Miss, or Ms.? Find out also an *inclusive job description* of the position, so that you know what details (qualifications) you should provide. Ask about the goals and the expectations of the company or institution. One phone call can sometimes yield this information. All of this should help you present yourself professionally and choose what to include in your letter and on your résumé. It will also help you in adopting a courteous and tactful tone. Remember: you need to show your reader(s) that you have *transferable skills* that can benefit the company.

Scope

Provide all details of your qualifications that you think will help you to secure the position. Doing your résumé first is often a very good idea so that you can make sure that the letter and résumé correlate; do not include in your letter things that you do not list on your résumé. Unless you obtain permission from your instructor to do otherwise, **limit your letter to one page and your résumé to one page**.

Schedule

See your class calendar.

Format

For your **letter**, you may use any standard format (straight block, modified block, left justified only, or full justification). You may create your own personalized letterhead for your letter and résumé. Experiment with different placements of your name and address and, if you wish, with appropriate color for the particular situation and choice of paper. Try out several font styles and point sizes for your letterhead. For the body of your letter itself, choose a font carefully. Avoid unusual fonts and very small or very large point sizes. Using a "serif" font makes a letter look more formal. Serifs are the tiny "adornments" or tails on each letter in a font. This paragraph, for example, is set in Palatino — a serif font — and is in 10 pt., while a non-serif font, like Arial, provides a more casual look, as you can see in this example. Keep this in mind, also, for your résumé. So, select a font or fonts and an overall design based on the situation and on the traditions in your field. For example, do you need a hard copy, an on-line, or a scannable product? Is your reader likely to want to see a creative or traditional approach? Exercise good judgment in your choices.

In your **résumé**, be aware of the principle of *accessibility*. For example, formats that include lists are much easier to read than those set up as paragraphs in each section (see student samples for list-type résumés).

Make sure that both your letter and résumé look professional in every way: proper choice of font styles and point sizes, use of appropriate and accessible information, selection of quality paper, and employment of good graphic design. Look carefully for any errors in grammar, usage, punctuation, or spelling.

Note: Submitting a letter of application and a résumé is not the normal way to apply for postgraduate programs or for medical, dental, or other professional schools, nor is this common for students in a performance major such as graphic design, illustration, theater, photography, or music. For this class, though, complete this assignment as if a letter and résumé were required as the first step of the application process. If you have questions, consult your instructor before beginning this assignment.

Helpful Hints for Writing Your Résumé

- *Everything listed on your résumé should define your ability to perform the particular job the employer needs done.* Show the skills that are *transferable* to the needs of the company.

- You have only about five to ten seconds to make a good first impression on your reader. When you consider that a company may receive up to 400 applications for a given position, that only five applicants are invited to interview, and that only one will be offered the job, that first impression becomes very important.

- *For each application,* make sure you structure your résumé so that you list the *most important qualifications first* (Education? Work Experience? Skills? Awards?) for that particular position.

- In today's job market, a new beast has emerged: the *scannable* résumé. While the traditional résumé "stressed strong action verbs, the key-word searches that hiring personnel will perform [today] will search for nouns. Students [who write scannable résumés] must focus their attention on the key nouns that are field and position specific. Some . . . companies . . . actually have lists of terms" (Hansen 5). Joyce Lain Kennedy provides a list of the differences between the traditional résumé and the scannable one:

TRADITIONAL	SCANNABLE
action verbs	nouns and labels
abilities in short, generic phrases	provable facts, measurable quantities
avoid jargon	use buzzwords and industry jargon
typically one page	can be more than one page
skills at end	skills at beginning
desktop publishing	no frills, plain format
serif fonts	sans serif fonts
larger fonts for headings	10–14 pt. fonts even for headings
bold, italics, underline	limit bold; avoid italics and underline
lines, rules, graphics, shading	text only
indents, some columns	left-justified, no columns
multiple copies	send original
static information	dynamic information (n.p.)

At the end of the Letter and Résumé section, you will find student samples that illustrate the difference between traditional résumés and scannable ones.

Helpful Hints for Writing Your Letter

Whatever the format you choose for your letter, remember to include

- *your address* (if you create a letterhead, include your phone number plus your e-mail address or fax number if you have one)
- the *date*
- a complete *inside address* (to whom the letter is addressed + his/her title + organization name + full street address + city, state, and ZIP code)
- and a *salutation* (Dear   :)

Before you begin writing the body of your letter, you may want to review the information on sales letters provided in the introductory material to this unit. Remember that you need to quickly capture the *attention* of your reader. To help achieve this, your introductory paragraph should include some or all of the following ideas. (Looking at the student samples and at the section on tone may help you in designing your first paragraph.)

- Who/what you are (*not* a "My name is . . ." statement)
- What you want (what is your **purpose**?)
- Make absolutely clear what kind of position you are applying for and be very specific—art historian, film editor, photographer, master's degree candidate, or such.[1]
- Refer to any previous correspondence or state how you found out about the position

Construct your second (and perhaps third) paragraph to *sustain the reader's interest* in you and your qualifications. Take care that you give an honest appraisal of your skills (neither underselling nor overselling yourself). Provide a *detailed* account of your qualifications, not your "philosophies." Remember, your experiences are what distinguish you from others. So, what, *specifically*, have you done to prepare yourself for this position? Make sure that this becomes apparent in the details you list in your letter.

In your last paragraph, graciously *ask for action*. Ask for an interview (where appropriate) and state when you are available for interviews; state how you can be reached; provide any other important items here. If your return address will change over the course of time it might take to get a reply, mention an alternative address where you can be reached after a certain date.

You may close with whatever seems most appropriate to you (Cordially, Sincerely, Respectfully; but not Sincerely yours, and certainly not Love!)

---

[1] Do a net search (see "Internet Resources" in this section for a listing of some sites). What's out there that you haven't seen anywhere else? What positions would you be interested in? Qualified for? Can you make important, reliable contacts through the network?

Tone in Letters of Application

Consider carefully the tone you use in your letter. Is it appropriate for the particular audience? Assess the appropriateness of the tone in each of the following excerpts from student letters of application. Compare Samples 1 and 2. Are there any similarities or differences that could affect the reader? Also look at the first two samples to see if the applicants provide details to support their claims. Sample 3 presents only the first paragraph of another student's letter. Does she "introduce" herself well and with a suitable tone? (The excerpts shown here are reproduced exactly as they appeared.)

SAMPLE 1: LETTER OF APPLICATION TO A MEDICAL SCHOOL

Life's success as well as movement into and up the professional ladder is as you know obtained through, first: who you know, and then what you know. In our previous meeting in November up at the Grand Hotel Hunt Club, we discussed my future in the medical field. The topic of recommendations from very prominent sources carrying such tremendous impact when applying for various medical schools was brought up. I am in my last year of undergraduate studies at Brigham Young University and will soon be applying to medical schools. Being as you are the Head Surgeon at the Des Moines General Hospital and on the Board of Directors of the University of Iowa's Medical School I would like to ask for your recommendations of me to be sent along with my application to the University.

A career in the medical field is my highest ambition. To become a surgeon in a specialized area and eventually have my own practice has been a goal since I decided to study in this field back in high school. Having played various sports from childhood up to the college level I have endured many injuries. During the treatment by surgeons, and vicariously obtaining information on those injuries an interest has spurned which leads me to believe I could be of great benefit to not only the University of Iowa's Medical School but to the medical profession in general. I enjoy working with people and know that helping patients through traumatic injuries would be very rewarding, physically to them as well as emotionally and psychologically to me. It is undoubtedly a very demanding career and therefore is suited to a special breed of persons; I believe I am one of those.

SAMPLE 2: APPLICATION FOR POSITION AS A "CULTURE BROKER" WITH McDONALD'S CORPORATION

This letter may sound extremely audacious to you. Good. It should, because it is about doing business in India, where audacity is essential in any business endeavor. I have followed with keen interest McDonald's recent developments in India. As any company going global will attest—McDonald's more than anyone else—there are some tough cultural problems to be solved along the way; and as you've probably already discovered, India is a minefield of such cultural difficulties.

Enter the minesweeper. My name is Karandeep Singh. I was born and brought up in a business household in New Delhi, India. But I decided to acquire skills in cultural anthropology so I could work in the challenging realm of international business. I am twenty-one years old and currently working towards a Bachelor's degree in anthropology at Brigham Young University (BYU), Provo, Utah. Given my background in India and my training in anthropology, I am confident that I can undertake a project for your company that will help establish a good cultural base for McDonald's in India.

Before coming to the U.S. I attended the College of Business Studies (CBS) in New Delhi for a year. This is where I was exposed to disciplines like Marketing and Organizational Behavior. In addition to these scholastic skills, I also acquired an access to the school's socio-political network, which, I believe, will prove indispensable while undertaking any project on the Indian market. Just before starting my education at CBS, I worked for Benetton, the Italian multinational apparel company, where I was responsible for introducing any new items in our product line. And then, the desire to acquire a liberal arts education drove me west.

While at BYU, I have been involved in research on the use of calculus. Those endless hours spent in the library have also taken me through many a failed inter-religious and intercultural dialogue, thus making me acutely aware of the challenge I will face in all intercultural business situations. Being a teaching instructor and assistant has not only helped me sharpen my presentation skills, but, more importantly, it has taught me the rigorous humility that is required of any person in a position of authority. This accumulation of achievements at BYU has led me to some lofty aspirations, not the least of which is to become a cultural broker in a marketing or manufacturing setting: a unifying nexus between the consumer and the company across cultural boundaries.

I wish to make myself useful to a company that I admire and appreciate. I can be reached at the Anthropology Department at (801) 378-3058 during the day (9am-5pm Monday through Friday), and at (801) 373-9968 at other times. Both phones are equipped with voice mail.

I look forward to our association in the near future.

(USED BY PERMISSION OF KARANDEEP SINGH.)

SAMPLE 3: APPLICATION FOR POSITION AS AN INTERNATIONAL TEXTILE BUYER FOR HARSEY FURNITURE CO.

After completing a field study research project in India this next semester, I will graduate in April 1994 from Brigham Young University with a B.A. in Social/Cultural Anthropology. I wish to pursue a career with your company as an International Textile Buyer. I became familiar with Harsey Furniture during a conversation with Laura McFerson and was informed that much of your purchasing takes place predominately in China and India.

(USED BY PERMISSION OF DANA BOWEN.)

A Final Checklist for Your Cover Letter

❏ Did you write in a clear, concise style that meets the needs of your **audience**?

❏ Does the letter reflect qualifications listed on the published job description?

❏ Did you begin your letter about 1" from the top of the page, regardless of whether you use a traditional style or a created letterhead?

❏ Is your letter centered on the page vertically? If not, do *not* use the "Center Page Top to Bottom" feature on your computer. Instead, add or delete line spaces between the date and the inside address.

❏ Did you put only 2 [HRts] (with line spacing set at 1) between the last line of the inside address and the salutation (Dear   :)?

❏ Did you put 4 [HRts] (with line spacing set at 1) between the closing (Cordially,) and your typed name?

❏ Have you used high-quality paper for both your letter and résumé? Do *not* use erasable paper. It smears.

❏ Some authorities question the use of postal abbreviations for states (UT, CA, OH, ME) in formal letters of application and in résumés. You must decide whether to use the abbreviations or spell out the state names. Either way, have you used them consistently?

❏ Have you put a date on your letter?

❏ Have you eliminated excess words and phrases? Don't use constructions like "I would like to take this opportunity to introduce . . . " Be careful that you use the accepted word order (not "on-hands experience" for example). And don't give your reader a way out with such phrases as "in any case" or "in any event."

❏ Did you remember to sign your letter?

❏ Reread your letter. Is the **tone** appropriately courteous and tactful?

A Final Checklist for Your Résumé

❏ Is the information gauged to your particular **audience**? Did you include everything that defines your ability to perform the work necessary (your *transferable* skills) and leave out all unnecessary information?

❏ Were you consistent in using either state abbreviations or full spelling of state names?

❏ Are your phone number (including area code) and email address on your résumé?

❏ Look objectively at your résumé. Is the information easily *accessible*? (See sections below for hints.)

❏ Did you put the most important section first? If **Work Experience** should come before **Education** in a particular application, put it first; if not, don't. Also, find a way to highlight the most important information in each section, by the use of **bold**, <u>underline</u>, *italics*, font size, or positioning. For example, if a job title is more important than the dates of employment, make sure that the job title is clearly and immediately seen. If your degree is more important than your university, make sure the reader sees that first.

❏ Did you list all data in each section of your résumé from *present to past*? Except in rare cases, this is standard.

❏ Have you been careful with your use of hyphens and dashes in certain constructions?

Use	May 2000-June 2003 (one hyphen; no spaces before or after)
not	May 2000 - June 2003 (space hyphen space)
Use	B.A. in Art Education--Brigham Young University (two hyphens; no spaces before or after)
Or	B.A. in Art Education—Brigham Young University (m-dash; alternate character set)
Or	B.A., Art Education, Brigham Young University, 2003 (commas acceptable)
not	B.A. in Art Education - Brigham Young University

❏ Have you been careful with the use of periods?

GPA not G.P.A.   MIT not M.I.T.

NATO not N.A.T.O.   BYU not B.Y.U.

Don't use a double period. For example: Compiled data, organized files, etc.. (Avoid "etc." anyway.)

❏ Did you list your GPA? If so, list standard also: 3.5 of 4.0 or 3.47/4.00.

❏ Have you left off your Social Security number? Unless specifically requested, it is *not* necessary on the résumé.

❏ Have you crammed too much or put too little on the page? Try adjusting format if you think you have a problem. *White space* (the space not used) is as important as the space you actually use.

Interviews

The letter and résumé can take you only as far as the interview. In an interview, the time you have to present a good first impression may be three to five minutes, so be prepared to answer a variety of questions *in a way that relates to your qualifications and how your skills can transfer to the position*. In order to do that, of course, you will probably have to do some research over and above that which you did before writing your letter of application. Become as familiar as you can with the operating procedures and personnel expectations of the particular company. You may also wish to review the job description thoroughly.

Remember that during interviews for positions, the interviewers represent their own company needs first and foremost. Most recruiters, then, focus on getting at whether you actually qualify for the positions they have open, whether you are motivated to work hard, and whether you can work well with others within the companies. They may also be looking for certain other skills and general character attributes, such as organizational skills, rhetorical skills (both oral and written), creativity, and initiative. Make sure that you present these to your interviewer by naming *specific details* of what you have done that reveal these attributes. Do not speak in generalities. As you have already noted in "Helpful Hints for Your Letter," it is the details of your experiences that make you unique.

You may also be subjected to some strategies designed to place some stress on you, so that the interviewer can see how you cope. These strategies could include the use of silence at various points during the interview or asking questions that seem to have a "double edge" (for example, "Can you tell me about a time during your college classes when you were not totally honest?").

In addition, carry with you a couple of quality copies of your résumé, paper and pen, names of references typed out on a separate sheet (list only those people who have consented to recommend you), your college transcripts, and appropriate personal documents.

Note: Be considerate enough (and wise enough) to send a thank-you note to your interviewer after your interview—regardless of what you think the outcome may be.

Internet Resources

Job Search & Employment Opportunities: Best Bets from the Net

FedWorld Information Network

http://www.fedworld.gov/

This site provides access to more than 130 U.S. Government dial-up bulletin boards, organized by subject. The employment link is to FedWorld Federal Jobs Search,

http://www.fedworld.gov/jobs/jobsearch.html

A database of open U.S. Federal Government jobs. This database is updated every Tuesday through Saturday and can be searched by state and keyword.

Career Mosaic

http://www.careermosaic.com/cm/

This site offers databases of employers that can be searched by job description, job title, geographical area, and company name; a search engine for regional and occupational news groups that can be searched by keyword and geographical area; a site that allows you to post your résumé online; a web site that links to helpful hints, networking opportunities, résumé worksheets, etc., for use by students and recent graduates; an International Gateway that links to other Career Mosaic sites around the world; a database of health care jobs;

a list of current job fairs on the web at which you can submit your résumé over the web, talk with company representatives, etc.; and a web site that provides tips on job hunting, résumé writing, and professional organizations.

Teachers.net

http://www.teachers.net/jobs/jobboard

A list of teaching positions by region of the U.S., plus Australia, United Kingdom, and other countries.

Monster Board

http://www.monster.com/

This site provides a database of over 50,000 jobs, an employer profile database, an online résumé posting service, and a job posting board. The job search engine can be searched by geographic location and discipline. The employer profiles can be searched by geographic location.

SAMPLE LETTERS AND RÉSUMÉS

Sample 1: Traditional Letter and Résumé

ANGELA PASKETT   1000 South Apple Lane ▪ Payson, UT 84651

(801) 444-4444 ▪ Fax: (801) 444-4000

E-mail: paskett@cougar.netutah.net

July 31, 1997

Mr. John Uibel, Art Director
Mastermind Film Productions
1000 West 2610 South
Salt Lake City, UT 84119

Dear Mr. Uibel:

I am very interested in working for Mastermind Film Productions as a Set Dresser. I will graduate from Brigham Young University in December 1997 with a B.A. in Theatre Arts, my personal studies focusing on set design and theater production. I learned of the Set Dresser position at Mastermind Films from Leadman Kee Miller, and believe I am qualified to fill this opening.

As indicated in my resume, I have been a set dresser on both *Promised Land*, a television series produced by CBS, and *Dojo Kids*, a series dealing with junior high students involved in karate. Although I do not have years of experience, the experience I have is extensive because of the responsibilities I was given. I have dressed a variety of sets including campsites, sheriff's offices, school rooms for all ages, hospitals, hotels, graveyards, a museum, homes, cafes and restaurants, bars, card and toy stores, a music store, an outdoor concert, a city street music festival, a wedding, a newspaper office, and the only standing set on *Promised Land*, the Green family's trailer (many times dressing this alone). I also took the initiative of organizing the purchases in the warehouse to be easily accessible for re-use in later episodes, saving large amounts of time and money for the production. Everyone in this business understands the demands of having a set ready for the cameras. I am able to locate and procure set dressing items to meet these deadlines, dealing with merchants and others to get what the script (and the Decorator, Art Director, and Designer) requires.

In addition to my set dressing experience, I have developed skills in other areas of production. In my years attending BYU I have designed and helped construct sets for theater, as well as learned the basics of lighting, hair and make-up, costuming, and scenic painting through courses and volunteer work.

Enclosed is a copy of my resume for your review. Please contact me at any of the numbers listed above so that we can arrange for an interview. Thank you.

Sincerely,

Angela Paskett

Enclosure

ANGELA PASKETT
1000 South Apple Lane ▪ Payson, UT 84651

(801) 444-4444 ▪ Fax: (801) 444-4000

E-mail: paskett@cougar.netutah.net

EDUCATION

B.A. Theatre Arts, Brigham Young University, Provo, UT, Graduation December, 1997
- GPA: 3.85/4.0
- Golden Key National Honor Society
- National Dean's List
- Dean's List of Honor Students
- Honor Society of Phi Kappa Phi
- Trustees Scholarship

Diploma, Skyline High School, Longmont, CO, 1992
- GPA: 3.9/4.0
- National Honor Society
- Presidential Academic Fitness Award

SELECTED EXPERIENCE

Construction, *Sesquicentennial Spectacular*, Signature Scenery Inc., Jun.-Jul. 1997
Construction Coordinator: Mike Magelby
- Construct set pieces for live performance at Cougar Stadium—experience in wood and metal

Set Dresser, *Dojo Kids*, Q.E.M. Trust Productions, Feb. 1997-Mar. 1997
Set Decorator: Kee Miller
- Dressed and wrapped junior high classrooms

Wardrobe Buyer, CBS, *Promised Land*, Merlot Film Productions, Dec. 1996-Feb. 1997
Costume Designer: LaWane Cole
- Located, purchased, and returned wardrobe articles
- Aged and made basic alterations to costumes

Shopper/Set Dresser, CBS, *Promised Land*, Merlot Film Productions, Aug. 1996-Dec. 1996
Set Decorators: Barbara Ward and Carol Taylor; Leadman: Kee Miller
- Dressed and wrapped sets
- Located, procured, and organized set dressing

Swing Gang, CBS, *Promised Land*, Merlot Film Productions, July 1996-Aug. 1996
Set Decorator: Les Boothe; Leadman: Kee Miller
- Dressed and wrapped sets

Set Designer, *The Arkansaw Bear*, Young Company traveling show, BYU, Jan. 1997
- Designed transportable set for elementary school audiences

Co-Set Designer, *Gadianton*, Margetts Arena Theater, BYU, Dec. 1996
Winner: Outstanding Set Design 1996-97

Task Force, BYU Theater Dept., Sept. 1995-June 1996
Scenic Studio Foreman: Frank Weight
- Constructed sets for theater—experience with wood and metal

Assistant Set Designer, *Jane Eyre*, DeJong Concert Hall, BYU, May 1996
Set Designer: Prof. Rory Scanlon

Laborer, April 1996
Construction Coordinator: Ray Versluys
- Constructed scenic facilities for seminar and corporate training videos

USEFUL SKILLS
- Knowledge and use of hand and power tools
- Hand and machine sewing and alterations
- Scenic art
- Office and organizational skills

References and Letters Available on Request

Sample 2: Scannable Résumé

CATHERINE MATTHEWS
163 S Sentinel Rd 147
Provo, UT 84604
(801)-370-0000

Employment Objective: Editor and magazine writer; experience in the entire publication process.

Skills:
Editor, proofreader, document designer, layout designer, layout editor, technical writer, creative writer, technical editor, teacher, software (PC): DOS, Windows, HTML, WordPerfect, Quattro Pro, German, online help, accurate, industrious, results oriented, team player, organizer.

Education:
Brigham Young University, B.A. in English, August 1996, *Magna Cum Laude*, GPA: 3.95/4.00.

Relevant Course Work: Technical Writing, Creative Writing, Critical Writing and Research, Rhetoric and Composition, Contemporary Literary Theory, Rhetoric and Teaching Writing, Editing for Publication, Advanced Technical Writing, Teaching Advanced Composition.

Academic Awards: Honorable mention in the Linda Hunter Adams Fiction Contest (1996), honorable mention in the *New Era* Essay Writing Contest (April 1995), Trustees scholarship at Brigham Young University (1993-1996), Mae Covey Gardner scholarship (1995), College of Humanities Dean's List (Fall 1994-Spring 1996).

Publications and Conference Presentations: "Pop Culture: Theory and Practice in the Composition Classroom" presentation at the Connections Conference in February, 1997; "A New Kind of Knowledge" publication in the *New Era* in August, 1994.

Professional Organizations: Society of Technical Communication.

Experience:
Composition Department, Brigham Young University, Provo, UT, 1996 to present: Graduate composition instructor for English 115 (College Reading and Writing) and English 316 (Technical Writing). Designer and implementor of innovative composition course in service learning. Team teacher for English 316 (Technical Writing).

Statistics Department, Brigham Young University, Provo, UT, May 1996 to present: Copy editor and proofreader for faculty publications, Masters theses, and student papers. Writer of faculty biographies and updater of faculty web pages.

Faculty Editing Service, Brigham Young University, Provo, UT, January 1996 to present: Copy editor, proofreader, formatter, and document designer of faculty publications, projects, and manuals. Indexer for a faculty member's book and writer of forwards recommending various books for publication.

Inscape, **Brigham Young University**, Provo, UT, January 1996 to May 1996: Copy editor, proofreader, document designer and layout designer of poetry pages using Quark.

Writing Center Tutor, Brigham Young University, Provo, UT January 1995 to April 1996: Peer tutor for all levels of students working on the writing process. Designer of handouts and class presentations on resumes, computer skills, and connectives.

BYU Studies, **Brigham Young University**, Provo, UT, May 1995 to April 1996: Source checker, copy editor, and final format editor.

References: Available upon request.

Sample 3: Résumé for Performance Major

ISAAC C. WALTERS

339 W. 1400 S. #19   (801) 371-0000 (home)
Provo, UT 84604   (801) 370-0000 (work)
E-mail: isaacwalters@aaaa.net   (801) 370-1111 (fax)

Directing Experience:	**The Great Divorce** by C. S. Lewis, adapted by DeLayna Anderson, produced at Brigham Young University (BYU), Provo, UT, April 1997 • Experimental project; explores how relationships in a company affect the audience in performance
	Quilters by Barbara Damashek, produced at Camp Rising Sun, Clinton Corners, NY, July 1996
	Medea by Jean Anouilh, produced at BYU, February 1996
	Sigh No More Ladies by William Shakespeare, produced at Camp Rising Sun, Clinton Corners, July 1995 • A collection of women's scenes from Shakespeare, with music of the period
	People of the Lie by M. Scott Peck, adapted by Isaac Walters, produced on film at BYU, April 1995
Acting Experience:	**Serebryakov** in *Uncle Vanya* by Chekhov, adapted by David Mammet, at BYU, April 1996
	The Father in *Six Characters in Search of an Author* by Luigi Pirandello, at BYU, March 1996
	SS Officer and **Doctor** in *Fear and Misery in the Third Reich* by Bertolt Brecht, at BYU, November 1995
	Graduate and **Father** in *Lighting the Way*, a BYU Fundraising Film, October 1995
	Old Siward in *Macbeth* by William Shakespeare, at BYU, November 1994
	Peter in *Wakefield Passion Play*, at BYU, March 1994
	Kent in *King Lear* by William Shakespeare in *Experiencing Shakespeare*, a made-for-PBS educational film, February 1994
Education:	**B.A. with Honors** in Theatre Arts, August 1997 Brigham Young University, Provo, UT 84602 GPA—Major 3.7/4.0, General 3.49/4.0
	C.I.C.T. workshop with Peter Brook National Theatre of England, June 1994
Community Service:	**A.C.C.E.S. Volunteer**, April 1993–November 1994 • Big Brother/Big Sister Organization

Writing Proposals

For many who work in the arts and humanities professions, proposals become a significant part of the workplace. Many institutions and businesses could not function without successful proposals. Most proposals offer to provide a service or accomplish a specified task at a specified cost. Others request approval to proceed with a project or seek donations of time, equipment, or supplies. Whatever the goal, carefully consider the ideas given below before writing any proposal:

Realize that your goal is to persuade.   Every proposal, regardless of its specific aim, is written to persuade someone else that you grasp the nature of the problem at hand and that you have a viable plan for solving that problem. This means that you must understand fully the needs of the proposal readers and address those needs in a clear, concise, well organized argument. Remember, too, that most proposals are submitted in a competitive environment, an environment that makes it necessary for you to be more persuasive than other writers.

Know what research is important in each situation.   Another way to convince your reader that you fully understand the problem is to use supporting evidence gathered from a thorough and substantial review of the published literature and from other sources (interviews, knowledge of like situations, and so forth) that have direct application to the problem you are offering to solve.

Adapt your proposals to diverse situations.   Some institutions and governmental agencies solicit proposals (called a Request for Proposal) in order to meet specific intra-organizational needs, to provide research opportunities, or to solve problems. In such cases, you may find that the requirements for writing and submitting a proposal differ significantly from each other and from other cases where proposals are not solicited. Think of some situations where you believe formal proposals have been used effectively. What has been accomplished? See if you can come up with actual examples for each of the following situations.

1. Request for funds for the construction or expansion of an art museum
2. Request approval of a new college course that deals with the problems of writing about the arts and humanities
3. Permission to set up a training seminar for teachers of art in the high schools of a district
4. Request for donation of facilities and equipment for a public forum addressing community problems and solutions to those problems
5. Suggestions for internal changes that could enhance productivity within an organization
6. Solicitation for computer equipment and appropriate software for a graphic design course

Would you write the same type of proposal for number 1 above as you would for number 3 or for number 5? What differences would there be and why? Would some general structures remain the same?

Adapt your proposals to diverse audiences.   An important corollary to recognizing the variety of situations for which proposals are written is knowing that each situation has a specific audience that your proposals must take into account. Look again at the examples above. In what ways do these audiences differ? In what ways are they the same? Despite the many differences you need to cope with, you will find that all proposal readers, regardless of the situation, look for certain common elements as they read. For example, they may question whether the proposal clearly

- declares what is being proposed
- recounts what the problem is (necessary to show that you understand the situation)
- discusses why the problem should be solved
- outlines the objectives in attempting to solve the problem
- enumerates what steps will be taken to meet these objectives
- indicates how much it will cost to solve the problem
- provides a time line for completing the project

These concerns should help you determine what you need to include in a proposal, and they will help you focus on something Arthur H. Bell addresses when he maintains that proposal readers "want more than a *general* reassurance. They want to know *specifically* how the proposer will solve their problem" (italics added) (296). Make sure, then, that each step above is concise and detailed.

Adapt your proposals to diverse formats.   Some proposals are brief; some are very lengthy. The proposal submitted for the construction of a new art museum took two years to research and develop. It included 146 pages of text that provided information on room sizes, shapes, capacities, and purposes; on types of exhibits to be housed; on lighting; on materials and equipment; on personnel; and on costs. On the other hand, the examples given for the training seminar for teachers and for the use of facilities and equipment for a community problem-solving meeting consisted of only a few pages each. Some organizations require that proposals be submitted on preformatted forms, while other agencies require only that certain concepts and sections be included in some logical order. Whatever the length or the format requirements for any given proposal, you must always make your proposal look professional, and you must make the information accessible to your readers.

PROPOSAL ASSIGNMENT (OPTION 1)

Purpose

Write a proposal that offers to complete a research paper related to a problem you are interested in solving. Make sure you read the research paper assignment before you begin work on your proposal. Also review the general information regarding proposals provided above.

Audience

For this assignment, your audience will be your instructor and the members of your class. Remember your overall goal: to convince your audience that you can actually complete the project you are proposing. To do this, you must persuade your readers that you

- have a well-defined concept/problem in mind
- know what resources are available to accomplish the task proposed
- have a valid plan for organizing the resources to accomplish your objectives
- can accomplish the task within the specified time

Remember that proposals are formal documents that center on the project itself, not on how you came to be interested in solving the problem. In other words, while it is appropriate to write "I propose to . . . ," it is not appropriate to say "I came to be interested in this problem when I enrolled in a humanities course in my sophomore year and I realized that . . ." Focus sharply on the problem and your proposed way of solving the problem.

Scope

Length: somewhere between three to six *double-spaced* pages. Do whatever it takes to convince your audience you can perform the task. The Guide for Proposal Assignment (Option 1) will help you organize the sections of the proposal and see what important information you should include in each section. (Remember also not to confuse the scope of this particular assignment with the scope of the research paper.)

Schedule

See your class calendar.

Format

See the Guide for Proposal Assignment (Option 1) below.

Guide for Proposal Assignment (Option 1)

Structure of Proposal

> Unless your instructor requires otherwise, set your proposal in *memo format*. Begin your proposal as follows:
>
> TO: (Instructor's name)
> FROM: (Your name)
> DATE: (See your course calendar)
> SUBJECT: Proposal to complete a research paper on . . . (describe exactly the focus of your research paper)
>
> Then include the following major sections:
>
> **PROJECT SUMMARY**
> **PRELIMINARY OUTLINE**
> **REVIEW OF THE LITERATURE**
> **SCHEDULE FOR COMPLETION**
> **PRELIMINARY BIBLIOGRAPHY**
>
> If your project consists of mostly original research, you may need to alter these headings slightly.

Contents of Major Sections

Project Summary

In this section, focus on the topic itself and on your objectives, not on what led you to want to do research on this topic. *Describe* the topic you propose to research, including a brief historical background of pertinent information. Then explain how you will limit that topic by showing the reader what point of view (what approach) you will take. In other words, identify your specific research question. Briefly tell the various subsets of that question (your outline can help keep you on track here). If you intend to do original research, or if your subject is unique (you haven't found someone who has done what you intend to do), indicate that to your reader. Show that you've thought *through* your topic — that is, that you know some of the points you want to make in your research report (again, your outline can help with this).

Keep in mind that describing your topic is just one of your goals here. You're also convincing your audience that what you propose to do is worth careful attention and that you can complete the project. And remember that proposals are formal documents; adopt an appropriate tone.

Here are two excerpts from Project Summaries from two student proposals. Which do you think is more convincing to you as a reader? Which better completes the assignment? Which do you think yielded the more focused research paper?

EXCERPT 1

Sam Shepard is one of the leading playwrights of our time and has been a major influence in shaping contemporary theater. More than any other artist in his field his work has remained outside the common classifications of today's critics. Sam Shepard's plays, although consistently popular internationally, have continually changed in their subject matter and method of presentation. I am submitting this proposal to prepare a research paper with the following purposes: to order and classify Shepard's work by style and content and to research and report Shepard's development as an artist.

EXCERPT 2

In Kenneth Branagh's film adaptation of Shakespeare's *Much Ado About Nothing*, Beatrice (Emma Thompson) recites the opening "Sigh no more, ladies" refrain, a refrain originally intended for a male. With a female reading the part, the connotations of the original words change. I propose to research the different effects of a feminine versus a masculine reader, drawing on both the gender relations of Shakespeare's time and of today, specifically looking at recent feminist criticism and how it pertains to the contemporary audience. Did Branagh change the orator of the text to appease feminist film critics as well as the feminist audience; and, if so, was it required? My research paper will attempt to answer this question. (*See the full text of this proposal in the student samples of this section.*)

Preliminary Outline

A carefully designed outline serves as another tool for persuading the reader that you can follow through on your proposed project. So, construct an outline for your research paper that shows the relationships, as you envision them now, between your research question and your categories of support. Make sure that the ideas within it flow logically.

Here are two outlines for you to compare. Do all the major sections lend support to the thesis for the paper? Do the subcategories support the major ideas? Does the information provided in each sample help you as a reader clearly understand how the resulting report will be structured and why? Does one or the other seem better suited for yielding a problem-solving report?

OUTLINE 1

I. Introduction
   Thesis: To discover how Katherine Kurtz, Robert Jordan, and Terry Brooks use J. R. R. Tolkien's element of "Recovery," as defined in his essay "On Fairy-stories."

II. Tolkien's Element of "Recovery"

III. Katherine Kurtz' Approach in *The Bastard Prince*
   A. Use of Recovery in description of clothes
   B. Use of Recovery in magical rituals

IV. Robert Jordan's Approach
   A. Use of Recovery in *A Crown of Swords*
      1. Example of wind
      2. Example of character behavior
   B. Use of Recovery in *The Eye of the World*
      1. Example of the garden and nature
      2. Example of the Eye of the World

V. Terry Brooks' Approach in *First King of Shanarra*
   A. Use of Recovery with the dark
   B. Use of Recovery with the castle Paranor
   C. Use of Recovery in nature

VI. Conclusion

OUTLINE 2

I. Introduction
   Research Question: Which photographic technique is best for photographing ballet?

II. A Brief History of Photographing Dance

III. Various Techniques Used to Photograph Ballet
   A. Multiple images
   B. Single image

IV. Analyzing Photographs
   A. First photograph
   B. Second photograph

V. Conclusion

Note: You may have more or fewer major categories (indicated by Roman numerals), and you may have more or fewer sub-ideas (A's and B's, 1's and 2's) in any given category. However you set it up, remember that outlines are based on categories of like ideas (the major headings) and on division of these ideas into sub-ideas. Because you are dealing with division, you may not, then, have an **A** without a **B**, nor a **1** without a **2**. You may, though, have a C without a D and a 3 without a 4.

Review of the Literature

Look carefully at your project summary and the support categories on your outline to determine what information you must present to your readers in order to convince them that you have a viable method for resolving the problem. Next, examine the published literature on your proposed topic. Make sure you do a *thorough* review of a variety of sources (books, magazines, journals, *reliable* internet sources, and so forth). Then write your Review of Literature according to the *ideas* (content) that you anticipate need to be included in your research paper. If you do this, you can "lift" this material from your proposal and, with some minor revisions (and some additional information you find after your proposal has been submitted), insert it into your research paper. If you organize your Review of Literature according to *sources*, you will probably face major rewriting tasks before you can transfer the information. The excerpts below should help you see the difference.

EXCERPT 1: ARRANGED ACCORDING TO IDEAS

Research Topic: Developing a Director's Concept for Jean Anouilh's *Antigone*

> *In her Project Summary, this student defines a "director's concept" and explains why it forms an important part of any production. She then claims that a director's "vision" for any production must be original. Because of this claim, she goes on to show how* Antigone *has been performed in Japanese, modern, and French theater. By knowing what has already been done, she believes she can create an original director's concept for the play, which she intends to direct in the near future.*
>
> *Study the excerpt below from her Review of Literature section of her proposal. Does she cover some of the essential concepts that she would need to know to solve the problem? As far as you can tell from this excerpt, are you convinced that she has a good grasp of what the problem is, what her objectives are, and the specific steps she will take to meet her objectives? Also consider whether or not this section can be "lifted" out of her proposal and used (almost word for word) in her research paper.*

The Japanese theater of Yugen chose to do *Antigone* in traditional Japanese "Noh" style (Fielder 411), which is similar to traditional Greek theater. It involves "masks, dance-like movement, a chanting chorus, punctuating flute music, sparse stage settings, and a compressed and sharply focused script dealing with mythic material" (Fielder 411). While it seems natural to perform *Antigone* in a style similar to the Greek, this performance didn't receive good reviews. Mari Fielder explains that this might be because the "inner emotional development of the actors and the charged energy created by formal restraint of such emotion are missing during much of this production" (413).

Another common choice for this play is to direct it in modern times, as was done at the Cottesloe in London. This performance also received poor reviews. Rosalind Carne believes that the directors of this production (Peter Gill and John Burgess) "have opted for the formalized, wooden approach, perhaps assuming that the use of austere modern dress will compensate as a signpost to drag the ancient world into the present. It doesn't" (25).

An even more modern version was performed at the Yale Rep. This version, called *Antigone in New York* and directed by Janusz Glowacki, changed various parts of the play to modernize it, which can commonly cause audience alienation. In regard to this performance, Robert King writes that "the gulf between *Antigone in New York* and the audience paralleled the one between Glowacki and Sophocles" (46).

In France, *Antigone* has been adapted by multiple authors and has even been made into an opera. . . . Of all the adaptations, the most popular one was Jean Anouilh's. . . . Anouilh has written a version of this Greek tragedy that neither alienates an audience, nor betrays what Sophocles intended . . . Mary Ann Frese Witt believes that "Anouilh's play is both darker, . . . and lighter than Sophocles' tragedy. Lighter, because of its self-conscious theatricality and its playing with modernity . . . ; darker, because the characters, by assuming their roles, are aware from the beginning of their inevitable doom . . ." (61).

For further research, I intend to interview two people who have direct-ed . . . Anouilh's version of *Antigone*. . . . I also intend to interview . . . audi-ence members to get their perspective on the play. From these interviews and the library research I have already done, I will be able to elaborate more on what has been done before, why I have chosen Anouilh's adapta-tion, and what my own concept will be.

(USED BY PERMISSION OF LISA HOLLIDAY.)

EXCERPT 2: ARRANGED ACCORDING TO SOURCES

Research Topic: How the Chinese republican poet Hsü Chih-mo's con-tact with the poetry of Sir Algernon Charles Swinburne influenced his late work

> *This student provides a significant background section on "the syntactical patterns of classical Chinese" writing and how those patterns changed over time. He discusses how artists "of the common speech school brought Chinese writing forward to the 20th century"; introduces one such artist, Hsü Chih-mo; and indicates his belief that Hsü Chih-mo's education at Cambridge greatly influenced this young Chinese scholar's later poetry, specifically with reference to Swinburne.*
>
> *Ask the same questions about this excerpt that you did for the previous one.*

Texts of Chinese poetry, especially in translation, are scarce at the Harold B. Lee Library. Even fewer are comprehensive analyses of this genre. There are, however, several excellent sources on which I have based my preliminary research.

The incomparable Sinologist Herbert Giles, in his exhaustive, 3-vol-ume reference, *Biographical Dictionary of Republican China*, briefly describes Hsü Chih-mo's activities at Cambridge in the context of his pro-lific career and acknowledges its effect on his decision to turn from eco-nomic and sociological studies to poetry. He also examines the effect of Swinburne in developing in Hsü Chih-mo "a taste for alliterative cadence and impressionism."[2]

A more elaborate, though by no means complete, analysis of the Cam-bridge period appears in Hsü Kai-yu's *Twentieth Century Chinese Poetry*. He asserts, ". . . Hsü did not find his voice until the atmosphere of aristo-cratic idealism at Cambridge helped him to cultivate his poetic sensitivity."[3] This author explores Hsü's quest for supreme individualism and romantic idealism and how it was germinated by the verse of Swinburne on the banks of the Cam. *Twentieth Century Chinese Poetry* also offers the only English translations of Hsü's poetry in the Lee Library.

What each work lacks, however, are examples of Swinburne's poetry that Hsü encountered at Cambridge and a comparison of these works with own later work. For this purpose, I will consult two collections of Swinburne, *The Works of Algernon Charles Swinburne*[4] and *Swinburne: The Portrait of a Poet*.[5] I will use collections of Hsü's verse, both in English translation and in the original Mandarin[6] for comparison. As a control to my conclusions, I will conduct interviews with native Chinese educators familiar with the Chinese literary arts and Hsü Chih-mo's work to determine which qualities in Hsü's work are truly revolutionary departures from Chinese convention and thus can be attributed to the influence of others. The result of such research using primary sources and checked with cultural ballast will be original and meaningful conclusions.

(USED BY PERMISSION OF ADAM JOHNSON.)

Even though both of these proposals ultimately led to the production of good research papers, which one do you think required the least amount of rewriting? Does one proposal strike you as being more persuasive than the other? Why?

Notice that these two students carefully cite their sources within the text of their proposals. Whenever you borrow specific information of any kind from someone else, you must provide a citation for that source within the text of this section *as well as* supplying the full bibliographic data, which appears in the Preliminary Bibliography. Also observe two other important things: (1) Lisa uses MLA documentation style in her text, while Adam uses a style current in his own field (see instructions under Preliminary Bibliography if you wish to use a style other than MLA). (2) Because the first student arranges her Review of Literature around the *ideas* she will focus on in her research report, she is better able to introduce or integrate the quotes and paraphrases into the context and structure of her own ideas. This is important because your instructor wants to know how the information from your sources connects to your concept.

Schedule for Completion of Project

Set up a realistic schedule for completion of the various tasks for the research paper. Don't underestimate the time it takes to revise.

TASK	COMPLETED BY
Complete Library Research & Note-taking	(provide dates for each task)
Analyze and Interpret Data	
Organize the Research Paper	
Write the Rough Draft	
Revise Subsequent Drafts	
Submit Final Copy of the Research Paper	

Preliminary Bibliography

Your preliminary bibliography should be on a *separate, attached sheet* and should include the works you cited in the Review of Literature section of your proposal plus any you think you will use in the research paper itself (somewhere around ten sources for papers based primarily on library research, five to eight for papers based primarily on original research). Some instructors will require a more comprehensive bibliography, and some will have you annotate sources you have found that may help you complete your research paper but which you have not cited in the proposal. If so, your instructor will guide you in preparing this.

Use MLA documentation format (the newest version) unless you are given permission by your instructor to do otherwise. You should have access to the *MLA Handbook*, either in hard copy or on MLA's internet site (www.mla.org). If you have permission to use a different documentation system, give the teacher samples of correct formats for the common types of entries, taken from a guide for the system you are using.

Denote the documentation system you use in the bottom right corner of the preliminary bibliography page of your proposal.

SAMPLE PROPOSALS FOR RESEARCH PAPER

SAMPLE 1: PROPOSAL. NOTE THAT REVIEW OF LITERATURE SECTION IS IDEA ORIENTED

TO: Dianna M. Black
FROM: Natalie Thompson
DATE: May 19, 1999
SUBJECT: Proposal to complete a research paper on whether or not the opening "Sigh no more, ladies" passage in Branagh's *Much Ado About Nothing* requires the change from masculine to feminine reader in order to appease contemporary audiences.

PROJECT SUMMARY

In Kenneth Branagh's film adaptation of Shakespeare's *Much Ado About Nothing*, Beatrice (Emma Thompson) recites the opening "Sigh no more, ladies" refrain, a refrain originally intended for a male. With a female reader, the connotations of the original words change. I propose to research the different effects of a feminine versus a masculine reader, drawing on both the gender issues of Shakespeare's time and of today, specifically looking at recent feminist criticism and how it pertains to the contemporary audience. Did Branagh change the orator of the text to appease feminist film critics as well as the feminist audience, and if so, was it required? My research paper will attempt to answer this question.

PRELIMINARY OUTLINE

I. Introduction
    Does the opening "Sigh no more, ladies" passage in Branagh's *Much Ado About Nothing* require the change from a masculine to feminine reader in order to appease modern audiences?

II. Modern interpretations of Shakespeare
    A. His intent—his patriarchal society
    B. Placing his words/works in a contemporary context
    C. Feminist Film Criticism
        1. Definition
        2. Different implications of this criticism

III. Specific look at the opening scene
    A. Emma Thompson's recitation
        1. Shakespeare's original denotations vs. contemporary denotations
        2. Differences in connotation and expression rendered by Thompson
    B. Balthasar's recitation
        1. Differences in inflection
        2. Differences in expression

IV. Evaluation of the overall project
    A. Was it necessary for Branagh to change the speaker?
    B. Does the modern audience expect the change? Would they be repelled by Shakespeare's original intentions?
    C. Does the difference in speaker make Branagh a feminist or simply contemporary?

V. Conclusion

REVIEW OF THE LITERATURE

Most modern interpreters of Shakespeare, when trying to appease Shakespeare's socio-historic context, place their interpretations in the present. As Susan Bennett says, modern "texts themselves display an obsessive interest in the past as a figure for the desires of the present" (3). Almost unwittingly, modern translators (e.g., directors, actors, and screenwriters) place Shakespeare's text in their own time frame: our contemporary society.

Because Branagh takes an older text and translates it into a modern movie, he faces the problem of interpreting old literature for today's audience. In an interview with Paul Meier, Branagh maintains that he "tr[ies] to be as real as possible" (88) when pursuing this goal. He also says that he feels as though "there must be some form of balance between a scrupulous observation of the text and a truly imaginative character" (82). In the film's depiction, Branagh addresses this issue by giving the "Sigh no more, ladies" refrain to a female character, which allows Beatrice to have a strong feministic tendency and eliminates the refrain's possibly sarcastic tone when Balthasar later sings it.

Both Shakespearean critics and feminist film critics express opinions about this type of exchange. In Shakespearean criticism, Claire McEachern talks about the distinct difference between the patriarchal society that Shakespeare wrote in versus the society we live in today. Because of this, she says it is difficult to apply feminist criticism to Shakespeare and to place the two in the same context (270). Sarah Werner says that women cannot act Shakespeare in a realistic manner because the universality and the subjectivity of his work apply only to men (250). The question arises, then, if a director should attempt to create a character where Shakespeare did not intend one. Is there any reason for Branagh to create a feminist character in his work? Does Shakespeare's text allow for this?

Feminist film criticism more specifically concerns itself with the role women typically fulfilled in the past and also with the presumed male "gaze" of the audience. Elizabeth Cowie discusses the role of women in the cinema as a result of this gaze, looking closely at the implications (15). If the crowd contains a proportionately high tendency towards feminist attitudes, casting Beatrice without feministic and strong-willed traits may cause the target audience to dislike the adaptation.

It is also necessary to look at this particular scene using a reader-response approach because the majority of the audience will respond with highly contemporary connotations and because modern denotations differ from the original Elizabethan Renaissance ones. Because of film (spoken rather than written) media, the words need a connotational analysis, with a specific look at the delivery of Thompson's performance through her voice intonation and facial expression. The information here primarily stems from a direct look at the movie, comparing Beatrice's rendition to Balthasar's.

SCHEDULE FOR PROJECT COMPLETION

TASK	COMPLETED BY
Research	May 24, 1999
Outline	May 28, 1999
Preliminary Draft	May 31, 1999
Rough Draft	May 31, 1999
Final Draft	June 7, 1999

PRELIMINARY BIBLIOGRAPHY

Belsey, Catherine. "Feminism and Beyond." *Shakespeare Studies* 25 (1997): 32–41.

Bennett, Susan. *Performing Nostalgia: Shifting Shakespeare and the Contemporary Past.* New York: Routledge, 1996.

Boston, Jane. "Voice: the Practitioners, Their Practices, and Their Critics." *New Theatre Quarterly* 13 (1997): 248–54.

Carson, Diane, Linda Dittmar, and Janice R. Welsch, eds. *Multiple Voices in Feminist Film Criticism.* Minneapolis: U of Minnesota P, 1994.

Cowie, Elizabeth. *Representing the Woman: Cinema and Psychoanalysis.* Minneapolis: U of Minnesota P, 1997.

Donawerth, Jane. "Teaching Shakespeare in the Context of Renaissance Women's Culture." *Shakespeare Quarterly* 47 (1996):476–89.

Light, Alison. "The Importance of Being Ordinary." *Sight and Sound* 3 (1993): 16–19.

McEachern, Claire. "Fathering Herself: A Source Study of Shakespeare's Feminism." *Shakespeare Quarterly* 39 (1988): 269–90.

Meier, Paul. "Kenneth Branagh: With Utter Clarity." *TDR* 41 (1997): 82–9.

Shakespeare, William. *Much Ado About Nothing.* Ed. Holger Klein. Lewiston: Edwin Mellon, 1992.

Sharman, Leslie Felpein. "*Much Ado About Nothing*—Review." *Sight and Sound* 3 (1993): 50–1.

Werner, Sarah. "Performing Shakespeare: Voice Training and the Feminist Actor." *New Theatre Quarterly* 12 (1996): 249–58.

(USED BY PERMISSION.)

SAMPLE 2: PROPOSAL. NOTE THAT REVIEW OF LITERATURE SECTION IS MOSTLY SOURCE ORIENTED

TO: Dianna M. Black
FROM: Benjamin Pew
DATE: October 12, 1994
SUBJECT: Proposal to complete a research paper on the languages of Tolkien's Middle-Earth

PROJECT SUMMARY

The trilogy *The Hobbit, The Lord of the Rings,* and *The Silmarillion* is widely regarded as one of the greatest fantasy epics ever written and influence a large percentage of the fantasy written today. J. R. R. Tolkien, the author of this epic, worked on his ideas and backgrounds for most of his life and thus was able to establish a realistic surrounding for his stories that is unparalleled. One aspect of this surrounding is the several languages that Tolkien developed. Most uses of different languages in fantasy consist of single words or phrases, or in borrowing an actual language that seems appropriate for the setting. Tolkien's languages, in contrast, though not borrowed from a living society, are detailed enough to include poetry, songs, and a distinct writing system.

I would like to examine the ways in which the languages of Tolkien's works resemble natural languages, as well as the "historical" development of his languages, which also parallels the development of natural languages. For my research paper, then, I propose to apply the principles of linguistic analysis to his languages in an effort to show the depth of the realism of these languages.

PRELIMINARY OUTLINE

I.   Introduction: Do Tolkien's invented languages show similar development and form as the natural languages of man?

II. Tolkien's conception of his languages as part of a whole.
     A. Languages show history of the people who spoke them
     B. Languages show character and nature of the people.

III. Aspects of Language in Tolkien's languages
     A. Morphology
     B. Phonology
     C. Syntax

IV. History of Languages of Middle-earth
     A. Relation of the Elvish languages
     B. Relation of other languages
     C. Influences and borrowings between languages.

V.   Conclusion

REVIEW OF THE LITERATURE

The first sources for understanding Tolkien's languages are, naturally, the books themselves. J. R. R. Tolkien includes several passages in various languages along with translations of these passages, such as this example of the language known as the "Black Speech": "Ash nazg durbatulûk, ash nazg gimbatul, ash nazg thrakatulûk agh burzum-ishi krimpatul! 'One Ring to rule them all, One Ring to find them, One Ring to bring them all and in the Darkness bind them'" (333-334). By examining this sentence, several different morphemes can be identified, such as ash=one, nazg=ring, dur=rule, ba=infinitive, tul=them, ûk=all, gim=find, thraka=bring, and krimpa=bind. Another valuable source is the book *The Road Goes Ever On*, which includes two Elvish songs along with word-for-word translations by Tolkien. These provide an important tool in analyzing the languages, as the word forms become evident. For example:

A Elbereth   Gil-thoniel,   silivren   penna
O Elbereth Star-kindler, (white) glittering slants-down

míriel   o   menel   aglar
sparkling   like jewels from firmament glory

elenath!   Na-chaered   palan-díriel
[of] the star-host to-remote distance after-having- gazed

o   galadh-remmin en-nor-ath, Fanuilos,   le
from tree-tangled middle-lands, Fanuilos, to thee

linnathon   nef   aear   sí   nef   aearon
I will chant on this side of ocean here on this side of the Great Ocean.
(Swann and Tolkien 72)

This enables an analysis of the syntax as well as the morphology of the language. Extensive notes on many of the languages are also provided in several volumes of *The History of Middle-Earth*, edited by Christopher Tolkien. These notes include an extensive etymology of the Elvish languages in an early stage of their development, which shows many of the phonological changes between languages, such as *b* in the proto-Elvish shifting to *v* in Quenya, as in *abar-* to *avar, bal- -Vala, bar- -varna*. Another interesting change is the loss of an initial *g* in Quenya. The other languages underwent other changes that differentiate each from the others. For example, in Noldorin, non-initial *b* shifts to *f*. Volume 5 of this series, *The Lost Road*, also includes a tree showing the relation between the languages (196).

Finally, *The History of Middle-Earth* also provides us with the background of the languages and their development, as well as insights into Tolkien's ideas about his own work. For example, Christopher Tolkien explains his father's conception of the difference between "invented" and "artificial" languages:

> Those languages were conceived, of course, from the very beginning in a deeply "historical" way: they were embodied in a history, the history of the Elves who spoke them, in which was to be found, as it evolved, a rich terrain for linguistic separation and interaction: "a language requires a suitable habitation, and a history in which it can develop." Every element in the languages, every element in every word, is in principle historically "explicable" — as are the elements in languages that are not "invented" — and the successive phases of their intricate evolution were the delight of their creator. "Invention" was thus altogether distinct from "artificiality." (341)

SCHEDULE FOR COMPLETION

Complete Library Research & Note-taking	1 November 1994
Analyze and Interpret Data	10 November 1994
Organize the Research Paper	14 November 1994
Write the Rough Draft	20 November 1994
Revise Subsequent Drafts	27 November 1994
Submit Final Copy of the Research Paper	29 November 1994

PRELIMINARY BIBLIOGRAPHY

Swann, Donald and J. R. R. Tolkien. *The Road Goes Ever On*. Boston: Houghton, 1978.

Tolkien, Christopher, ed. *The History of Middle-Earth, Vol. V: The Lost Road and Other Writings*. Boston: Houghton, 1987.

Tolkien, J. R. R. *The Fellowship of the Ring*. New York: Ballantine, 1965.

PROPOSAL ASSIGNMENT (OPTION 2)

Purpose

Write a proposal that seeks funding for a specific project. Select a project that would actually require *resources* from a granting agency. You may wish to use the following ideas as springboards as you think about proposing a worthwhile project.

- Propose to do a service project or a seminar for a particular agency

- Propose to include an additional course in a curriculum (be sure it will require additional resources)

- Propose to complete a creative project for a city park (sculpture, architecture, landscaping, a concert platform, or even a fountain)

- Propose to write a children's storybook (along with illustrations by an illustrator you know)

- Propose to film a documentary based on the life of a famous artist or humanitarian

- Propose to set up a day-care center for employees of a large corporation

- Propose a sabbatical to do research on an ad campaign that will run in countries other than the United States

- Write a prospectus for an undergraduate honors thesis

After you select a focus for your proposal, make sure you review the information supplied previously about the nature of good proposals. Think carefully about how to make your document as persuasive (and competitive) as you possibly can given the situation, the audience, and the format.

Audience

Unlike Option 1, your audience for this proposal is not your instructor and members of your class. For this assignment, research the various granting agencies, foundations, and corporations that are concerned with the kind of thing you are proposing. For example, if you propose to present a one-man or one-woman show in a reputable theater in a midsized city in the U.S., to which agencies would you submit your proposal? What kinds of projects have they funded in the past? What are their goals for the future? What kind of people staff these agencies (who will be your audience)? When you have your audience firmly in mind, provide specific, detailed information that supports your proposal and convinces your readers that your project has value. Remember to focus tightly on the project and your objectives; still, it is not only your project that you must "sell." Convince them, too, that you *fully intend* to complete the project responsibly and that you *have the capabilities* to complete it well.

Scope

Length: somewhere between four to seven double-spaced pages (see Format section below). Consider the situation, the audience, and the format; then do what it takes to make your proposal persuasive.

Schedule

See your class calendar.

Format

Your instructor may ask you to locate a specific form from a granting institution and work within that format. If so, make sure you understand what the grantor expects and complete each section fully and meticulously. On the other hand, your instructor may ask you to use a format similar to the one shown at the end of this section. In the structure below, keep your **Project Summary** very concise and short, giving a full and specific **Project Description** in the next major section. (Pay attention to the subheads here. Don't neglect to add the details necessary to show what has been done, what you want to do, why you want to do it, how and where you will carry out the work, and what benefit your work may have.) You will "defend" yourself in the **Qualifications** section, provide a clear and well conceived **Budget**, and then attach any **Appendices** to the end of the proposal. Again, remember that when you show what others have done, you must supply citations to the source material. Here is an outline of the structure:

Project Summary

Project Description

> **Introduction**
>
> **Rationale for and Significance of Project**
>
> **Plan of Work**
>
> **Facilities and Equipment**

Personnel Qualifications

Budget

Appendices

In the future when your proposals get funded, you should carefully document the progress of your project—a history of how you spent the grant money and what you accomplished. Most grantors will require you to write progress and final reports.

EVALUATION SHEET: PROPOSAL

Author _____   Date _____

Reviewer _____

1. How specific and direct is the subject line? Does it clearly indicate the selected topic?

2. Does the Project Summary offer engaging background to the project?

3. What specific questions does the Project Summary detail?

4. Does the proposed Outline directly reflect the Project Summary and the Review of Literature? Does it show how the author will proceed in this research? Does it suggest that the research project has been thoroughly planned?

5. Is the information in the Review of Literature sufficient for the readers to evaluate the original source and connect it to the proposed research project? Is the source clearly introduced and cited? Has the author integrated source material effectively into his/her concept for the research project?

6. How many sources — and *what kinds* of sources — are listed in the Preliminary Bibliography?

7. Overall, does the proposal reflect a unity of purpose and content?

Writing Recommendation Reports

This kind of analytical report arises as the result of specific needs: to make changes in workplace procedures; to accept an ad campaign aimed at generating revenue; to purchase one new computer system over another; to invite a particular artist to exhibit in a gallery; to make personnel policy; to choose plays, concerts, or dance revues (and which specific ones) for an upcoming season; and so forth. Recommendation reports help organizations make important decisions. Many of you in the arts and humanities will write these reports or make decisions based on them. The best recommendation reports contain

- a clear purpose
- well-defined descriptions of possible solutions and the standards for comparing those solutions,
- good collection of relevant data
- careful analysis (free of personal bias) of the data in relation to the criteria
- conclusions based on the data
- recommendations that stem naturally from the conclusions

This assignment will help you *write* solid recommendation reports and also *read* them carefully, with a critical eye. Remember that it may seem easy to describe a situation as it currently exists, but getting from there to recommending *one* possible solution to a situation requires careful planning. The old adage "You can lead a horse to water, but you can't make it drink" has meaning here: you must find a way to allow your reader to "drink" your solution. This probably can't happen if any of the sections of your report prove faulty or illogical. If you find faults in another's report, you, as a decision-maker, may quickly dismiss the recommendations made.

Given the information above, here are some questions to help you begin the process.

- What is the overall goal here? How does the goal fit into the structure of the organization?
- Which solutions are possible here? And how many should you consider?
- What data will you need to gather for each solution? What kind of data would be relevant?
- How will you interpret the data? Will you need to set up standards (criteria) by which to judge? What will your standards be? Do your standards affect the type of solution possible?
- What biases, if any, does your employer (and, hence, the reader of your report) have? Will this matter? Will the information in any of the sections of your report need to be altered if there are biases? How much data will you have to present in order to convince your employer you have a valid recommendation?
- What outcomes are possible should your recommendation be accepted?
- What kind of structure and format will you use?

Like every other writing assignment in this class, consider carefully who your audience is and how that audience will react to your recommendation. What audience characteristics would make it easy to convince your readers? Which characteristics would make it difficult? How could you overcome some of the difficulties?

RECOMMENDATION REPORT ASSIGNMENT

Purpose

To write a report recommending a course of action (in this case, making *one* choice or selection from among several choices) to be taken by an individual, group, committee, or organization. In your opening paragraph, you establish the need for such a recommendation report within the context of a rhetorical situation. In the body, you present your criteria (standards of judgment), then *fairly* represent the strengths and weaknesses of each choice and demonstrate, given the standards, why one choice is best.

You may wish to organize your report in one of the following ways, each with its advantages: (1) You may organize it as a *series of reasons* why one choice is better than the others; (2) You may devote a section to *each choice*, arguing its strengths and weaknesses and making sure the best choice shows the greatest strengths and fewest weaknesses; or (3) You may devote a section to *each of the standards* and show how each choice measures up to that standard. With any of these strategies, you will be constructing an argument for your choice, developing it section by section for your reader. Remember to offer choices *that can be subjected to all the standards.* You cannot include a choice that can be dismissed because it does not fit into one or more of the criteria (for example, choosing something that does not fit into your "cost" limitations in the first place and then simply dismissing it). As you analyze your data, you will probably find that even what appears to be the best choice in most categories does not "show" well in one or two categories. Be prepared for this eventuality. You may have to rate or weight the criteria (and assign appropriate points for those ratings) to reflect what you feel are the most important ones for the situation.

To effectively carry out your purpose, make sure that you

- clearly outline the established criteria that guide your decision
- clearly explain the choices available
- make a sound choice from the alternatives
- tell your audience what that choice is
- communicate persuasively your reasons for selecting that course from among available alternatives

Audience

You should write to the audience specified in the rhetorical situation you choose. (See "Rhetorical Situations for the Recommendation Report" for more details.)

Scope

This depends on a number of things; e.g., the criteria you use, your audience, the graphics you will need, the rhetorical situation, your format, the limitations set by your instructor. Generally, three to five pages, double-spaced.

Schedule

See your class calendar.

Format

Most instructors will require that your report follow memo format. You may wish to incorporate different types of fonts and point sizes, colors, bolded headings, indenting, bullets and icons, or charts and graphs—anything that will make your report more visually scannable and enjoyable to read.

Rhetorical Situations for the Recommendation Report

Read the rhetorical situations described below. You may choose one of these or you may create your own situation. If you create your own situation, please talk it over with your instructor before you begin your report. Together you will need to discuss the feasibility of the situation and the intended audience.

Important Tips for Successfully Completing Your Report

- For any rhetorical situation you choose, *use four choices.* Evaluate those choices according to *three to six criteria* (standards of judgment).
- Clearly delineate your criteria.
- Locate or invent the "data" you will need for your situation. Remember to present good concrete details about the situation itself and about the choices.
- Carefully consider the audience implicit in your situation and meet the needs of that audience.

Situation A

Assume that you are serving as a member of the curriculum committee in a department within a College of Fine Arts or a College of Humanities, and that the committee has asked you to recommend *one* of four courses being considered for addition to the department's curriculum. Create four courses you think could actually be considered, evaluate them against realistic criteria (consider departmental limitations and needs), and recommend one. Your audience is the chair of the department and the other members of the curriculum committee.

Situation B

You are the managing director of a small theater group. You are facing a serious budget shortfall this year and must choose which *one* of four advertising campaigns submitted to you will result in the greatest intake of funds. Think about your needs and predicament, set up criteria by which to judge the ad campaigns, and present your findings to the Board of Directors. Cost should be a factor, but each of the four campaigns must be "affordable."

Situation C

Assume that the last time you were home, your grandfather said to you, "That old Dodge I gave you when you graduated from high school is no longer reliable. You need a better car. I know you don't have much money, but I have some put away for you kids when I die. Still, you need the money now, and I might live ten years. Let me give you $20,000 now to buy a new car. Get what you can from the old Dodge."

Select *four* alternatives that fit within your price range (the $20,000 plus whatever you can get out of the old Dodge plus any small amounts of savings you have). Set up criteria that reflect your particular needs and lifestyle. Then evaluate all choices according to these criteria and choose *one.* For this situation, you will not have to "invent" the details. You can visit local car dealerships to pick up brochures or talk to sales representatives. You can also get good information on criteria from various magazines in the library. Because you should be selecting alternatives that you can afford with the money you have, using the initial cost of the vehicle as a criterion is discouraged.

Write your report to grandpa explaining how you arrived at your decision.

Situation D

You are on the staff of a small art museum in the western United States. Given the museum's evaluation criteria for selecting new pieces (printed below), select *one* piece from among four new works of art and write a report to the Board of Directors recommending the piece the museum should acquire. The Board consists of nine people, some of them opinionated and headstrong. Several members have been lobbying you and other board members to buy each of the four pieces under consideration. Your report must be convincing enough to win a two-thirds majority.

Evaluation Criteria for Acquisitions: Museum of Art

In devoting the Museum's financial resources, exhibition space, and manpower to the growth and improvement of the permanent collection, the Board and Museum Director must be guided by two criteria: areas of emphasis and measures of quality. All acquisitions recommendations should be made in light of them.

(1) Areas of Emphasis
- Works by in-state artists or depicting scenes or history of the state.
- Works of regional fine art. The Museum will strive to obtain quality examples by representative western artists in all styles: painting, watercolor, sculpture, drawing, prints, and photography.
- Nonwestern art that has relevance to the existing collection or that directly influenced the art of the region.
- Nonwestern art that is of such high quality that it may be considered to be a masterpiece.

(2) Measures of Quality
- Works of great artistic and historical value. These can be considered the finest pieces in the collection and may justify moving or removing other pieces in order to be displayed.
- Works of good quality and high historical value. These are of the sort that can be moved or even sold later to provide space and funds for first-rate works.
- Works of average quality that are important to fill in the history of the art of the West or that of a particular artist important in the entire collection.
- Works of low quality but which are judged so essential to the permanent collection, for sentimental or historical reasons, that they should be acquired. An example may be "primitive" art done by early painters who lacked technique but were among the first in the area to paint seriously.

Remember that for each of the pieces below, you must invent the "data," e.g., provide the artist's name, the title of the piece, and details about the work itself. Be careful not to distort the basic problem of selection.

- *The first piece is a work of sculpture of a mother and child by a well known Western artist. Revered by local people, he has received several sculpture commissions from local churches and organizations. The museum owns four of his works. This one represents a phase of his work not in the collection, but you and several others consider the piece to be sentimental and artistically below standard. Price: $3,500.*

- *The second piece is a painting by a young female artist not represented in the collection. In fact, she is something of an unknown. Her painting depicts two young women examining paintings in a gallery that can be positively identified as the museum you work for. You don't know whether the artist's other work will measure up to this piece, but everything you know about art says, "This piece is good. I want to have it around." Price: $2,500.*

- *The third piece is a painting by a female artist from Boston who specializes in abstracts. Her work is valued across the country. You have a chance to pick up one of her works at well below its art-market value. You know a good buy, and this is one. If the museum decides later not to keep it, it can probably be sold for twice what you paid for it, assuming her popularity holds. Price: $3,000.*

- *The fourth is a set of photographs of early frontier life. The set has importance both as historical documents and as samples of the history of photography. The set is owned by the Metropolitan Museum of Art in New York but is now for sale. Your museum has very little photography at present, although its objective is to represent all the visual arts. Your own evaluation goes like this: aesthetically, the photos are not particularly striking. They were taken by five photographers, only two of whom are distinguished. But the set is of great interest historically. Price: $4,000.*

If you choose this situation, you may either use the two criteria (with all or some of their subsets) given in the box above, modify the criteria somewhat, or develop your own criteria. If you use "cost" as a criterion, assume that all of the pieces under consideration fall within the museum's acquisition budget of $4500.

Other Situations

For any of the situations given below, invent the details for *four* choices, provide criteria appropriate to the situation, and take audience factors into consideration.

- Selection of *one* genre of art (oil, prints, sculpture, installations, or such) for exhibit in *one* of the internal galleries of a new art museum
- Selection of *one* play for performance in a repertory theater (or *one* musical composition for a concert, or *one* novel for review at a book club, or *one* ballet for a dance revue, or . . .)
- Selection of *one* book, essay, poem, philosophical treatise, or such for addition to the Great Works list at a major university
- Selection of *one* site for a family reunion of about 300 people
- Selection of *a* site for a new business (restaurant, clothing outlet, art supplies shop, dance gym, theater, hardware store, computer store, or . . .)

Again, you may make up your own situation. If you do, clear your project with your instructor before you begin.

SAMPLE RECOMMENDATION REPORTS

SAMPLE 1: RECOMMENDATION REPORT

TO: Dr. William Solti, Keyboard Head, Department of Music

FROM: Sarah Patterson, Assistant to Dr. Sam Beck

DATE: September 21, 1994

IN RE: Recommendation to include Chopin's Valse in A Major, opus 42 in Myra Carr's senior recital

Myra Carr's senior recital is scheduled for December 17. She has a number of works ready to perform and will be perfecting several others of her choice to include in her program. She has room on her program for one more piece. Last week, Dr. Beck asked me to analyze the three compositions that Myra has expressed a desire to play, to select the one that would be the most valuable for inclusion in her recital, and then to indicate that choice to you. The three pieces Myra considered are Beethoven's Sonata No. 8 in C-sharp Minor, Anton Webern's opus 27, and Chopin's Valse, opus 42 in A Major.

As you know, in any recital, and especially in a senior recital, specific requirements are set by the Music Department. In addition to these requirements, certain unspoken stylistic traits are automatically in place. Based on these considerations, I set up the following criteria in order to judge which of the three pieces would be best:

- Technical Difficulty: On a scale of <u>M</u>oderate, <u>D</u>ifficult, and <u>V</u>irtuoso, prefer <u>D</u> to <u>V</u>.

- Musical Genre/Period: Composers from Baroque, Classical, Romantic, and 20th-century periods must be represented.

- New Material: New material must be learned before the scheduled recital.

After analyzing the three pieces according to the criteria, I recommend that Myra include the work by Chopin. Below is a report on my analysis.

Technical Difficulty

Any musician who has played Beethoven knows how demanding he can be. Sonata No. 8 is especially difficult to master. The accents and consistent octaves in the theme along with the turns and trills in the development serve as reminders that Beethoven was quite a showman. For these reasons, this piece is extremely difficult, even to the point of deserving a Virtuoso rating.

Anton Webern's opus 27 is also quite exacting, but in a different manner. The harmonies are not as obvious as in the Beethoven, and this makes it appear difficult at the outset. Nevertheless, it is very slow, which helps the pianist to adjust. It rates a Moderate on the scale.

Chopin has always incorporated good technique with difficult passages. Edited fingerings in many of his waltzes are evidence of this. The particular waltz is brilliant and exciting, as if it were a race to the finish. It is not so difficult that it loses that enthusiasm by being overdone. It earns a Difficult rating.

Musical Genre/Period

To understand this particular requirement, it is necessary to know the program and see it from a vantage point of looking at the whole. I have included a list of the other works Myra will be playing, along with their periods.

Bach	Prelude and Fugue No. 23 in B Major	Baroque
Haydn	Sonata in D Major No. 19	Classical
Mozart	Sonata K.381 in G Major	Classical
Debussy	Voiles	Romantic
Schumann	Papillions, op. 2	Romantic
Bartok	Two Roumanian Dances, op. 8a SZ43	20th-century
Copeland	Scherzo Humoristique	20th-century

As you can see from this inventory, each of the time periods is represented by two pieces except the Baroque. Indeed, it would seem best to consider another piece from the Baroque period and make the recital completely balanced. Still, it is not unheard of to have more of one genre than another in a particular recital. Here then, are the other three possible selections with their respective periods:

Beethoven	Sonata No. 8 in C-sharp Minor	Classical
Webern	Opus 27	20th-century
Chopin	Valse, op. 42 in A Major	Romantic

Because Mozart and Haydn are both Classic composers and wrote in almost the same time period, it would seem much too redundant to use Beethoven, as he composed only a few years later. In concert, some 20th-century music has not been well liked by the audiences, and considering that Myra already has prepared two good 20th-century pieces, it is probably best to not include another. The Chopin was written in the Romantic period, yet contains many facets of Classical music, thus serving as a perfect connector between the Classical and Romantic composers.

New Material

Myra learns fast and memorizes quickly. Nevertheless, with the credit load she is currently taking and with perfecting some of her other choices, she does not have as much time as she would like to devote to a new piece. Myra does not yet know the Beethoven, but because of its level of technical difficulty, it would be likely impossible to perfect before her recital. She knows the Webern very well and used it for her jury a few semesters ago.

Myra has played through the Chopin a few times, and although she does not have it all learned, she is at least familiar enough with it to comprehend the nuances that must be achieved.

Conclusion

In the three areas of consideration, it seems clear that Chopin's Valse, opus 42 in A Major is the only work that can fulfill the priority requirements for the senior recital. The summary chart below shows the criteria as related to each selection.

	TECHNICAL DIFFICULTY	MUSICAL GENRE/ PERIOD	NEW MATERIAL
Beethoven	Virtuoso	Classical	Yes
Webern	Moderate	20th-Century	No
Chopin	Difficult	Romantic	Familiar

The technical level of the Chopin is rated Difficult, a requirement by the Music Department. The musical genre of Chopin is Romantic, but it serves as a connector from the Classical to the Romantic. This shows style and creativity within the regulations the Music Department has set. Finally, the Chopin piece is new, but not completely new for Myra, which will give her the opportunity to stretch herself as she has done so well in the past. My recommendation, then, is that she include the Chopin in her upcoming recital.

(USED BY PERMISSION.)

SAMPLE 2: RECOMMENDATION REPORT

Canine Consulting

We provide the dog, you provide the bone.

TO: Sam and Mary Stevens

FROM: Anne Black, Liz Hutchings, Michael Johnson, Ben Mackay, and Jeff Thompson, Consultants

DATE: 5 March 1998

RE: Choosing the right dog for you

Thank you for entrusting us with choosing the right breed of dog for you. As you requested, we have considered your living arrangements and your wants. As we understand your situation, you have a one-bedroom apartment with a small fenced-in yard. You would like a dog that is active but can go a couple of days without being exercised. The canine candidate must be moderately sized, good with your nieces and nephews, and not too much trouble to take care of. Using your specifications, we broke down the criteria into four main groups:

1. **Size**   Is the dog small enough to be content in a small house with a small yard?

2. **Activity**   Is the dog active and energetic enough to take jogging every once in a while?

3. **Maintenance**   How much attention must be given to cleaning up, grooming, and medical needs?

4. **Temperament**   Does the dog have a friendly disposition, and is it gentle with children?

With these categories in mind, we researched the different breeds of dogs and narrowed our choices to the following four:

- The Dachshund (Smooth-haired)
- The Labrador Retriever
- The Cavalier King Charles Spaniel
- The Cairn Terrier

We then rated these breeds against each criterion on a scale of one to four, with 4 representing the highest possible score and 1 representing the least. The results for each category were then tallied, the highest score indicating the most suitable breed for you.

The Dachshund (Smooth-haired)

The Dachshund, sometimes referred to as "the wiener dog" for its likeness to a hot dog on legs, is a short, long-bodied animal, originally bred in Germany as a hunting dog (*dachshund* literally means "badger dog," named so for its hunting instincts). The average Dachshund stands about 9 inches tall and weighs about 25 pounds. The Dachshund's size makes it ideal for the small home and yard. Because the Dachshund was bred originally as a hunting dog, it is energetic and lively, but it is not an ideal running companion due to its short legs. An attractive feature of the Smooth-haired Dachshund is its coat—it is odorless, impervious to mud and rain, and requires virtually no grooming. On the other hand, the Dachshund's long body makes it prone to back injuries that may require occasional medical attention. Finally, we must consider the Dachshund's temperament, which is usually agreeable with familiar adults but tends to be disagreeable with young children.

TABLE 1. SCORES FOR THE DACHSHUND (SMOOTH-HAIRED).

Criteria	Score
Size	4
Activity	2
Maintenance	3
Temperament	1
Total Score	**10**

The Labrador Retriever

The Labrador was originally bred in Britain and is a real "people dog." The average Labrador stands 22 inches tall and weighs about 66 pounds. Because of its large size, this dog may feel confined in a small house and yard. Although the Labrador may seem too big for your living and playing area, it would make an ideal exercise companion. Unfortunately, missing a few days of exercise during those times when your schedule proves hectic would not serve the dog well. The Labrador requires daily vigorous exercise. The dog is easy to maintain as far as grooming goes, but its large size and active personality might lead to muddy footprints and spilled Kool-Aid. Unquestionably, the Labrador's love for people makes it a strong contender. It is gentle with children and would make an excellent playmate for your nieces and nephews.

TABLE 2. SCORES FOR THE LABRADOR RETRIEVER.

Criteria	Score
Size	2
Activity	3
Maintenance	3
Temperament	4
Total Score	**12**

The Cavalier King Charles Spaniel

The Cavalier King Charles Spaniel belongs to one of the "toy" dog breeds and will only grow to be about 18 inches tall. This compact size makes it an excellent choice for a small home and yard. The Cavalier King Charles Spaniel is surprisingly active for its small size and would make a delightful jogging companion. The dog does not tire easily and loves the outdoors. The only major drawback of the spaniel is that it demands a fair amount of grooming; its long coat requires regular washing and brushing. The spaniel also has notoriously weepy eyes that must be constantly cleaned. Despite the trouble of maintaining this dog, its temperament is excellent. It is gentle, affectionate, obedient, and loves being around people of all ages. Unfortunately, your needs require lower maintenance than this breed demands.

TABLE 3. SCORES FOR THE CAVALIER KING CHARLES SPANIEL.

Criteria	Score
Size	4
Activity	4
Maintenance	1
Temperament	4
Total Score	**13**

Cairn Terrier

The Cairn Terrier is a relatively small dog with an average height of about 15 inches, making it a perfect size for your living space and yard. This Scottish hunting dog (immortalized by Toto in *The Wizard of Oz*) is active, enjoys the outdoors, and has a natural sporting instinct. The Cairn loves exercise and would make an energetic jogging partner but would suffer no ill effects from occasionally missing a daily outing. The Terrier requires little maintenance, except an occasional haircut to keep it in good "shape." Finally, the affectionate and loyal dog adores people, making it ideally suited for your situation.

TABLE 4. SCORES FOR THE CAIRN TERRIER.

Criteria	Score
Size	4
Activity	4
Maintenance	3
Temperament	4
Total Score	**15**

Recommendation

The Cairn Terrier rates highly in all four categories, scoring a total of 15 points. It meets all of your requirements in a way that the other breeds do not: it has appropriate size, its activity patterns fit your lifestyle, it is practically maintenance free, and it is gentle and affectionate to people of all ages. Please refer to the table below for a summary of all breeds and their scores.

TABLE 5. SUMMARY OF TOTAL SCORES FOR THE DIFFERENT BREEDS.

Breed	Score
The Dachshund (Smooth-haired)	10
The Labrador Retriever	12
The Cavalier King Charles Spaniel	13
The Cairn Terrier	15

Thank you again for your business and enjoy your new pet!

Instructor's Note: The graphic illustrations — of the four different breeds of dogs — submitted originally with this report have been removed to conserve space.

(USED BY PERMISSION.)

Making Oral Presentations

Oral presentations, briefings, and demonstrations are as important in work situations as written reports, and sometimes more so. They give people a chance to hear a living, breathing person, sense personal attitudes, see samples of items being discussed, and ask and answer questions.

Writing Versus Speaking

Good oral reports borrow some features of good writing, but not all. Good reports, both written and oral, share these features:

- they are clear in purpose
- they are adapted to the audience
- they are clearly organized

However, an oral report designed as a spoken version of a written report can be very ineffective. Consider these differences:

- Readers can handle higher levels of complexity in content, organization, and language than listeners.
- Readers can tune out and tune back in without losing content. They simply review, then pick up where they left off. When listeners tune out, they can't go back.
- Readers have visual clues to organization and to connections between details through headings, paragraph breaks, and white space. Listeners have none of these. They rely on the presenter to give cues to connections and emphasis.

Even so, speakers have advantages that writers don't have. The physical presence of speaker and audience; the speaker's voice, gesture, manner, and movement; and visual aids such as physical objects, charts, transparencies, posters, computer presentations, and slides all create opportunities for effective communication that can't be duplicated in writing.

Guidelines for Successful Oral Presentations

To utilize the above advantages and make up for the difficulties audiences have paying attention and comprehending, follow these guidelines:

- *Relate your purpose to the audience.* Audience can influence purpose. Consider your audience's wants, interests, expertise, attention span, and age. Then find ways to make your purpose clear and pertinent to that audience.
- *Know the constraints* of time, location, room size, and equipment.
- *Plan a simple structure.*
- *Give listeners an opening* that identifies the problem or background, states your purpose, and forecasts the points you'll cover.
- *Use aids to memory, understanding, and attention.* Use **transitions** so that listeners can follow the progression of your presentation. Use **visual reinforcements** such as charts, overhead transparencies, handouts, drawings, physical objects, computer demonstrations, slides, and graphs. Choose these visuals for each presentation carefully; a variety of factors — room size, light levels, noise levels, type of information to be shown, colors used, and so forth — can, and do, influence the effectiveness of these aids. Put complex material in handouts or charts so listeners can survey it, but interpret such materials so listeners notice the main conclusions to be drawn.
- *Rehearse your presentation* so you can know exactly what you'll say and how long it will take (leave a little spare time — you'll ad lib under the pressure of the real thing). Make sure that all audio-visual devices are working properly and that seating arrangements are appropriate. A rehearsal will help you overcome content anxiety and help you talk like a real person to real people.
- Remember that *you are the most important visual reinforcement* the audience has. Pay attention to your dress, grooming, voice, and eye contact. Without overdoing it, use eye contact, voice, and movement to engage the audience and emphasize your points.

Delivery

Most presenters feel nervous, but the best presentations are given by people who appear to be relaxed and confident. Thorough preparation reduces nervousness. Rehearsing also does so. Ironically, sheer anxiety keeps some people from rehearsing; but after good preparation, no other factor can improve your presentation more than a run-through can.

Last-minute nervousness can be released by inhaling and exhaling deeply a few times.

Dress to the occasion. Clothes convey subtle messages to the audience about your character, your respect for them, and your social sensitivity. If you're in doubt, wear something that can be made more or less formal by adding or removing accessories such as a coat and tie for men, scarf or jacket for women.

As a presenter, you are not the topic of your briefing, but the medium through which your topic is conveyed. Immerse yourself and your audience in your topic. Avoid theatricality, irrelevant humor, and cheap gags.

INSTRUCTOR'S GRADING SHEET: ORAL REPORT

Reporter or Group #_____

Subject of Report _____

CHARACTERISTICS	EXCELLENT	GOOD	POOR
APPEARANCE: appropriate dress and grooming			
BEHAVIOR: confident attitude, effective use of hands, natural movement, good eye contact			
VOICE: proper pitch, volume, tempo, enunciation			
ORGANIZATION OF REPORT *Introduction:* clear indication of the subject and how the material regarding that subject will be presented *Body:* clear pattern of development, main points clearly distinguishable, effective and logical transition between main points, significance of facts and inferences shown *Summary/Conclusion:* clear, concise, drawn from information presented			
AUDIO-VISUAL AIDS: sufficient number, size, quality, clarity; relevance to subject; proper type			
AUDIENCE: relevance of subject to audience, awareness of level of knowledge, use of appropriate language, response to questions			
TIME: subject was properly limited for the allotted time			

ADDITIONAL COMMENTS:

GRADE: _____/_____ = _____
         (points)   (A, A-, B+, etc.)

Working in Collaboration

Why Collaborate?

Some instructors of this course may ask you to do a project that requires collaboration. For students of the natural and physical sciences, this seems a logical requirement — after all, much of their work and the resulting reports can be and are completed collaboratively. Students of the humanities, though, may find it difficult to give up autonomy; indeed, the creative nature of the work at times demands that you work alone. Nevertheless, much of the work in the humanities gets accomplished when the ideas, experiences, skills, and direction of many are brought together. Graphic designers must often work with advertising writers and marketing strategists; teachers of art should certainly seek the input of others in the field to develop new teaching strategies; and those in theater and film can hardly work independently from directors, actors, and technicians.

The collaborative process may vary from one work place to another. It can include writing, but does not necessarily have to. Because this is a writing class, however, your instructor will probably require you to produce a report as a result of your collaboration. If so, you and every member of your group will most likely complete some of the writing tasks.

Some brief ideas from educators on why we should engage in collaborative experiences follow:

- Lisa Ede and Andrea Lunsford, in reporting on the results of their writing survey of men and women in the sciences (admittedly, not the humanities), claim that of the 44% of the time these people spent in writing-related activities, 87% of that time was spent working as a team member (60). They also say that their research "could not tell [them] why prohibitions against collaborative writing in the humanities have remained so strong or why the assumption that writing is a solitary activity has been so deeply and broadly accepted by English teachers" (12).

- Kenneth Bruffee believes that we (and our knowledge and feelings) are a product of how we interact with our community and that because of this, writing is indeed a collaborative venture (640–42). Linda Brodkey concurs: "Writing is a social act," and "People write to and for other people," and yet, we still "do not easily picture writers in social settings" (54).

- M. L. J. Abercrombie, a British researcher, discovered that when students participated in groups, they learned "faster and more reliably" than students who worked individually (qtd. in Weiss 33).

What Can Collaboration Accomplish?

Many who have participated in collaborative learning list the following as some of the advantages:

- producing a high-quality document
- spreading the workload
- obtaining and using joint knowledge and experience
- having a variety of approaches
- acquiring a better audience awareness
- writing a more accurate text

What Problems Can Collaboration Present?

Not all collaborative experiences end in success. The very nature of collaborative writing creates some problems, including:

- the lack of a consistent style throughout the document
- the need for additional time (because with a group it simply takes more time to coordinate and carry out different phases of the project)
- a nonequitable division of work (and even a *perceived* notion of unequal work loads)
- getting bogged down in minor points and problems
- getting caught up in personality conflicts
- a poor performance by one or more members of the team

How Can Collaborative Groups Be Organized?

Different groups function differently. A strategy that works well for one group may not work at all for another. Be that as it may, you may wish to consider some suggestions about group structure and writing patterns before you begin your project. Ede and Lunsford set forth two *modes* of collaboration (Killingsworth and Jones designate these as *models*). These are the

- *dialogic mode or integrated-team model*: all group members participate fully in the writing process; process is interactive; roles remain flexible; the writing process is recursive rather than linear.
- *hierarchical mode or division-of-labor model*: all work is parceled out and supervised by a group leader; group members perform prescribed tasks; the writing process is linear rather than recursive. (qtd. in Morgan 540)

In addition to these two modes, Meg Morgan suggests four *organizing patterns* to draft a collaborative document:

- The group divides the task, and each member assumes responsibility for drafting a different part of the document.
- One member assembles group discussion notes and materials and drafts the entire document.
- The group decides that each member will draft a complete document; group members then choose the best draft or parts from the best drafts.
- Group members draft the document together. (540–541)

Morgan points out that "students may fall into organizing patterns rather than choose them" (543). She also stresses that all members of the group *"should be encouraged to participate knowledgeably in the decision-making process, not simply respond to situations or to other group members"* (italics added, 545). This, then, is perhaps the ideal place to talk about how group members should respond to one another in order to achieve the collective potential of the group.

Rebecca Burnett suggests three categories of conflict that arise in collaborative work and tells us which one works to a group's advantage:

- *Affective Conflict*, where disagreements between personalities cause problems
- *Procedural Conflict*, where disagreements about how the group should function cause conflict
- *Substantive Conflict*, where disagreements arise concerning content and rhetorical elements of the project and document (533)

Burnett defines substantive conflict as *"considering alternatives and voicing explicit disagreements* about both content and rhetorical elements such as purpose, audience, organization, support, and design" (534). If group members tend to focus on personality differences (affective conflict) or if they get caught up in arguing over who should do what (procedural conflict), the project can quickly become derailed, create stress, and cause delays in meeting deadlines. On the other hand, substantive conflict, if handled well, can enhance the success and quality of the project and the document.

How Do You Proceed with a Collaborative Project?

In many ways, the collaborative writing project will proceed in much the same way as any individual writing project. You must

- select an appropriately focused topic
- determine what your exact purpose is
- tailor that purpose for your audience
- brainstorm
- map out what you think you will need to support that purpose
- ask yourself if this report will be based on original research (survey analysis, an original analysis of a work of art, an analysis of one's own creative work, etc.) or on library research (exploring comparative meanings in two works of art, an exploration of the historical perspectives present in an art form, etc.)
- gather evidence and data through research (even original research projects have some research involved, perhaps for use as background material)
- analyze and interpret the data
- draft, revise, and edit the paper
- present the final document

The collaborative project will differ in that you will

- organize (or "fall into") a structure for the group
- meet with other group members on a regular basis
- confer in selecting and planning the project
- share responsibilities for a part or all parts of the project as determined by the group
- present one document at the end of the project that represents the efforts of the group as a whole

How Do You Evaluate a Collaborative Project?

During this class, you will probably be required to complete at least one collaborative assignment. At the completion of these tasks, you will evaluate your collaborative experience and the work of other members of the group. To do this effectively, you should consider the ideas listed below before you begin to fill out the Peer Evaluation form that follows this section.

Sharon Brehm and Saul Kassin present some interesting theories on the social/psychological behavior of individuals when they find themselves involved in community or group situations. While these authors apply *bystander effect* ("the more bystanders there are, the less likely the victim will be helped") and *diffusion of responsibility* ("the belief that others will or should intervene") specifically to situations related to victims of violent crimes (315-318), they seem relevant to collaborative functions also: the more group members there are, the less likely it is that all students will participate in the group project or take responsibility for group functions.

Brehm and Kassin discuss *social loafing* — "a group-produced reduction in individual output on simple tasks where contributions are pooled" — when they talk about collective processes. They find social loafing to be "alive and well." They believe, though, that "social loafing is reduced or eliminated entirely when participants believe that their individual contributions are identifiable . . . or if they think their effort is uniquely necessary for the group to succeed . . . [or if] people regard the task as personally relevant, [or] challenging" (493–94).

These authors also talk about *cooperation vs. competition*, saying that "in general cooperation is matched by cooperation in return, while competition provokes competitive reactions" (517). Even though your group may, indeed, be "cooperative," you still may have to develop *bargaining and negotiating skills* (but to a lesser extent, perhaps, than if your group functioned only competitively).

M. M. Bahktin talks about how a "struggle between different conceptual systems . . . creates new elements and . . . understanding"; Olga Dysthe calls this *"dialogism,"* and extends this to include writing in the classroom, where "the interaction of writing and talk facilitates learning" (Dysthe 391).

Recency effect, or the focusing on what happened most recently to the exclusion of what happened some time ago, tends also to bias an evaluation. You may need to think carefully of the "big" picture (what did a group member do over the entire course of the project?).

What Are Your Responsibilities?

In addition to the information you read above, please consider the following concepts.

J. Blake Scott links *ethics* to writing (a form of rhetoric), pointing out that we make more of (he quotes Ornatowski) "efficiency, effectiveness, and usefulness" in our writing to produce action, while making little of "responsibility" (190). He gives Steven B. Katz's example of how Hitler used rhetoric to produce action in a very expedient way, and then asks if this is the kind of action we should have in mind. He believes, like David Dobrin, that ethics must be inherent in the writing curriculum (189).

Your collaborative experience(s) are not only about writing, but also about your interactions with your group. Please consider that you have an *ethical responsibility* to your team *in all of its functions.* Remember that *you,* as a member of a group, are in large part responsible for the success or failure of the entire group. Remember that your presence, your ideas, your guidance, and your work are absolutely necessary to other members of your group.

PEER EVALUATION FOR COLLABORATIVE PROJECT   Your Name _____   Date_____

Evaluate the other members of your group; do *not* evaluate yourself. Do so honestly, carefully, and ethically, and consider the concepts given in the collaboration section of your text as you complete this evaluation.

QUALITIES TO EVALUATE	PTS POSS	NAME OF PEER ___	NAME OF PEER ___	NAME OF PEER ___	NAME OF PEER ___	NAME OF PEER ___	NAME OF PEER ___
Attended **all** *scheduled meetings*	4 ▶						
Active **contributions** *to group project:*							
• helped solve problems	3 ▶						
• helped introduce new concepts/ideas	3 ▶						
• accepted/carried out responsibilities on time	3 ▶						
• understood own role/function in group	3 ▶						
• understood group priorities/processes	3 ▶						
Interaction *with group members*							
• understood others' viewpoints	3 ▶						
• negotiated differences	3 ▶						
• helped in making decisions; supported them	3 ▶						
• allowed for the input/ideas of others	3 ▶						
Attitude *toward project/group members*							
• enthusiastic, motivated, cooperative, pleasant	3 ▶						
• helped *you* to remain motivated	3 ▶						
• helped *you* understand new concepts	3 ▶						
Based on **overall** *performance throughout project, would you want to work with this person again?* No = 1-4 pts.; **Maybe** = 5-7 pts.; **Yes** = 8-10 pts.	10 ▶						
ENTER TOTAL POINTS GIVEN PER NAME ▶	50 poss						
If you answered "no" or "maybe" to the last question above, please provide specific reasons why (in 2-3 sentences).							

PART 2

Problems in Aesthetic Discourse

People who write about the arts and humanities have more credibility when they understand the core problems in art discourse. These problems involve the nature and status of art, the nature of interpretation, theories of art's value, and issues of critical evaluation. The following discussions are designed not as exhaustive treatments, but as starting points for thinking carefully about these problems.

Interpretation

Interpretation Is Many Things

Interpretation is one of our most common and inescapable activities. A friend interprets a remark that could be taken in several different ways, readers interpret passages in the Bible, a judge interprets the law, actors interpret characters when they enact a play, a market researcher interprets results of a survey, students interpret what a professor really wants in an essay question, other students interpret a difficult passage in Kant, and a pianist interprets a composition in playing it. Obviously, the term *interpretation* means different things, but most of these involve perceiving complex data, seeing relationships, and inferring meaning. In this light, few things we do are free of interpretation.

Few tasks seem to make students more nervous than to be told to interpret something. Why such anxiety? Probably because they feel put on the spot and believe their teachers are looking for one correct, hidden meaning. Perhaps students sense that interpretation involves seeing all the possibilities in a text or art work and synthesizing them into a single distillation. Perhaps they sense that discussions of interpretation often involve power struggles over who thinks correctly and what view of things will prevail.

Interpretation and Possibilities

Even a short poem like this one by William Blake can stump anyone who wants to come up with one meaning.

> O Rose, thou art sick!
> The invisible worm,
> That flies in the night,
> In the howling storm,

Has found out thy bed
Of crimson joy,
And his dark secret love
Does thy life destroy.

Is the poem about a real rose blossom that, on closer inspection, Blake found to be infested? Even if so, what makes it interesting—the single instance or the implication that the instance stands for a pattern of disillusionment in life? Is the poem a curse hurled at life, or at a particular person, or at a concept that Blake distrusted (rationality, perhaps)? Is it about the worn-out conventions of poetry, here symbolized in the rose, together with an implicit call for a new kind? Is it a rejection of the late eighteenth-century reverence for nature, the speaker now seeing nature itself as fallen and diseased? Is it a rejection of romantic love as a richly deceptive kind of beauty? A rejection of sexuality? A record of a bad dream? A depiction of British society and institutions in the 1790s, or of European civilization, or of the French Revolution and the ensuing terror?

In light of Blake's thinking, his historical situation, and the circumstances of the poem's composition and publication, some of these interpretations are more probable than others. But quite often, the correctness of one interpretation over another can't be demonstrated. Even a simple text is really many different ones.

Perspectives and Dimensions

Let's view the act of interpretation from several viewpoints to help us understand it better:

1. As with the term *art*, *interpretation* refers to different things, and we might be better served by having different terms for them. It can mean translating from one language to another, analyzing data from an experiment, getting a sense of what a poem literally says (who is the speaker, and what is he or she saying to whom?), inferring the implications, perceiving a symbolic or covert meaning in a poem, playing a musical number, assessing clues to a crime, and gazing at an abstract painting.

2. Most of these have one thing in common—the solution or meaning isn't immediately obvious to everyone. Interpretation must take into account the obvious but tries to go beyond it. That being the case, interpretation will involve inferences based on evidence. Given the nature of the guesswork, inferences, and evidence in art, interpretations *will* vary from one person to another.

3. Interpretation looks in two directions through the medium of the person interpreting: it looks at the artifact or text, and it looks at the audience for whom the interpretation has been formulated. All of these elements—artifact, interpreter, audience, and also occasion—affect interpretation, although much interpretation pretends that only the artifact governs the process.

4. We can differentiate kinds of meaning-making by stipulating that *personal significance* refers to private feelings, thoughts, and associations that a work of art triggers in a person. While these thoughts and feelings can be communicated to others, others can't be expected to share them. *Interpretation* refers to those meanings that can be substantiated by evidence in the art work itself, the artist's thought, the times, and other sources of verification. As soon as such interpretations have been spoken to others, they are no longer simply private—they become something for the community to think over, respond to, and evaluate; therefore, interpretation may require that we make our thinking and our evidence clear to others.

5. The possible interpretations of a single work of art reside on a spectrum somewhere between two extreme propositions: *The work or text means only one thing* and *The work or text means all things and everything.* The fact that real readers, including trained critics, disagree destroys the first possibility. The fact that no one consults T. S. Eliot's poem *The Wasteland* to adjust the brakes on a bicycle destroys the second. But deciding which meanings of a single artifact are valid has proved a most difficult problem.

6. Those who argue that interpretations come from people and not from art works tend to forget that art works set limits on viable readings. Interpretations come from the complex relationships *between* people and art works.

7. That being the case, to learn to interpret art is to learn to perceive, analyze, and discuss in a community in accordance with the conventions of that community.

8. The community is not one unified thing. It is made up of practitioners, teachers, patrons, critics, and students, with many points of view. But the community usually has much to teach the amateur about the kinds of interpretation it values and its standards for presenting one.

9. Interpreting according to an artist's or author's intention is, for many contemporary critics, highly problematic on the following grounds. First, we have no direct access to an artist's intentions; rather, we infer them from the work of art. Second, even biographical statements may carry no more weight than inferences drawn from the work of art. Be cautious, then, about making simplistic assumptions about what the biographical artist thought or felt, except when evidence for connecting the two is very strong. Third, when an artist displays or sells a work, he or she places it in a public arena and gives up control over how it will be received. It must stand on its own. Even granting these points, it is still very difficult to construe meaning without saying that it is *someone's* meaning. To solve this dilemma, it is often best to view the artist's intention not as something the artist consciously wanted to accomplish, but something we construe as we read the text, view the art piece, or watch the performance. This *hypothetical intention* sums up, from all the evidence of the piece itself, what the piece seems designed to do. It provides a

whole in terms of which the parts make sense. Then we needn't quarrel over what the actual artist wanted.

10. Interpretations vary not only among individuals and communities, but they vary according to the context in which one places the object to be interpreted. A work of art may take on very different meanings when we first view it knowing very little of its historical background and then see it after having gained much knowledge of the artist's life, other works, and times. Similarly, different theories and schools of art criticism pose different types of questions and draw different corresponding meanings from a text or piece of art. For instance, we can discuss a single painting (or building, sculpture, musical composition, or novel) very differently if we are looking for connections to

- the psychology of the artist
- the materials and techniques common at the time it was created
- the conditions and politics of the social classes that produced and supported it
- the movements, theories, and styles prevailing when it was created
- the social relations of men and women of the time as these appear in the work or as they conditioned the work
- the philosophical, social, political, and religious beliefs of the artist
- the history of the art piece itself—its emendations, corrections, and revisions, as well as its showing, acceptance, and ownership
- historical events, controversies, or other pieces to which a piece responded
- the form or genre of the piece, together with how it maintained or varied the form

11. Each of these approaches may lead to a different interpretation, yet it is possible that none of them may actually conflict with other interpretations. They may be different but complementary. Some pieces, of course, evoke conflicting interpretations, each with well-developed evidence.

That's a lot of information to keep straight. To simplify it, think of the process of interpretation as four elements that influence each other:

- an artifact that lends itself not only to several meanings, but to several kinds of meaning, and which also imposes limits on what one can responsibly say of it
- the interlocking worlds or contexts in which the artifact exists historically (how it refers to the time of its creation), biographically, politically, socially, artistically, economically, and technologically
- an interpreter who brings to the task his or her unique experience, feelings, knowledge, skills, and preferences, as well as the prevailing attitudes and interests of his or her time. Our individual and historical limitations open up potential interpretations, but they also limit us. That is why wide knowledge, honed skills, self-understanding, and awareness of assumptions make us better interpreters.

- a purpose for which, and an audience for whom, the interpretation is offered

Immediate Versus Contextual Interpretations

Your instructor may ask you to write either an unresearched or a researched interpretation, so some discussion of these types may help you. The **immediate interpretation** involves only you and the work itself. This type emphasizes your own interpretation, not the historical and biographical contexts that conditioned the work. Since we experience many works first-hand, without any information other than that provided by the work itself, and with no tools but those we bring to the moment, the immediate interpretation is a common experience and makes a valid assignment.

The term "immediate" is misleading if you think it means instantaneous or uninformed. Your interpretation should result from sustained attention to your subject. Additionally, your interpretation will be already somewhat contextual in that it is influenced by your present knowledge of the art work and artist, as well as by your level of education, family background, national or ethnic culture, age, and gender. But unlike interpretation based on research, an immediate interpretation will draw only on careful examination of the work at hand. Nevertheless, it will still strive to provide the best insights possible.

The **contextual interpretation** involves research into one of the contexts that lend meaning to a piece of art. Let's consider some of the ramifications of historical interpretation. All art is generated within a specific cultural and historical context. To avoid simply catering to our own current needs or biases, we should extend our awareness of the original historical and cultural contexts. Granted, our knowledge of history is not a pure, unmixed set of verifiable facts, any more than our response to a work of art is universal and impersonal. Nor does a historical context lead to only one interpretation. Spectators at the Globe Theatre differed just as much as we do in their response to Shakespeare's plays. Those differences don't negate our need to hear the past speak; rather, they justify us in extending our interests and knowledge. As we expand and listen we gain deeper understanding of the works we enjoy and even of our own place in history. As Northrop Frye explains: "The culture of the past is not only the memory of mankind, but our own buried life, and study of it leads to a recognition scene, a discovery in which we see, not our past selves, but the total cultural form of our present life" (346).

In the contextual interpretation you will explore an art work (or series) from the perspective of its maker, the historical conditions that shaped it, or a framework of interpretation. You will be asking questions like these: Why did this piece appear at this time in history or at this phase of the maker's life? Why did it take the form it did, given these conditions? How does the work reflect the age in which it was created? How does it reflect the man or woman who created it? What was its meaning or value to its original audience? How was it received and what influence did it have on people in general, other artists of the time, or later artists and thinkers? Given a specific theory or school of interpretation, such as Jungian psychology or feminist theory, what meaning does the work carry?

A number of approaches exist for relating an artist to his or her work. Each approach implies theories of history, of psychology, and of art's nature and function. The more you know about the author, the times, and the work, the more possibilities will present themselves as worth pursuing.

Recognize, too, that any work has many contexts, and the contexts you choose will lead toward or away from different kinds of meaning. A reading carried out in terms of aesthetic history will often reveal an artist's intention to follow, vary, refine, or challenge the conventions practiced by other artists at the time. A psychological reading might look for symbolic manifestations of the mind and feelings of the artist. A political reading will reveal class, gender, and racial conflicts that the politics of the time may have ignored or attempted to smooth over. Marxist historical interpretation is especially concerned with the ways in which art expresses and perpetuates the interests and ideologies of both the dominant and struggling classes. Various other historical approaches will show how the work manifests the intellectual, cultural, or religious climate of the day. Or a reading might treat the work as a force in history and show what effect it had. All useful theories lend themselves to richness and subtlety — or to flatness and reductiveness — depending on how thoughtfully and fairly we employ them and how thoroughly we know the work.

Interpretation Problems for Discussion

1. Here is a sonnet, "Surprised by Joy," by William Wordsworth (1770–1850). Would it be possible to interpret this poem more fully if you knew that Wordsworth had a daughter, Catherine, who died June 4, 1812, at the age of four?

> Surprised by joy — impatient as the Wind
> I turned to share the transport — Oh! with whom
> But thee, deep buried in the silent tomb,
> That spot which no vicissitude can find?
> Love, faithful love, recalled thee to my mind —
> But how could I forget thee? Through what power,
> Even for the least division of an hour,
> Have I been so beguiled as to be blind
> To my most grievous loss! — That thought's return
> Was the worst pang that sorrow ever bore,
> Save one, one only, when I stood forlorn,
> Knowing my heart's best treasure was no more;
> That neither present time, nor years unborn
> Could to my sight that heavenly face restore.

Much later, C. S. Lewis wrote *Surprised by Joy*. Do you think he was influenced by Wordsworth? If so, could you explore those influences?

2. Defoe's novel *Robinson Crusoe* has usually been read by boys eager for adventure. It tells of a shipwrecked man on an island who must survive alone for over twenty years. Many Defoe scholars are interested in Crusoe's religious, economic, and political views. They see Crusoe's religious awakening, mental and emotional maturation, and acquisition of wealth on the island as indications of Defoe's opinions. Defoe lived at a time of religious controversy and had convictions of a particular sort. How would you go about ascertaining what kind of religious doctrine and devotion Defoe favored in this novel? How would you determine his views on the respectability of the merchant as a calling in life? How would you substantiate that Crusoe's views reliably represent those of Defoe?

3. Shakespeare's plays have been produced in all kinds of historical dress, including authentic Elizabethan, modern urban, Calypso, African tribal, British Edwardian, cowboy, circus, and futuristic. Each such production lights up different aspects of a play's characters and speeches. Are these productions essentially different plays? Are they Shakespeare? Can any enacted drama avoid being one possible interpretation of a dramatic text, given that every line, character, and event depicted in the text can lend itself to different interpretations?

Defining Art

"I like it, but is it art?"

Which of the items below do you want to call "art," and which do you want to call something else? Can you explain why?

- ❏ a child's sand castle
- ❏ a bronze sculpture in a museum
- ❏ souvenir figurines of Michelangelo's *David*
- ❏ an African mask
- ❏ cave drawings
- ❏ a Rembrandt painting
- ❏ acupuncture
- ❏ a half-time marching band
- ❏ paper airplanes
- ❏ a hummingbird nest
- ❏ a person practicing the piano

- ❏ a piano
- ❏ a concert pianist performing in a hall
- ❏ a quilt on display at a craft show
- ❏ a quilt on a bed under a bedspread
- ❏ a dance performed before an audience
- ❏ dance movements by a person at a dance
- ❏ a Lexus ad on TV
- ❏ paintings on black velvet
- ❏ T-shirt logos

We generally use the term *art* in our conversations to refer to a finely made artifact or skilled performance. The term allows us to communicate readily without having to explain in detail what we mean. Yet when we slow down to specify what we mean, we often find the following problems.

1. Others don't use the term exactly like we do.

2. Our definitions not only favor one kind of artistic medium over another, they differ in the types of definition devices they use (see next page for definition strategies).

3. Historical eras and cultures have differed in what they mean by *art*, and some cultures haven't even had such a term.

4. One may at some point suspect that the category "art" is an artificial mental construct made to designate something upon which we have determined to bestow honored status, and there are both positive and negative consequences of doing so.

The Trouble with Definitions

It helps to know that these problems affect all kinds of definitions. For example, when we speak of *love*, what, precisely, do we mean? And why do we have only one word to designate so many different experiences? Don't the affections and commitments of a parent for an infant differ markedly from those of a brother for brother, daughter for mother, newly-wed wife for husband, fifty-five-year-old husband for wife, thirteen-year-old girl for sixteen-year-old guy, teacher for student, person for God, God for person? Shouldn't there be different terms for each of these? One may also ask, if love exists, where does it exist? If love occurs only in the individual human beings who feel it, doesn't each individual experience love in ways that are to some degree unique to that individual? Then what allows us to apply *love* to all these? We could look for common threads in the experiences mothers have with their children, fiancé with fiancée, and adolescent for movie star; but even then, who gets to say which threads are really common? By the time we're finished, we may end up with a definition so general that it fits other experiences that we don't call *love*. Perhaps we don't really want to develop a precise vocabulary of love because we might lose the flexibility and vagueness the word allows us. Perhaps *art* is the same way.

The purpose for asking these questions is to bring you to a different level of participation in art discourse. At this level, you can recognize the problems of defining ideas, see the strengths and weaknesses of your own point of view, acknowledge the merits and flaws of others, and still make commitments to the kinds of art you value most.

Does Art Exist? Nominalist vs. Realist

So, to begin with, we acknowledge the possibility that there may be no such thing as art, apart from our determination to have such a category of thing in our minds. To grant this possibility moves us toward the position of the *nominalist*, who believes that such ideas are only mental conveniences for talking about things generally, even though no such general thing truly exists.[1] The

---

[1] Our discussion here and of the strategies for defining has been influenced by Margaret Battin and others, *Puzzles about Art* (New York: St. Martin's Press, 1989), 4–8.

nominalist would argue that there is no such thing as "love" or "sports" or "crime," only many individual ideas in individual minds for which we have, for our convenience, created names. The individual examples of these things share only the name we have assigned. The name essentially creates the category.

Suppose we agree with the nominalist. Does that mean that our ideas make no difference? On the contrary. Ideas we create can greatly affect our lives. "Democracy" may not be tangible, but there are nations that follow democratic political principles; and their citizens enjoy very different kinds of lives from those lived under harsh, authoritarian regimes. Might the made-up category "art" also affect how we live and interact? The fact that we have such a concept may be seen as evidence that our culture has determined that art does have a separate existence and important effects. Figuring out when, how, and why the term "art" began to occur in Western civilization is a matter for separate, and very fruitful, discussion.

One advantage of the nominalist position is that it frees one to stipulate definitions. That is, one can say, "All right, perhaps no such thing as art exists out there in such form as we can all agree upon, but I still have an idea of it, and in the present discussion, I shall define it as . . . "

The *realist*, on the other hand, believes that categories like "art" exist in the world and that the mind discovers rather than creates them. For the realist, *art* denotes certain features of objects made or viewed in certain ways. The problem for the realist, of course, is this: if such a general category of thing really exists, why haven't we reached satisfactory agreement on what it is? Perhaps, as in the case with *love*, we have only one word to cover many different concepts. Or perhaps human life is so subtle and complex that we should expect to have difficulty deciding on the precise nature of what we do, see, and know.

Strategies for Defining

Once we have recognized the possibilities in the nominalist and realist positions, the next hurdle is to gain some sophistication in the techniques of defining. If you believe that a dictionary definition says it all, it's time to get a clue. Dictionaries don't pretend to have captured the real nature of the terms they define. What they do offer are concise formulations of how people *use* words.

Definitions differ not just in methods used, but also in assumptions about the nature of reality. For our purposes, we will outline three methods of defining.

Formal Definitions, or Defining a Thing's Nature

The first strategy seeks to identify the essential qualities of a something. *Essential* here refers to qualities that are part of a thing's inner nature. To accomplish this a person examines carefully a number of samples of art and then distills the features that set art apart from other kinds of objects. Suppose we define art this way: "Art refers to objects made or activities performed with great skill for the sake of their beauty rather than their utility." This definition first places art in a class — objects made or activities performed — and then differentiates it from other objects and performances.

Even though formal definitions offer concise and powerful tools for conveying meaning, they often raise problems. The easiest way to expose these problems is to show that

- the definition applies to things known to be outside the topic. For example, an NBA basketball game, a child blowing bubbles, or a good bedtime story could fit the definition above.
- the definition doesn't cover things known to be within the category. For example, primitive art or folk art may not be executed with great skill; a driftwood sculpture isn't "made" in the same sense as a marble statue; a great speech is given for a practical purpose.
- the definition begs for further definition. For example, who gets to say what counts as "great skill," "beauty," and "utility"?

Defining by Trait Sets or Family Resemblances

Those who want to offer formal definitions and find snags like these might give up. What then? The philosopher Ludwig Wittgenstein discovered that people don't define terms with the care that formal definitions imply, yet they still use general terms usefully and skillfully. To do this they seem to have working sets of conditions or traits in mind; when a sufficient number of these have been met, they apply the term. We may call this manner of defining the nonformal or family-resemblance type. It has the advantage of flexibility. Let's say that out of ten commonly accepted conditions for art, four apply to an item under consideration. Then people may feel justified calling an improvisational dance, a painting, an antique hunting horn, and a pile of scrap metal on the floor of a gallery "art," even though there are radical differences in occasion, medium, form, skill, and technique.

One disadvantage of the family resemblance definition is that it gives up the rigor of the formal definition. In its truthful reflection of how most of us use words with a certain degree of play, it seems to forego the possibility of being precise about what a word means.

Here is a short list of traits or conditions we associate with art. Using the family resemblance type of definition, we may exclaim, "Ah! Art!" if, in a given circumstance, only a few of these traits occur:

- well-made
- beautiful
- not mass-produced
- designed to be contemplated rather than used or used up
- set on a pedestal, hung on a wall, or otherwise placed apart for viewing
- performed before an audience
- involves known media or materials: painting, sculpture, drawing, dancing, vocal or instrumental performance
- taught by art teachers, featured in art books, or reviewed by art critics

- indirectly critical of society or expressive of an unusual point of view
- produced by a known artist

Ideological Definition

Let's return now to the nominalist, who holds that "art" merely names an idea that we have determined to make visible in our culture. Let's say that this nominalist looks around the globe and finds that even though every nation, tribe, or culture produces decoration and fine-quality crafts, a given culture may not have concepts or terms coinciding with what we call "art." Our nominalist then argues that understanding the way people define "art" provides only a half step toward full comprehension of the term. To take the full step, we must know why it matters to a culture to have a term such as "art" and what groups and classes benefit from the concept and practice of art. We then notice that not all groups benefit from or take part in art to the same extent. These groups and their incentives have changed over time. In Renaissance Europe, the fine arts of music, sculpture, and painting were largely commissioned, either by the church or by the social and political elite. Today the world of art has expanded to include corporations that sponsor and buy art, universities that teach and promote it, foundations that fund and promote it, and governments that offer grants, but art discourse still serves the purposes of those most involved in promoting and preserving the arts. At any given moment, art is whatever the art world thinks it is.

Have you ever wondered whether the best artists are really the best known, whether there are discrepancies in the prices placed on one artist's works over those of another, whether it's not what you know but who you know, whether movements and counter-movements are ever created from economic or egotistical motives? If so, you have been thinking about the art world's making—we might even say manipulating—of the category "art."

Of course, not all participants in the art world agree with each other. They hold all kinds of contrary definitions, and they use all the techniques of defining we have covered in this discussion. One of their most important activities, however, is the actual production of whatever they conceive of as art. The goal of their discourse is to keep the public receptive to the importance of art (and so guarantee a market) and to the changes of direction, movements, manifestoes, traditions, rebellions, conventions, and excesses of the contemporary scene.

Ideological approaches to the definition of art help us understand how art discourse functions within a society, but it has its drawbacks. In focusing on commercial and class interests it can shrink art into a crass business. Yes, art is business, and art means money. But is that all? The ideological approach has difficulty explaining why, in different societies, men and women have been passionately devoted to the arts when their passions have often led to poverty and neglect. It also has difficulty accounting for the continuity in art criticism—the fact that in spite of some obvious differences, thinkers from Aristotle to today have discussed art in similar ways.

Does Defining Art Matter?

If you aren't bothered by what others think of your taste in wall decorations or music, art's definition won't matter to you either, unless you start to defend your choices. You might insist that to worry about taste reveals more snobbery than aesthetics. If you sit at home and say, "I'll put whatever I want on my walls, and that's that," then talking definitions won't matter much. With any luck, people will leave you in peace. But once you start explaining why you like your soda-can pop-top wall hanging, your definitions of art will matter. You'll be taking part in the art world, and you might as well know what you think art is and why so many opinions are possible.

In the community sphere, the way people define art has great impact. Who selects the art that will be displayed in galleries, performed at the opera house, featured on TV programs, placed on city hall's walls, taught in schools, reviewed in magazines and newspapers, funded by grants, and bought for display in public buildings? Someone does. Whenever committee members select art for display in a building or support an artist with money (perhaps from your taxes), they bring their criteria into play. If you believe that the art a society sponsors reflects that society but also affects it, then defining art certainly does matter.

Critical Evaluation

In the last section we considered what qualifies an object as a work of art. In this one we focus on how we decide how good a piece of art is. Notice that when many people call something art, they already imply that it is of a certain quality. But in this section we assume that there may be good and bad art. On what basis do we evaluate?

In some cases, our judgment occurs so immediately and instinctively that conscious reflection seems unimportant. People will say, "I can't explain why; I just like it." To enter into conversation about such judgments, we must interrogate our responses and ask what assumptions they reflect about aesthetic accomplishment. Critical evaluation ranges from the strictly personal preferences to those intended for dissemination and discussion in the art world. At the one extreme, you have the right to like whatever you want and to state your preferences. In this class, we want to elicit the reflective response intended for dissemination and discussion because this kind generally must take into account a deeper knowledge of art, art history, and art theory.

Critical evaluation may involve many factors, including individual taste, our own level of skill and education in an art form, awareness of the difficulty of working in certain materials, knowledge of the history of an art form, knowledge of the current state of an art form, intuitions about what is original and what is merely conventional, and evaluation of the personal and social effects of a piece of art.

Where Is Beauty?

We can't consider in detail the difficulties posed by each of these factors, but we can discuss one standard of critical evaluation, beauty, that reflects the problems we have in applying other standards.

If you've ever stopped liking a piece of music after being passionately fond of it, what has changed? Is the difference only in you? Or has the piece changed, too? Do you really listen to the same thing now that you heard before? Suppose you lived in a remote village and thought the homes there unremarkable and even ugly. A famous architect travels through your village and declares that your houses are a major contribution to domestic architecture in their synthesis of form and function. After several books feature photos of your village, you and your neighbors begin to admire your homes and talk proudly of the local heritage. What has changed? Are the houses more beautiful than they were?

These questions involve the nature of beauty. Some philosophers view beauty and ugliness as intrinsic and enduring elements within things, created by proportion, unity, harmony, and magnitude. Other thinkers have argued that beauty and ugliness refer to a response within us which may change from time to time as we respond to sensory stimuli. Do beauty and ugliness designate something in objects and in nature, or do they merely convey our approval or disapproval? The question is a tricky one because neither can exist without the other: beauty and ugliness are relative terms and entail each other. Besides, an inner response needs some kind of stimulus to trigger it, and not all kinds of stimuli evoke a response we feel like calling beauty. If beauty exists in certain kinds of order and harmony in external objects, what would be the point of saying so if there weren't a faculty in us that responded with pleasure to such order and harmony? It would be rather like saying that something has two cubic feet of volume or that its temperature is 102 degrees.

A clearer view of beauty emerges when we consider both aspects, the internal aptitude to respond with pleasure to certain kinds of stimuli and the qualities of objects that trigger the response and make it possible to talk of the piece itself without continually mentioning the pleasure it evokes. A similar dynamic relation between perceiver and object occurs in other ways of asserting art's quality and importance.

Art for Art's Sake

Another way of valuing art is to detach it from all functions and practical applications. The phrase "art for art's sake" expresses this view. It was coined in the nineteenth century by those who wanted to keep society (anyone who didn't already agree with the artist's freedom) from imposing its expectations on art. Rather, artists declared that they must be free to produce art without interference from those who wanted it to teach conventional morality, instill respect for authority, and uplift with safe beauty. These proclamations placed the artist in a privileged position. Since those others, who mustn't interfere, were still expected to pay for the art and thereby provide financial support for artists, it seemed rather arrogant for artists to insist on having this freedom. So what does "art for art's sake" mean? If it means that art should be produced without any market influences, then perhaps it is fair to request that artists not benefit from the market, either. If artists want to insist on their freedom, it is fair to ask them how their freedom benefits society in less direct ways.

If "art for art's sake" means that art has value apart from reference to the humans who make, enjoy, and learn from it, we are led into an absurdity, since humans make art because they like to. So perhaps we should start by finding out how one can say that art exists for art and not for some other end. Some theorists would say it means that art has a special kind of utility that can't be measured by ordinary standards of usefulness: it feeds innate human desires for beauty and for representations of all facets of experience—whatever humans see, think, imagine, and feel—and it creates cultural excellence, the kind by which a society will be measured by future generations.

In some cases the phrase means that art gives a special kind of enjoyment called aesthetic pleasure, which is asserted as something other than mere enjoyment. If we could say precisely what enjoyment is and why we have it, we might be able to solve the problem. Theories of aesthetic pleasure exist because we don't know with certainty what enjoyment is. Even if art brings enjoyment above all, the question remains, what is the value of this kind of pleasure?

Art and Other Values

We can also evaluate art by its ability to strengthen other values. Does art teach like a good role model, shape perception like a literal change of vantage point, illuminate like a lamp, reflect like a mirror, adorn like a fine paint job on a classic car? Does art actually convey a higher perception of truth than we ordinarily have? Does it provide unique insights into ourselves or into historical periods from which it dates, and if so, what kind of insights? These questions help us to identify the values by which art can be evaluated. Among the values extrinsic to art itself but which justify it are the following:

The Artist's Feelings and Perceptions

This value entails two propositions: that certain people who become artists have feelings and perceptions that deserve wider dissemination than those of ordinary people, and that some people have greater skill in creating artifacts that express feeling or create it in the viewer. These two areas of skill may or may not be related. The proof lies partly in what the art communicates and partly in how well it does so. The latter is, more strictly speaking, a matter of aesthetic judgment. Of the former, who can say whether a piece actually expresses a particular feeling of the artist? To say so presumes that we know the feelings of the artist and have ascertained that a piece actually does express them.

Truths about the World

Since much art represents human conduct and thoughts in various locations and events, it can safely be asserted that art has all the power to convey the truth of these matters that any representation has. Seldom, though, do art critics pause to mention a corollary—if art can convey truth, it also has the power to distort and falsify. Some would argue that its ability to mix these—fiction, imitation, and distortion on the one hand, and shrewd perception of things as they really are on the other—is the hallmark of art. Allegory, for example, claims to depict general truths through particular stories that are often extremely unrealistic in their makeup. But not all art makes this claim. A painted portrait can certainly convey subtle clues as to character. It is difficult to generalize about the kinds of truth art expresses because each medium has its unique potential for representing (or not representing) the world around us. Stories can convey certain kinds of truth, while a giant mock-up of a hamburger, a prelude, an abstract sculpture, and a ceramic vase can convey others.

The Truth of Perception

Those uncomfortable asserting that the novel *Catch 22* offers a truth about people in general or World War II specifically may be more receptive to the idea that it offers the truth of how World War II appears to a certain group of people as told from a given point of view. Art, then, expands our horizons by helping us perceive as others do. We no doubt benefit from seeing the world from other people's points of view. This experience should make us more tolerant. However, the mere proliferation of points of view may or may not make a person better. At some point, the mature thinker will start to evaluate points of view for their comprehensiveness, accuracy, and usefulness.

Aesthetic Experience

Many artists say there is unique kind of value in hearing a favorite Beethoven symphony, viewing a van Gogh painting, or reading Henry James. We can call this the aesthetic experience. When a person's thoughts and feelings are wrapped up in experiencing a work of art, the fusion of content and form influence that person positively. If that is so, may some artworks also disharmonize a person? Or is there some intrinsic and simply positive relation between aesthetic structures and their effects on viewers?

Art and Society

How do art and artists contribute to society apart from the functions of teaching, beautifying, and contributing to economic exchange, as discussed above? Should everyone consider himself or herself an artist, or is it natural and good for certain people to form a separate class of artists? How, apart from the ability to support themselves by producing art that others buy, does one qualify as an artist in the eyes of society?

Art and History

The art of the past provides historical understanding. When we study past societies, particularly those that left no written records, we depend largely on their carvings, pottery, weaving, drawings, and statuary. Even when we have written records, as in the case of classical Greece or medieval Europe, we derive additional understanding from painting, music, and architecture. Additionally, present depictions of history have power to shape our awareness of the past and keep it alive. But, as with art and truth, that power works both ways. Oliver Stone's movie *JFK* distorts many of the documented facts of

Kennedy's assassination. What value does the film have as history and as art? What if we then move to the idea that history itself is not one thing but competing, selective representations of past events made for their usefulness to the present? Then both art and history share in being "made" things that give partial glimpses of a complex world that eludes a single attempt to represent it.

Art and Religion

Although many art lovers despise didactic art, some of the most treasured art of medieval and early modern Europe was produced under religious sponsorship for the purpose of teaching church doctrine and instilling reverence and faith. Churches today also commission murals, paintings, choral works, and buildings to reinforce the beliefs of their followers. And, of course, many artists and writers of deep religious conviction reveal their beliefs in their works. Both church-sponsored and privately initiated artworks vary greatly in the degree to which they express religious belief. Some artists cannot imagine doing anything else; others believe their art suffers when they make it conform to their beliefs or reflect the expectations of other believers, so they immerse themselves in the aesthetics of their creations and let the art take them where it will. The variation raises legitimate questions about the relations between aesthetic form and expressive intention and about the relative superiority of didactic and non-didactic art. It also raises questions about the role of conviction and inspiration in artistic integrity. Does a person who feels moved upon by a divine spirit produce superior artifacts? Or is the talent for artistic creation quite a separate matter from inspiration? And what about sincerity and integrity? Contrast two painters, both monks. One lives a scandalous life and has a son, the other observes the rules of his order. Which one paints more sublime religious art? There actually lived two figures, Fra Filippo Lippi and Fra Angelico, father and son, respectively. Could the fact that Fra Angelico lived a more saintly life have affected the reception of his paintings as more excellent portrayals of religious subjects and religious conviction?

Art and Morality

The central concern here is how art affects the ethical standards, attitudes, and actual behavior of individuals and society. One aspect of this concern takes us back into the relations between art and what it expresses. Another takes us into the question of appropriate content. Compare today's PG-13 film with a film of the 1950s and you'll notice quite a difference in language, display of the body, and treatment of physical affection between people. Do the changes simply reflect changes in society's sexual morality, or did films help bring about changes in society's standards? How would you explain art's role in suggesting and preserving correct moral standards and, at the same time, serving as critique of society's morality?

Occasionally, an artist will disavow all the high-sounding, trendy talk about his or her art. Giovanni Papini records an interview in which Pablo Picasso, looking back over his career, reflected:

The "refined," the "rich," the professional "do-nothings," the "distillers of quintessence" desire only the peculiar, the sensational, the eccentric, the scandalous, in today's art. And I myself, since the advent of cubism, have fed these fellows what they wanted and satisfied these critics with all the ridiculous ideas that have passed through my head.

The less they understood, the more they admired me!

Through amusing myself with all these farces, I became celebrated, and very rapidly.

For a painter, celebrity means sales and consequent affluence.

Today, as you know, I am celebrated, I am rich.

But when I am alone, I do not have the effrontery to consider myself an artist at all, not in the grand old meaning of the word: Giotto, Titian, Rembrandt, Goya were great painters.

I am only a public clown, a mountebank. I have understood my time and have exploited the imbecility, the vanity, the greed of my contemporaries. It is a bitter confession, this confession of mine, more painful than it may seem, but it, at least and at last, does have the merit of being honest. (qtd. in Garth)

What qualities do you think Picasso saw in Giotto or Rembrandt that he didn't see in himself?

Cases for Discussion

1. Recently, Salt Lake City installed near its downtown library a sculpture designed by a group of high school students and their instructor. The piece depicted the funeral scaffold of the Plains Indians. On top of the scaffold, old rifles were placed with a red sheet folded over them. The group wanted to make a statement against violence and bloodshed. Immediately after its installation, American Indians protested that the sculpture made a sacrilege of their burial customs. Within a week the sculpture was removed. Given the intentions of the designers to recommend the death of firearms, was the protest justifiable? Religious doctrines, leaders, buildings, attire, and symbols such as the cross have often been used in secular art and are often depicted with ridicule. Should all such depictions be protested? When are they legitimate? Did the fact that a student group designed the sculpture make it easier for the city to remove it? What if a well known artist had been paid $100,000 to create it?

2. Colleges have been hotly debating the kind of curriculum they ought to have. Some say that the curriculum has favored the culture of dead, white European and American males. This group wants students to study the art and literature of women, the poor, minorities, Asians, Africans, and others so they learn that no one group has all the answers to life's deep questions. The more traditional camp admits

that the curriculum is selective, and that given all the possible things one might study, all of them with value, colleges have to make a tough choice. The European tradition is the most influential on American culture, and it has extraordinary insights, art, beauty, and wisdom to help students form their opinions and character. Both camps see the power of art. They disagree on how that power should be used. How would you contribute to the debate?

3. In her essay "The Cultural Importance of Art," Suzanne Langer says,

> But art is not practical; it is neither philosophy nor science; it is not religion, morality, or even social comment (as many drama critics take comedy to be). What does it contribute to culture that could be of major importance?
>
> It merely presents forms—sometimes intangible forms—to imagination. Its direct appeal is to that faculty, or function, that Lord Bacon considered the chief stumbling block in the way of reason, and that enlightened writers like Stuart Chase never tire of condemning as the source of all nonsense and bizarre erroneous beliefs. And so it is; but it is also the source of all insight and true beliefs. Imagination is probably the oldest mental trait that is typically human—older than discursive reason; it is probably the common source of dream, reason, religion, and all true general observation. It is this primitive human power—imagination—that engenders the arts and is in turn directly affected by their products. (91-92)

What kind of defense of art's importance is Langer making? Much seems to be riding on the phrase, "It merely presents forms . . . to imagination." How would you explain this phrase?

4. Aristotle pointed out that representations of unpleasant things can please. A painting of a dung hill can please. And what about representations that are themselves deliberately ugly, whether or not the object portrayed is? For example, the twentieth-century painter Francis Bacon depicted scenes in grotesque shapes and in garish colors. Do these paintings have their own kind of beauty? What would make them different from simple ugliness? Does ugliness have its own aesthetic standards?

5. A known poet patches together a series of phrases picked almost at random from articles and ads in one issue of a weekly news magazine. The poem is published. A student does the same thing and receives a low grade in a creative writing class. Who is creating art? What art or skill is at play? What ground rules? What power relationships?

6. A janitor in a modern art gallery leaves a pile of rubbish—bricks, broom handles, mop bucket, and other odds and ends—in a corner of the gallery. A patron sees the pile and hastily makes a sign for it calling it "Swashbuckler." Because of the sign, the other gallery workers leave it there for weeks, where thousands of patrons pause to view it. Is this inadvertent art? When the gallery management find out, what should they do? Remove it? Commission more pieces by the janitor? What is at stake? How would other artists whose works are on display likely respond?

PART 3

Interpreting and Evaluating Art

Introduction: Writing as an Expert

Have you thought of yourself as an expert in your major? In this section we will assume you are one. We don't mean that you need to know everything or that you may adopt a commanding or condescending tone. We do assume that you know enough to contribute to the dialog in your field.

If you think about the types of writing you do in most classes, what we are asking is quite a shift. Even though your major professors want you to become an expert, in college they function as the experts with you as apprentices. They ask you to write not so they can learn from you but so they can evaluate your mastery of their subject matter. In the writing assignments that follow, we ask you to write as one who knows more than your readers. And in fact, because your writing teacher can't master the major fields of all students in your class, you will often know more than he or she does about your topic. The same applies to your wider audience: your fellow students and, beyond them, an intelligent and curious public, may know only modest amounts about music, dance, film, theater, design, and literature. To succeed in these assignments, take seriously your obligation to provide readers with valid, significant, and thoughtful content expressed in ways that average readers can grasp—plainly, concisely, and creatively.

Don't assume that because you know more than your readers do about film directing or Portuguese literature, you can bluff, talk down, get by with easy generalizations, or hide behind difficult vocabulary or technical analysis. Because most people can comprehend much more than they can perform (appreciating a fine poem doesn't mean you can write one), they can easily spot a phony who fails to give clear, informative, and significant knowledge.

In providing significant knowledge to intelligent readers, you face four challenges that all careful writers share.

1. **Depth of knowledge**. When you set out to write about even a single composer or choreographer, much less about a movement or style or

artistic school, you may have to do research in encyclopedias, books and periodicals, textbooks, lecture notes, and the Internet to top off your knowledge before you have enough to offer others.

2. **Perspective**. Your paper will have little reason for existing if you simply repeat and repackage others' ideas. Achieve your own insights and feature them in your paper. And make sure always to give credit to those whose ideas you borrow.

3. **Clarity**. Strive to express information in simple, clear language, so that those who lack knowledge and specialized vocabulary can understand even the most sophisticated and technical content.

4. **Quality and correctness**. Strive to write organized, concise, and coherent essays. Your audience will pay closer attention if you express yourself plainly and economically, and if you use correct grammar, spelling, and punctuation.

The Importance of Audience

Writing must be tailored to its audience. Vocabulary, style, tone, purpose, length, organization, and format must all reflect an awareness of who readers are, what they already know, and what they need. In component one you tailored your writing to audiences in work situations; in this component you'll write as an expert in the art world for the general public. You'll need to keep in mind the knowledge, attitudes, and interests of people who know much less than you even as you hold the interest of those who know more.

This kind of arts and humanities writing varies markedly (a museum art show catalog will sound more objective and formal than a current review). These differences spring from purpose and audience. Whereas readers in academic and work settings usually have to read to do their jobs, public audiences don't. They can choose to skim through a piece of writing or not read it at all. Many students, when asked to write for general audiences, immediately relax and think they can skim the surface. In doing so, they make a big mistake. Readers want depth, but they want it clear, not murky. Don't sacrifice one iota of content, but develop a concern for readers who can throw your work on the floor and watch TV or make a snack instead. This concern shouldn't lead you into sensationalism and sentimentalism but should give you a determination to offer new knowledge, expressed in a manner readers can enjoy.

Some publications contain only writing in which experts talk to experts. In these cases writers can assume that readers already know the vocabulary and background pertinent to a specialized field. The readings in this section come from a different, much more common type of publication, those that cover the arts and humanities for general audiences. By contrast with those publications serving experts only, these publications often maintain a high degree of sophistication in content but adapt it for less expert readers. In reading them, watch for how they express significant content and adapt their material to their audiences.

Brochure Assignment

Arts institutions face a constant struggle—how to lure an often indifferent public, without whose presence the ballet, collection of paintings, lecture series, or concert will fail. And if one event fails, there won't be money to produce the next one. An attractive brochure provides one means of attracting audiences and, once attracted, educating them so they feel they have spent their time wisely. To achieve these goals a brochure must combine substantial content, plain language, and appealing layout.

Purpose

Write a brochure for an actual or projected show, play, exhibition, program of study, museum, collection, conference, or performance. The purpose of the brochure is to invite, inform, and promote. Here are some ideas for a brochure:

- Promote yourself or some project in which you are involved or might become involved.
- Promote a workshop to train others in your performance skills.
- Advertise your services as a producing artist.
- Promote a museum, performing arts program, or course of study.
- Make a brochure to raise funds for a theater, institute, or museum.

Audience Considerations

Your audience will be those who might be enticed to support the activity by attendance and further study. Some of them already have inclinations toward, and some knowledge of, what you are promoting; others need to be attracted to a first-time visit or attendance.

Length and Scope

List all relevant information and details, including contact information (don't forget web sites) and, if pertinent, give a return address and leave space for a mailing address so the brochure can be mailed. Your brochure must include one hundred words of text expressing some type of background, content summary, significance, or interpretation relevant to the project. The brochure should also be your original work, created for this occasion.

Format

Must be a bi-fold, tri-fold, or a brochure with pages. Strive for accessible and eye-appealing format and effective use of white space. Consider employing lists and boxes to convey information, but keep the design simple and open. Organize information according to importance, interest, and logical order. Page layout must make sense to a reader who looks at the first page and then unfolds the brochure. Use fonts (two or three at the most) and font sizes that look good together and signal relevant levels of importance. Photos, illustrations, or other types of graphic support are encouraged. If you borrow graphics, make sure you provide credits and sources somewhere in the brochure.

SAMPLE STUDENT BROCHURE

LEARN THE ART OF
Watercolor

Instructor

Anita Robbins

www.artography.org

2003 COURSE
STEP BY STEP
INSTRUCTION

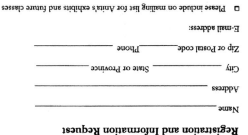

Art Originals, Instruction, Photography
4515 N. 3500 E.
Provo, UT 84604
Phone (801) 310-0000
www.artography.org
Artography@yahoo.com

Cut along dotted line

Registration and Information Request

Name _____

Address _____

City _____ State or Province _____

Zip or Postal code _____ Phone _____

E-mail address:

☐ Please include on mailing list for Anita's exhibits and future classes

Classtimes Planning to Attend:
☐ Tuesday evenings 7-9 pm
☐ Friday mornings 10-Noon
☐ Saturday mornings 10-Noon
Information Requested for
☐ Original Art
☐ Commissioned Art

WATERCOLOR CLASS INFORMATION

Fundamentals of Art through Watercolor Techniques – *Anita Robbins, Instructor*

All levels of skill welcome

Class times:

- Tuesday evenings 7-9pm
- Friday mornings 10-noon
- Saturdays 10-noon

Location:

Classes held in classroom above

Provo Art and Frame

201 W. Center Street, Provo.

Cost:

$40 a month, students can attend as many of the classes they wish in that month. Prepayment of three months is $100.

Enrollment:

Fill out information on back and turn into cashier at Provo Art and Frame with payment or mail payment and information to:

Artography
4515 N. 3500 E.
Provo, UT 84604

Suggested Supplies:

- Brushes: 2-#8 rounds, one needs to have a *great paint* (synthetic works). The second should be made of natural hair for blending. Also a ¾ inch flat brush and a 1½ inch flat brush or mop for wetting large areas.

- Paper: Arches 140 lb cold press watercolor paper.

- Paints: Tube paints preferred. Grumbacher Academy or Graham provides quality at a good price. Suggested colors: **Ultra Marine, Alizarin Crimson, Quinacrodone Gold, Burnt Sienna, Paynes gray, Sepia and Deep Hookers Green**

- Pallet: Pallet with large mixing areas and a lid.

- Accessories: Sponge, blow dryer, mechanical pencil, kneaded eraser, paper towels, and two water containers.

Watercolor Instructional Book

A tutorial page is provided each class session along with personal instruction. Demonstrations and step by step instruction are provided. Guidance centers on personal artistic goals of the students. Students can follow along or work on individual projects. Drawing skills, composition and color theory are discussed in each lesson. The book, *The Work of Art*, can be purchased separately.

Biographical Information

Anita Robbins has studied with watercolor artists: Willie Wong, Marilyn Kinsella, and Tony Couch. She provides art for book covers, cards, and private collections. Robbins works in a variety of mediums particularly enjoying the spontaneity of watercolor. Currently completing study at Brigham Young University for a BA in Visual Art and Minor in English. Her instruction includes a copy her book *The Work of Art*. Her work can be viewed at various exhibits and is sold on ebay.com. Robbins emphasizes techniques in watercolor, drawing, composition, and color theory. She nurtures the personal interpretation and rendition of each student along with support in their own artistic goals.

Personal Narrative Assignment

In this assignment you reveal what happened when you encountered an art work that, in retrospect, helped make you what you are now. The assignment also sets before you a fundamental challenge of good art writing: how to translate the nuances of inner experience into meaningful images that others can share.

Just about anything you write about the arts — reviews, historical interpretations, and formalistic analyses — will indirectly express your inner response to the art piece that is your subject. How else can you make statements about what is important, how a piece engages people, or how its design works to fulfill its purpose or intention?

You also know that others' inner responses to the same art work will differ. Personality traits, levels of education, thinking styles, cultural background, political values, sensitivity, and technical training all subtly influence our experience of the same artistic stimuli (or does each person in a sense encounter different stimuli?). A person who writes about the arts ought to become aware of his or her response tools and the patterns they create, as well as of the way in which others' responses lead to different versions of the same art work. In this way, a writer will express his or her views persuasively and honestly, yet at the same time will show awareness and tolerance of other views.

You can probably think of a novel, musical performance, or art show that gave your life new focus or direction. When you start to describe your feelings and thoughts, though, you may find it difficult to convey them with freshness and authenticity. Write a hasty first draft. By all means write out all you think and feel when you experience a work. Then go back and look for issues and insights that you can expand and express more convincingly. Often, our deepest responses hinge on feelings that others share with us. If you can uncover and express these, you become the link through which others can find greater meaning in the art work.

Purpose

Tell how a piece of art—a poem, dance, sculpture, film, musical composition, or other art piece—affected you at a certain point in your life or how an art work's effect on you has changed over time. Perhaps as you've grown an art work has taken on surprising new meanings. Perhaps it has lost its impact.

Audience Considerations

Address yourself to classmates or to readers of the arts section of a sophisticated magazine or newspaper.

This assignment raises interesting audience issues. You're writing about yourself, so what do you offer other readers? It all depends on what you have to say and how well you say it. Be true to your experience, but keep in mind that others must be able to share in the experience and what you learned from it.

The first time people write this sort of paper, they have a tendency to write "purple patches" loaded with intense effusions of feeling. There's nothing intrinsically wrong with such writing, but it is self-reflective and rarely rewards others' attention. Such writing can be a first step toward a more effective draft that can *elicit* a strong response without the intense vocabulary. Revise, so that your reader responds to the work more than to your feelings. For example, when you want to frighten your friends, you don't tell them how frightened you are. You relate the details of what frightened you so they become frightened also. If you want them to appreciate the beauty of a sunset, you don't simply keep repeating "awesome" and "gorgeous." You paint the scene: "silver trumpets of light pierced the clouds." Keep readers focused on events, people, and the work. Evoke the response.

After selecting the work you want to write about, your next challenge will be to plan how you'll write about it. You might want to describe your life before you encountered the art work, then describe your encounter with the work and finally trace its effect on you. Some narratives concentrate on "life before" and conclude with a powerful discovery; others lead up quickly to the transforming incident so they can concentrate on the work and its effect. Either way, be sure to give the reader enough details and interpretation about the work to make its effect on you understandable.

In planning your essay, use the Personal Narrative Observation Sheet on the next page. It will help you generate images and memories of your encounter with art.

Length and Scope

Consult your instructor on length and deadlines.

PERSONAL NARRATIVE OBSERVATION SHEET

This exercise should help you write your personal narrative or interpretation paper.

Name _____ Date _____

1. Describe briefly your situation. (What work of art? Where and when did this occur? How did you come to be there?) Describe also what your five senses "told" you was present.

2. List *several specific details* you noticed about/within the work itself. Are there any details "missing" in the work that you would expect to be there?

3. Describe your feelings as you experience the work.

4. Write down some important questions that you (or someone else) might ask about this particular work of art. (Explore various questions/approaches. Reach deep.)

5. Make two lists, one of traits of your life before, and one of traits after you encountered this work.

6. Jot down some possible interpretations or *meanings* based on the work itself, the situation, the details, and the impressions mentioned above.

7. If you were to write a narration paper based on the above, what context or contexts (e.g., historical, biographical, aesthetic, philosophical, psychological, or such) do you think you might use to frame it? Which of the details you listed could be *meaningful* given the context(s) you chose? Which could not?

8. Compare this experience to a *dissimilar* experience you have had. Can you find any similar meaning(s) in these disparate experiences?

SAMPLE STUDENT ESSAYS

SAMPLE 1: PERSONAL NARRATIVE

A River Ran Through Me

TIM C. BLACK

Norman and Paul sat on the banks of the Blackfoot River in upper Montana and discussed what they wanted from life. Norman wanted to become a professional boxer. Paul, the younger and more adventurous brother, decided that fly-fishing would suffice. This was the beginning of two boys' lives growing up during the early 1900s. When I watched the portrayal of these two fictitious characters in *A River Runs Through It*, I didn't expect them to affect my reality. I watched the movie only because my friend Greg loved the "awesome" fishing scenes.

During daily fishing lessons, the boys repeatedly heard the words of their father: "Casting is an art that is performed on a four-count rhythm between ten o'clock and two." Their father, a Protestant preacher who believed that even the twelve apostles of Christ fly-fished, professed that fishing was second only to religion in importance. Every day after school the two boys scampered off to tackle the "big water" in order to test their father's instruction. Day by day the brothers grew closer as they fished the river.

* * *

Greg stopped by my house and said: "Hey bro! Let's go slay some fish!" Almost before I could close my books, he dragged me out the door, saying confidently how unlucky the fish must feel. I responded: "You know I can't fish. Why should I tag along?" He ignored me and began babbling something about how "casting is an art form that is performed on a four-count rhythm." I had heard this before. While he assured me that the hip-waders he brought for me would keep me warm and dry, my mind wandered. "I got it!" I exclaimed. "Norman and Paul, right?" Greg smiled.

As we drove up Fairview Canyon, I thought about Paul and how he always repeated, "Nobody who didn't know how to catch a fish should be allowed to disgrace a fish by catching it." I didn't ask Greg what he thought. He possessed the same enthusiasm as Paul. I didn't want to douse his hopes with my negative attitude. He explained to me that sometimes you have to do a roll cast in order to get the nymph right where you wanted it. My ignorance surfaced when I told him that when I fished I used the largest lure I could find so that if I couldn't catch the fish, at least I would scare the hell out of it.

We stepped out of the car into an early fall drizzle. The canyon dripped boredom. I argued that we were the only creatures brainless enough to be out in the rain. Greg shivered with excitement. I shivered with cold. He caught two fish and searched out other prime "holes" before I put on my waders. He asked how long I was going to be "broke down," and then he continued fishing. I cautiously stepped into the water and felt the cold, brisk current. I caught up to Greg. He muttered something about how Paul could shadow cast. I grumbled: "Thank you, Oh Merciful Professor of Trout." He responded by quoting from the movie: "Shadow casting is where he [Paul] could keep his line above the water long enough and low enough to make a rainbow rise." I pictured the scene in the movie.

I remember that while Paul was shadow casting, Norman observed—much like what I did with Greg. But while Norman looked on in awe at Paul's artistry, I looked on with only impatience. Yet the movie stuck in my head. Only then did I recall what Norman said of Paul: "I realized that my brother had become an artist." I thought about this statement and again my mind wandered. My attitude about this fishing trip started to change. I quit thinking about the rain and the cold river, and I was amazed at the new cinematography in front of me.

My pessimism washed away and I valued the company of not only Greg, but Nature as well. I saw how the water cascaded and meandered down the canyon. I smelled the clean, damp air. Raindrops splashed rainbows. And I shared my sunflower seeds with a squirrel. Greg bragged about needing only three more years to learn how to think like a fish, while I offered to unhook the fish so that they could swim free. Greg asked if I had taken the hook from my own mouth. I smiled.

(USED BY PERMISSION)

SAMPLE 2: PERSONAL NARRATIVE

Sunday With Caesar

JEFF WIRTHLIN

Sometime springtime past: amid carnage of unwashed laundry, lying corpse-like, almost dying, filling the room like some cadaverous blanket, a few bodies draped over the desk chair, vining down into the contorted layers like some strange ivy—crumpled cloth.

It doesn't smell bad. Does it?

A small room, clean lines, tan walls warmed yellow by light falling from huge opposing windows. Yes, a pleasant place, when clean. Then the desk surface would make a neat perpendicular, its wood smoothness somehow recalling science fiction. But it now lay buried. Pencils, curling columns of paper, forgotten receipts faded slightly purple, unstamped envelopes, and the harsh creases of institutional statements, turned face down mostly, had seized the surface for days now. They spilled themselves over it. They covered it, seeming almost to replicate themselves in time like some mutant strain of poking, paper-cutting bacteria and unanswered letters.

Where was it?

Somewhere it lay. Somewhere, under the pointed papery layers, lay a bit of colored paper. And perhaps it too had reproduced itself in recent days; now three scraps, yellow, pink or blue, bore the same forgotten wisdom. The kind of scrap that usually bears the scratching of a hurried reference;

the kind that infuriates you sometimes as only it can, causing you to swear violently under your breath, amid rows of books, hushed and dusty, when you realize it forgot to record the call number. The kind of scrap you might have to spit into, should you need to clear your throat, amid the dust and the books, and didn't have a Kleenex.

Where is it?

An empty box of Kleenex sat askew above the paper garbage. Beneath the paper riot, set astir by nervous fingers, near the bottom lay the crunched paper shred. Smeared lead read: To Do—change oil, study physics, O chem, mail letters, Call Sit, read Caesar, clean room, bank, MCAT.

Read Caesar.

Important things bobbed among the wrinkled sea of neglected cloth. Sitting on, almost swallowed by, a too old bed. Scanning the three week clothes for useful flotsam. Important things bobbed up. Reaching: a crumple of green graph papers, stapled thick together, scrawled with formulas and forced conclusions about electric field fluctuations, black dots on a white board, and lines of force drawn backward, which, were they correct, might indicate life as we know it has ceased to exist. And others floated to the surface, bearing markings of the same dull pencil, covered with arrays of spiking carbon backbones and benzene hexagons living between addition signs, following the arrows into greater geometries—sinister markings that resurrect specters of standardized tests. And a crumpled carbon copy, the kind you save someplace in case your car breaks down again within the next 90 days, reminding you about changing oil and overheating in the desert or breaking down on some Nevada highway; the kind of thoughts that set gastric juices stirring in empty stomachs causing breath worthy of divorce or exile in foreign cultures. And at the brown briny carpet bottom, a variety of tax forms, miraculously forming with their layered grey tones a kind of anti-rainbow.

Which one do I use anyway?

Then, there among the jostled tax forms and mixed gastric juice, popped up the little black book. My hands recovered it. Lying back, sinking into the bed, held aloft partly by the elasticity of the blue bed sheet, one corner unhooked, stretching as a tight hypotenuse across the saggy mattress. Then— after repeating in my mind a professor's recent warning—the reading began.

Yeah, this isn't a class in secondary classical criticism!

And, suddenly sometime past summertime: all of Gaul is divided into three parts. The Belgians are the fiercest, being the furthest from Roman culture. But the Helvetians present a problem. They have burned their own villages and are migrating towards farther Gaul. The Alpine lands and passes will now be open to Barbarian invasion. This poses a threat to the Roman people. Caesar will not allow it. He summons Dumnorix, their leader. Caesar demands a change. Dumnorix defies him, reminding him Helvetians are accustomed to take, not give, orders. Caesar rushes with his legions to thwart the migrations. He overtakes the tribe at Bibracte. There he draws up the battle line. Caesar sends away the horses. Soldiers and commander now share the same peril. Suddenly the Helvetians attack. The Roman line begins to give way. M. Crassus reinforces the weakening line. The Helvetians make a forced march back to their burnt alpine villages.

But the increasing numbers of Germans are also slipping across the Rhine into Gaul. Caesar knows they must be dealt with. Their growing numbers threaten Rome. He announces his intention to the troops: they will march on the Germans the next morning. His soldiers have heard of the immense size and ferocity of German warriors. Everywhere in camp wills are being signed. Subordinate officers make presences for their fear. Some complain of the grain supply, others of the forest narrows, a few even suggest the standard bearers will refuse to move.

Caesar holds a war conference. He inspires his men. Then he orders an immediate march. After enduring long marches and insulting peace talks, Caesar engages the Germans. The Germans are deployed according to ancient custom. The men stand in battle line before their parents, wives and children. The women and children will watch the battle from their wagons. They will urge with cheers their fathers and husbands. But Caesar has learned the oracle of the German prophetess: before the new moon there is no hope of victory for the German people. Caesar orders immediate attack. Though standing on higher ground, the German warriors are no match for Roman arms. Routed, they leave their women and children, arms outstretched and hands pleading, to the mercy of their captors. All are thrown into chains.

And so pass the summers of summers past. Caesar subjugates the Belgians. Crossing the channel in a crude fleet, he defeats the blue painted warriors of ancient Britain. Caesar crosses the Rhine and strikes fear into the war councils of Germany. With waste and fire, he avenges the annihilation of his seventh legion.

Finally, all of Gaul insurgent, Caesar pursues their united army. He surrounds them at Alesia. He himself is suddenly surrounded by enemy reinforcements from farther Gaul. He is besieged within his own siege works. A pitched battle begins. Enemy hordes pouring at them from within and without, Caesar inflames the bravery of his men. Labienus is sent to reinforce a weakening Roman line. Labienus fails. The battle hangs in the balance. Then Caesar himself, accompanied by his strongest men, wearing the scarlet cloak that marked his person in battle, breaks the Gallic charge. The Gauls are captured. Insurgent leaders are punished with death. And all of Gaul lies prostrate at the feet of Caesar.

!

It is said Caesar as a young man, upon reading of the conquests achieved by Alexander the Great at the same young age, despaired of his situation. Myself, reading Caesar, I felt only the violence of his decision. Outside, the day was alight with afternoon's springtime green. Mountain scenes hung over apartment tops. Against the clean tan walls the windows seemed more like some organic painting, breathing and alive, nature's masterpiece. And into my mind, surrounded by self-made battle squalor, besieged by schoolbooks, assailed by repressed responsibilities and half-forgotten tasks, embattled with all the uncertainties of today's tomorrow, came a thought from farther Gaul:

Hell, I just need to be more decisive.

SAMPLE 3: PERSONAL NARRATIVE

Hospital Art

DONNAE TIDWELL

I have spent too much time in the hospital and not because I had to. Dad was the first to go. I didn't go see him in the first weeks after his trip in the dark to the emergency room. It would have been pointless anyway. After he died and they brought him back he couldn't remember anyone who had visited and argued with his brothers and sisters over who had come and who had not.

Leith was next. A ruptured appendix, and a good thing they caught it or he would have been gone. Leith was in high school, but he was still young enough to be placed in Pediatrics. The room had happy prints and a pair of soft sculpture dinosaurs on a shelf. He liked it because he could play Nintendo on the T.V.

We had a few months of occasional visits to Radiology and friends until December. Drannan describes the car as not being much wider than his hips. I saw him in Emergency before they cleaned him up. Troy was with me and tried to make me laugh before we reached the car. I wanted to hit him, but I was grateful anyway.

Drannan's room was in the tower. You rode the elevator up and walked past a bunch of rooms and a plaque from Kenny Loggins. Drannan looked better than the first time I saw him, but there were still little red blotches that would be there for a while. A quilt hung on the wall. The hospital's attempt to give life to empty spaces. It was small, maybe two and a half by two and a half. The colors were cool blues and greens with a few slashes of an out-of-place purple. Triangles of fabric representing neat rows of ships, sailing in multiples of three. I looked at it a lot when I came. Drannan was tired so we only laughed half as much as normal and I would look at the ships.

I was headed towards Baja when I found out he had broken his leg for the second time. Falling off the couch, how poetic. Turning around sounded good and I wish I had, but I had real sails to deal with and Troy was there.

A quilt may have been on his wall the second time around, I don't know. I hope it wasn't the ships because then he would have thought of me and been jealous. There wasn't anything to be jealous of: the wind never stopped, I got sick of eating sand, and Troy wasn't speaking to me. A stupid quilt in a hospital room is what I wanted to look at.

It's been a year since the night I woke up and waited for the call to give CPR to my father. Now half of my sister's face doesn't move and we canceled Dad's first-year second-birthday party. I spent time Saturday in the Radiology waiting room while Larissa had another CAT Scan. There was a picture on the wall. I think it was a bunch of lines arranged into a sunset. Anyway it wasn't a quilt. So I sat and stitched to myself and thought maybe someone will look at this and know that I am sick of the hospital.

(USED BY PERMISSION)

SAMPLE 4: PERSONAL NARRATIVE

A Winter With Sylvia Plath

JULIE TAYLOR

> Dying
> Is an art, like everything else.
> I do it exceptionally well.
> –Sylvia Plath

It was a dramatic performance. Mozart's *Requiem* was playing in the background as I turned on the hot water in the tub and pulled my package of Gillette razor blades from beneath the bath mat. Under my breath I repeated quotes from Sylvia Plath like offerings to the patron saint of suicide. "I am afraid. I am not solid but hollow. I feel behind my eyes a numb, paralyzed cavern, a pit of hell, a mimicking nothingness . . . I want to kill myself, to escape from responsibility, to crawl abjectly into the womb. I do not know who I am, where I am going, and I am the one who has to decide the answers to these hideous questions." I pressed the blade into my skin and pushed it across my wrist. Three cuts–each one deeper–and then I laid my cheek against the cool tile and, shaking with sobs, I closed my eyes and waited for the relief to wash over me like a wave.

It's hard to say when it all began. Fall semester was hard and lonely and, as usual, I buried myself in homework. When grades came out, the cold row of black A's stared up at me from the paper with severe indifference. The winter arrived with a vengeance, and the bitter wind which froze the pipes in buildings and broke power lines like brittle bones also stung the air as it entered my throat and turned the tears on my cheeks to ice. Slowly I began to realize how tired I was . . . tired of slipping up the hill to class, tired of looking at my own face in the mirror, and tired of waking up in the morning.

In February, after a particularly depressing day of generic existence, I told my roommate I was going to go hang myself from the Tree of Life, and I wandered out into the falling snow. Somehow I ended up at the library. I have always found comfort in the musty smelling shelves of the library. As a little girl I would run my fingers down a line of books, pull out one I had never seen before and sit on the floor between the towering shelves and begin to read. I wanted that same comfort now, so I wandered down an aisle, pulled off a thick grey volume, sat down on the carpet and began to read. The book was the journal of Sylvia Plath. The words were pure and passionate; they seared through my eyes and burned their impression onto the back of my brain. I absorbed the words until they began absorbing me; they sucked me in and soon I was behind the horizontal bars of backwards letters staring out from the page at myself. When I finally closed the book hours later and I tried to stand up, my legs were paralyzed with stiffness.

I spent the next two weeks copying and memorizing poems and lines from Sylvia's letters and journal entries. I taped sections of her writing all around the walls by my bed like a cave of paper. Sometimes I read quotes to my roommates but no one seemed to appreciate the bleakness of her art as I did. Like a secret possession, Sylvia's emotional and mental suffering was understood by me and me alone.

As my depression worsened and my isolation deepened, I stopped going to class and seldom left my apartment. I didn't sleep anymore. I would stare at the darkness that filled my room and think about my failures and my sins and imagine how I could escape from myself. I wallowed in the drama; I would light candles and stare at the flame or burn incense while I cut entire magazines into piles of shredded glossy paper on my bedspread.

The day I finally gave in to the pleading of my roommates and visited a psychiatrist, I took along one of my favorite quotes from Sylvia:

> Eddie wrote me after my last honest letter saying I had better to get psychiatric treatment to root out the sources of my terrible problems. I smile, now, thinking: we all like to think we are important enough to need psychiatrists.

My visit of course was a waste because I was convinced before I walked in the door that it would be. Who was I to think I needed a psychiatrist? I didn't need someone probing into my psyche and analyzing my childhood. What I really needed was an escape from my self-created hell of pity and isolation into a nirvana of nothingness. What I really wanted was to not exist. Later that day, I bought a package of razor blades.

I find it ironic that I have never thought more clearly in my life than when I was tottering on the line of unconsciousness in a pool of blood on my bathroom floor. I thought about everything I had ever done in my short 19 years of life and I thought about what I would find if I let myself die. And I wondered if non-existence was even possible. As the bathroom light was forming dark red spots across my eyes and the walls were turning to grey fluid, I was rationally weighing my desire for relief against the fear and doubt that were seeping from my mind. I lifted my head with my shoulder and I reached for a towel.

I spent a couple of weeks in the hospital where the doctors without scalpels tried to cut out the sickness which had grown inside me like a tumor. But the real healing began when I left to spend the summer in California. In the warmth of the constant sun, I began to soften and thaw. I discarded Sylvia Plath for a while. I recognized how I had used her writings in my self-destruction and I did not want to step again into that cave of paper where I used to sit and pour depression over myself like a thick acid.

I bought *The Bell Jar* by Sylvia Plath on my last day in California to read on the trip back home. I hadn't even begun reading the novel during the winter because quite honestly, I hadn't wanted to commit myself to life long enough to finish it. But things changed, and as we traveled along the highway towards Utah, I read. When I finally set the book down, I waited for the dark, cold feeling to come, but it never did. I had just read a depressing book that could have been my life story, and yet I was only content. It was then that I recognized how all winter, I had seen only what I had wanted to see. What I had taken from Sylvia Plath may have been parallel to what she put into it, but it was still only my interpretation, and I had chosen both the meaning and how it affected me. I didn't have to feel her pain, and I didn't have to stand in her shadow of gloom. As I relaxed back into the seat of the car, I glanced down at the scars on my wrists and I noticed they were fading to thin pink lines. I looked out the window at the heat rising up from the sage of the desert, and I felt warm.

(USED BY PERMISSION)

Creative Process Assignment

Creativity is a mysterious thing. Readers like to know how people get ideas for new pieces, what a work means to its creator, how a fine piece evolves in stages, or how events in the maker's life help shape a work.

Purpose

Describe your own creative processes. In preparing to do so, consider the following questions: What is your usual manner of working in your medium? Are there stages? Do breakthroughs happen? If so, how? What do you do to stimulate them? What do you do when you face blocks or staleness? What samples and details show how you produce your best work?

Audience Considerations

To give vitality to your processes of creation, use descriptive language that allows readers to see how you create. Illustrate your processes with your own work, keeping in mind that readers will need to find the work and its stages interesting enough to hold their attention.

Length and Scope

Consult your teacher.

SAMPLE STUDENT ESSAY

SAMPLE: CREATIVE PROCESS ESSAY

The Mystery of Creation

KRAIG VARNER

What is it in my life as an artist that causes this creative spark to ignite, pro-pelling me forward in a burst of materialized creation? In a way, making art is like a rocket thrusting out into some unknown space: I am never quite sure what I'll find. The question of creation is often as great a mystery to the artist as it is to others. Mozart said of his ideas, "Whence and how they come, I know not; nor can I force them." The purpose of this essay is to explore this mystery of creation in my own experience as an artist and how it has developed.

I do not believe that this creative spark can be learned or even taught, although a good art education can help in cultivating and refining creativi-ty. Mozart's statement implies that there are unconscious and mysterious sources of inspiration that cause the artist to create. When I am in the act of creating, I find myself yielding to moments of inspiration, risking the known to achieve a felt aesthetic of beauty or expression. I don't know what it is; I only feel what a work needs to have as I'm working.

Part of the challenge of creating art is the state of constant flux the artist must maintain. In a sense, the artist doesn't know from one moment to another exactly how a work will turn out. He only knows for sure when it feels right. From my own experience, this is a delicate process the artist has to discover from within. It is like reaching deep into your own galactic space, that unfathomable universe, and mysteriously uniting subconscious and conscious in a way that brings forth a magical and sensitive creation.

Of course, there are other forces within to explore: the need to com-municate and interpret by visual means the experiences, communions, feel-ings, even groanings, that words seem inadequate to express. I try to express these things through sculpture.

Many artists, myself included, are reluctant to analyze too carefully these forces within that surge forth like a tide moving us to create. There is a fear that as soon as you try to logically examine these forces, measure that which cannot be measured, you've lost them. Then your work becomes mechanical and dead. The arts and their creative processes do not lend themselves easily to be analyzed without so endangering. At the same time I don't want to give all the reasons for doing a particular work of art because I want the viewer to participate as much as possible from his own experience.

This leads me to another personal area to explore. How does an artist find out he's an artist? For me it was a discovery that did not come until late, but looking back now I realize I was always an artist. How did I make this journey of realization and begin to create art? I could say that my life has been shaped by many experiences and events; however, none of them are so different than those of others. What then? Part of the answer lies in how I responded to those events and experiences.

For example, I can still recollect how a scene appeared to me as a child of three or four years of age. I remember the young figure of my mother ironing clothes at night under an eerie yellowish light coming from one low-watt bulb. We lived in a small roof-tar shingled house in the railroad town of Havre, Montana. As my sister and I were playing, I would notice the shapes and patterns of our shadows moving across the wall, and we tried to make them into animal silhouettes with our hands. It was hot inside and the smell of crisp freshly ironed clothes permeated the summer air. My mother had opened the door and I remember looking out into the pitch black night. I was afraid of the dark. It seemed impenetrable and ominous. It was through images like these that the realization came that I saw things a little differently. I would notice things others paid no attention to.

Drawing was another response to the sensory perception of shapes, colors, patterns and textures in rich variety of life around me. It seemed as natural as breathing. It is still one of the most important factors in my creative process.

Finally, one of the most important facets in the process of creation, and it cannot be taken too lightly, is that it is not convenient. By this, I mean that ideas or inspiration come at odd times and sometimes very quickly. If I don't immediately stop and respond, I lose them. They are such momentary glimpses. Sometimes I'll awaken in the middle of the night with an idea or solution to a work. I've learned that an idea can come from any source at any time.

In conclusion, even after creating many works of art, when all is said and done, my creative process is still a mystery. There is this felt phenomenon among many artists that a work of art almost seems as if it were to create itself. It is like a work reveals how it is to be even before you finish. And in this indefinable aspect of art lies the mystery.

(Used by permission)

Artist Profile Assignment

Nearly every arts magazine and newspaper arts section carries artist profiles. These pieces inform the public of artists who deserve attention by discussing connections among the artist's life, character, opinions, and the work he or she creates. Sometimes the connections are aesthetic only — that is, the writer tries to convey the artistic intentions without reference to life experiences or messages and themes. In this case the background becomes not the artist's experiences but the surrounding art community in which the artist sees himself or herself in dialog.

A good profile requires a sense of how much detail will demonstrate the ruling patterns and show meaningful variations. The core of a profile can be formed from information of different kinds — education, views, influences, attributes, art work, and interpretation — woven together into a unified portrait. Focus may vary between the personality of the artist and the art work itself, but usually you should pay most attention to the work of the artist.

Purpose

Write a profile of an artist. You may write about a past or present figure, famous or obscure. Consider writing about an artist of your acquaintance, even a student. Why not discover someone?

Audience Considerations

Depending on the artist and medium you write about, your audience may need background in movements, terms, styles, and genres in order to comprehend the artist's context and contribution. Keep readers hooked with informative, lively writing.

Length and Scope

Address items from the following topics as you prepare your profile. Not all of them are mandatory, but you should include balanced attention to some.

- Family, regional, and ethnic background
- Education
- Early art — how the artist got started
- Mentors and teachers
- Phases of development
- First exposure — where the artist's work was first published or shown
- Traits of the art work
- Themes, concerns, and issues the artist raises
- Artistic context — other artists and thinkers your subject views as his or her artistic community
- An interview, if possible, on the above topics

While using these building blocks to add significant content to your essay, remember also to build around a single main theme, which should usually appear in the introduction and be visible in the sections of the essay's body.

Read several published profiles to see how information from different aspects of the artist are woven together.

Your profile should be four pages, double-spaced.

READINGS

Georgia O'Keeffe

Joan Didion

FROM THE WHITE ALBUM (NEW YORK: FARRAR, 1979)

"Where I was born and where and how I have lived is unimportant," Georgia O'Keeffe told us in the book of paintings and words published in her ninetieth year on earth. She seemed to be advising us to forget the beautiful face in the Stieglitz photographs. She appeared to be dismissing the rather condescending romance that had attached to her by then, the romance of extreme good looks and advanced age and deliberate isolation. "It is what I have done with where I have been that should be of interest." I recall an August afternoon in Chicago in 1973 when I took my daughter, then seven, to see what Georgia O'Keeffe had done with where she had been. One of the vast O'Keeffe "Sky Above Clouds" canvases floated over the back stairs in the Chicago Art Institute that day, dominating what seemed to be several stories of empty light, and my daughter looked at it once, ran to the landing, and kept on looking. "Who drew it," she whispered after a while. I told her. "I need to talk to her," she said finally.

My daughter was making, that day in Chicago, an entirely unconscious but quite basic assumption about people and the work they do. She was assuming that the glory she saw in the work reflected a glory in its maker, that the painting was the painter as the poem is the poet, that every choice one made alone — every word chosen or rejected, every brush stroke laid or not laid down—betrayed one's character. *Style is character.* It seemed to me that afternoon that I had rarely seen so instinctive an application of this familiar principle, and I recall being pleased not only that my daughter responded to style as character but that it was Georgia O'Keeffe's particular style to which she responded: this was a hard woman who had imposed her 192 square feet of clouds on Chicago.

"Hardness" has not been in our century a quality much admired in women, nor in the past twenty years has it even been in official favor for men. When hardness surfaces in the very old we tend to transform it into "crustiness" or eccentricity, some tonic pepperiness to be indulged at a distance. On the evidence of her work and what she has said about it, Georgia O'Keeffe is neither "crusty" nor eccentric. She is simply hard, a straight shooter, a woman clean of received wisdom and open to what she sees. This is a woman who could early on dismiss most of her contemporaries as "dreamy," and would later single out one she liked as "a very poor painter." (And then add, apparently by way of softening the judgment: "I guess he wasn't a painter at all. He had no courage and I believe that to create one's own world in any of the arts takes courage.") This is a woman who in 1939 could advise her admirers that they were missing her point, that their appreciation of her famous flowers was merely sentimental. "When I paint a red hill," she observed coolly in the catalogue for an exhibition that year, "you say it is too bad that I don't always paint flowers. A flower touches almost everyone's heart. A red hill doesn't touch everyone's heart." This is a woman who could describe the genesis of one of her most well-known paintings—the "Cow's Skull: Red, White and Blue" owned by the Metropolitan—"as an act of quite deliberate and derisive orneriness." "I thought of the city men I had been seeing in the East," she wrote. "They talked so often of writing the Great American Novel—the Great American Play—the Great American Poetry. . . . So as I was painting my cow's head on blue I thought to myself, 'I'll make it an American painting. They will not think it great with the red stripes down the sides—Red, White and Blue—but they will notice it.'"

The city men. The men. They. The words crop up again and again as this astonishingly aggressive woman tells us what was on her mind when she was making her astonishingly aggressive paintings. It was those city men who stood accused of sentimentalizing her flowers: "I made you take time to look at what I saw and when you took time to really notice my flower you hung all your associations with flowers on my flower and you write about my flower as if I think and see what you think and see—and I don't." *And I don't.* Imagine those words spoken, and the sound you hear is *don't tread on me.* "The men" believed it impossible to paint New York, so Georgia O'Keeffe painted New York. "The men" didn't think much of her bright color, so she made it brighter. The men yearned toward Europe so she went to Texas, and then New Mexico. The men talked about Cézanne, "long involved remarks about the 'plastic quality' of his form and color," and took one another's long involved remarks, in the view of this angelic rattlesnake in their midst, altogether too seriously." I can paint one of those dismal-colored paintings like the men," the woman who regarded herself always as an outsider remembers thinking one day in 1922, and she did: a painting of a shed "all low-toned and dreary with the tree beside the door." She called this act of rancor "The Shanty" and hung it in her next show. "The men seemed to approve of it," she reported fifty-four years later, her contempt undimmed. "They seemed to think that maybe I was beginning to paint. That was my only low-toned dismal-colored painting."

Some women fight and others do not. Like so many successful guerrillas in the war between the sexes, Georgia O'Keeffe seems to have been equipped early with an immutable sense of who she was and a fairly clear understanding that she would be required to prove it. On the surface her upbringing was conventional. She was a child on the Wisconsin prairie who played with china dolls and painted watercolors with cloudy skies because sunlight was too hard to paint and, with her brother and sisters, listened every night to her mother read stories of the Wild West, of Texas, of Kit Carson and Billy the Kid. She told adults that she wanted to be an artist and was embarrassed when they asked what kind of artist she wanted to be: She had no idea what artists did. She had never seen a picture that interested *her*, other than a pen-and-ink Maid of Athens in one of her mother's books, some Mother Goose illustrations printed on cloth, a tablet cover that showed a little girl with pink roses, and the painting of Arabs on horseback that hung in her grandmother's parlor. At thirteen, in a Dominican convent, she was mortified when the sister corrected her drawing. At Chatham Episcopal Institute in Virginia she painted lilacs and sneaked time alone to walk out to where she could see the line of the Blue Ridge Mountains on the horizon. At the Art Institute in Chicago she was shocked by the presence of live models and wanted to abandon anatomy lessons. At the Art Students League in New York one of her fellow students advised her that, since he would be a great painter and she would end up teaching painting in a girls' school, any work of hers was less important than modeling for him. Another painted over her work to show her how the Impressionists did trees. She had not before heard how the Impressionists did trees and she did not much care.

At twenty-four she left all those opinions behind and went for the first time to live in Texas, where there were no trees to paint and no one to tell her how not to paint them. In Texas there was only the horizon she craved. In Texas she had her sister Claudia with her for a while, and in the late afternoons they would walk away from town and toward the horizon and watch the evening star come out. "That evening star fascinated me," she wrote. "It was in some way very exciting to me. My sister had a gun, and as we walked she would throw bottles into the air and shoot as many as she could before they hit the ground. I had nothing but to walk into nowhere and the wide sunset space with the star. Ten watercolors were made from that star." In a way one's interest is compelled as much by the sister Claudia with the gun as by the painter Georgia with the star, but only the painter left us this shining record. Ten watercolors were made from that star.

The Bond in Bronze

Patti Jones Morgan

FROM ARAMCO WORLD, JANUARY–FEBRUARY 1989

Their hoofbeats echo rhythmically through the centuries, age passing into age on their strong backs. Their wind-whipped manes and flared nostrils promise conquest to the strong hearted. Born 3000 years ago in Middle Eastern deserts and inextricably bound to humankind in war and peace, the legendary Arabian horse, the "drinker of the wind," shares a spiritual bond with humans which continues to fascinate people all over the world.

Dr. Hussam A. Fadhli felt this fascination for the Arabian horse as he grew up in Baghdad, Iraq; years later it surfaced again as a desire to portray the horse in bronze.

"I'd always loved animals, especially the horse, and I loved art," he explains in his husky, distinctive accent. "In museums and galleries all over the world I'd always go straight to the equine sculpture. I'd say to myself, 'I can do that!'— but my career as a surgeon didn't leave me the chance to get involved in it."

Artistic from childhood, and one of Iraq's top students academically, Fadhli turned down an art scholarship in favor of medicine. "From seventh grade, I wanted to be a doctor and help people," he says. Later, after coming to the United States in 1957 to complete his postgraduate work, Fadhli opened a Texas practice in thoracic and cardiovascular surgery; his artistic impulse expressed itself only in occasional oil paintings.

It wasn't until 1980, when Fadhli's wife, Brigitte, began raising Arabian horses, that the surgeon's dormant talent was woken, his imagination and his eye were captured by the magnificent, affectionate animals, and the seed of his determination to commemorate them in bronze was planted.

From the outset, Fadhli approached sculpture very methodically. "I am the type of person who tries to be precise. My medical colleagues tell me I am a perfectionist. I'm not successful all the time because I am a human being, but I like to prepare things ahead of time." Accordingly, Fadhli began by learning all he could about sculpture before he started. "I thought, 'I have the talent— maybe, maybe!— and I have the desire, definitely, but I don't know the technical aspect of it,'" he says. After intensive reading of many books on sculpture, and particularly sculptural technique, he felt confident enough to start.

Finally, in 1986, the surgeon produced his first equine bronze sculpture of an Arabian at full gallop; its title was "Racing the Clouds." It was followed in rapid succession by several other pieces, and Fadhli had plenty more in mind. "The ideas had been bottled up and the moment I opened that cap, everything just exploded!"

The surgeon's sculptural theme, the Arabian horse and the culture and history of the Middle East, has carved him a unique niche in the art world and accounts, he feels, for his success: works sold for large sums in several galleries and displayed in the center arena at major Arabian-horse shows. "An artist has to do what he is familiar with and what he loves to do," Fadhli says. "From childhood, I was fascinated with the elegance and grace of the Arabian horse and the emotions they can create when they move, their expressive faces and their closeness with human beings. And that's what I'm after in my sculpture, the interrelationship between the man or woman and the horse, something that has existed for centuries, especially in the Arab countries."

"This interrelationship is so valuable, sensitive and intimate. And it is so typical of the exchange of love and affection and closeness between two creatures, human and horse," Fadhli says.

Observing life in its most touching and basic moments, and translating those perceptive glimpses into bronze, makes Fadhli a passionate artist. Yet his instinctive veneration for people and life guides him always to give priority to his career as a doctor over his work as an artist—although he enjoys both. "I have a first responsibility as a surgeon, and love what I do, although I wish I had started sculpting many years ago," he admits.

Committed to his adopted country, the United States, Fadhli nevertheless maintains strong ties with his Iraqi homeland. He occasionally ships Fadhli Arabians to Iraqi breeders, and his regular visits there include consultations with medical colleagues and some surgery, balanced by raids on Baghdad music stores for Umm Kalthoom tapes. For the future, Fadhli dreams of one day sculpturing monumental works — perhaps even one to be placed permanently in the land that nurtured him.

"I feel a sense of responsibility to pay back what I have gained," he says, "and I feel you must still communicate with the 'old country' and keep that emotional feeling nourished. This does not detract from loyalty to the new country—but I believe that if a person doesn't have a sense of responsibility to something in the past, to some important part of himself, then he will never have a sense of responsibility in the new country he lives in."

Fadhli's philosophy has found expression in his storytelling bronzes of Arabian horses and other Middle Eastern subjects, and he admits that the desire to share his heritage in this way is a conscious one. "I know people who came to this country who try to ignore their past, and don't even say where they are from. But not me. I am proud of what I am, of my background and where I'm from. I'm always ready to show people, through my sculpture, part of the culture of the Middle East."

A comfortable home on a quiet, tree-lined lane a few miles from the Gulf of Mexico is the center of Fadhli's creativity. A dining table is his working surface and shelves bulge with art books. A pot of sculptor's tools includes several retired pieces of surgical equipment—"Sometimes I just go and see what is being thrown out," he chuckles—now used for texturing, marking and scraping the Italian clay that Fadhli uses in the first stage of creating a sculpture.

Fadhli always looks forward to making time for what he calls his non-scientific side, when he can relax and refresh his mind after the tension of busy days as a surgeon. It is a time that invigorates him. Since sculpture can be taken up and put aside as his professional schedule demands, yet continually challenges his abilities, he feels it's a perfect medium.

In the evenings, often still dressed in the loose, green surgical scrubs, which reveal a small replica of the Qur'an on a chain around his neck, he works while his family gathers in the living room. "I don't like to work in a separate studio," he says, "because I like to be with my family. I don't even mind their criticisms of the sculptures I'm working on. They might say there's something wrong with a piece, and I'll look at it and maybe change something."

Fadhli's creativity is all-consuming once he is working on the clay; he is able to close out everything around him. Music stimulates his thoughts and imagination. "Beethoven makes me feel I am climbing a mountain and reaching the top," he says, while famed Egyptian singer Umm Kalthoom brings his

Middle Eastern heritage to the forefront of his mind. "When I'm sculpting an Arabian horse or Arabian subject, Umm Kalthoom's songs affect my mental attitude," Fadhli says. "This transfers into the piece through my hands."

His Arab heritage, never far from his consciousness, is an integral part of his attitude toward his art. Sitting at a delicate, handmade Syrian table in the "Middle East corner" of his living room, Fadhli points to an elegantly written verse from the Qur'an. It is from the *sura*, or chapter, called *al-'Adiyat*, "Those that Run," and it confirms Fadhli's belief that even the Creator found the Arabian horse admirable. "By the war-horses that run swiftly, panting, to the battle," Fadhli interprets, "and by those whose hooves strike fire from the stones, and by those which press home the charge upon the enemy early in the morning, raise clouds of dust, and penetrate into the midst of the foe. . . ."

"The horse is an important part of Arab culture and history," the surgeon explains. "It gave man a chance to broaden his scope of life, and to travel. It has made it easy for the human and that's why I think humans owe the horse a lot. The Bedouins, for example, value their horses so much that they bring them inside the tents when the weather is bad.

"What I try to show in my sculptures is the culture of the Middle East," he says. "People are afraid of, or not interested in, things they don't know about. Hollywood projects such a bad image of the Middle East, so with my art, I will show the real heritage and culture."

A prime example of this effort is Fadhli's sculpture "Guarding the Master," which depicts a mare standing quietly on a small hill next to her master, who is at prayer. In consideration of his horse, the rider has removed the tack and placed it on the ground. Kneeling in prayer, he bows his head, while the horse watches the surrounding area, ready to alert him to any danger. "This happens," says Fadhli, "since Muslims are required to pray five times a day." The sculptor points out the details which complete the story: the raised index finger of the man's right hand as he prays to God, the sandals neatly placed by his side. "He is saying the creed, 'There is no God but God and Muhammad is the prophet of God.'" And the depiction of a female horse is deliberate, Fadhli adds. "The female is preferred for traveling since she won't whinny and make a lot of noise when she hears another horse, like the male will," Fadhli explains.

Such concern with authenticity extends to using actual Iraqi saddles and bridles as models for his sculptures. The bridle displays the crescent and star of Islam, he notes, and is set with a "seven-eyed" turquoise jewel. "The saddle and bridle were used by us to show our national champion native horse, Eclipse," he says.

One of Fadhli's bronzes, "The Bonding," is the result of what he saw and felt as one of his wife's mares foaled, and emphasizes the close and complementary partnership between the Fadhlis where their horses are concerned. When it became apparent that the mare was in trouble giving birth to her first foal, Fadhli checked with his wife, then stepped in to help the horse.

"I tell you, when I saw that—the birth—and, after that, the care and the attempts of the mother to clean the baby and to make it get up and suck, all this process of caring really affected me," he says. "I thought about my mother and, although I loved her very much, I realized I never had given her enough in return for what she did. When I saw this, and how the mare just has her God-given instinct to try to help her baby, it was such a dramatic experience for me. I already respected life, but this affected me very deeply, and I really knew I wanted to show it in a sculpture."

Visibly touched by the memory of the event, Fadhli steps back from "The Bonding," a piece that subsequently took shape very fast and spontaneously, because his soul was in it. "You can quote me now," he says fervently. "Every child, boy or girl, must show more affection to their mother, because we don't realize what they did to bring us to this world."

The sculptor recalls that a life-sized edition of this piece, entitled "Time-less," stirred the emotions of many at an outdoor art show in Loveland, Colorado. "People liked it and came and looked at it quietly," he recalls. "Some thought it was real, and touched it!"

Part of Fadhli's skill in evocatively depicting horses and humans is a result of his doctor's expertise in anatomy, he feels. Much of the accuracy of his equine portraits comes from his practice of sketching his Arabians in the pasture, where he can touch them, combined with his strict adherence to what he terms "the basics" in art. Fadhli believes that the tendency to produce something that looks pretty and aesthetically pleasing cannot be carried to extremes. He is wary of over stylization in his work. "It must not look like a Disney cartoon," he says. "Art must reflect an idea and what the artist wants to say. I want my work to reflect reality, with a little of my feelings."

Thus, if Fadhli chooses to represent a male horse, it is first of all because it is appropriate to the sculpture he has in mind. The stallion's larger head, more abundant mane and tail, flaring nostrils and muscular neck set the mood of the piece. "It will present a more macho image, kind of, 'Here I am.' You know, like men," says Fadhli, comparing the stallion in "Racing The Clouds" with the gentle refinement of the mare in "The Gift." "She will have a smaller head and muzzle, less protruding ears and her neck and head will be in a more relaxed position," he says. "Actually, I do more females, horse and human, I think, because of my deep appreciation of them," he muses, somewhat surprised by his own conclusion.

The tender reality of his wife's love for her horses inspired a Fadhli bronze which he feels symbolizes all he's trying to say about the special relationship between the Arabian and the human. In "Magic Moment," a near life-size work, a woman gently winds her fingers through her horse's mane as the horse nuzzles her.

Formal Analysis Assignment

Why Do Formal Analysis?

Formal analysis refers not to writing that is stuffy and solemn, but to writing that analyzes form. It is the arts counterpart to taking apart clocks and engines to see how they work. Formal analysis helps us understand the internal architecture of a piece of art — its structures, devices, techniques, and distinctive use of its materials — in order to appreciate it, explain it, interpret it, and clarify why it affects us the way it does. Some college instructors refer to this type of writing as critical analysis.

For many arts students, analyzing or criticizing seems harder than creating. The concepts behind analysis and criticism are easy enough: *Analysis* and *critical* come from the Greek words *analyein*, to unloose, and *krinein*, to separate or choose. Simply put, the term *critical analysis* means to carefully take apart, examine, and judge a thing's parts. These activities seem to require more detached states of mind and abstract thinking than does creating.

Or do they? The process of taking apart is less methodical than it seems. Analysis requires imagination, just as does creation. For example, to analyze a novel, we want to see it in numerous perspectives, each of which reveals its parts to us in ways not evident while we are reading for pleasure. We can see its characters as ways of thinking and behaving, its episodes as stages in a journey, its settings as indicative of different personal or social problems or world views, its chapters or divisions as steps in a logical argument, and its events as links in a process bringing understanding out of misunderstanding or harmony out of confusion, or vice versa. Each of these imaginative revisions of a novel shows a structure where none may have been evident before, and formal analysis is exactly that — the perception of structure.

What is the difference between interpretation and formal analysis? In practice, formal analysis and interpretation often overlap. Formal analysis might be considered either a special class of interpretation, or it might be considered a separate activity quite distinct from the act of interpretation that occurs when we relate the results of formal analysis to some end. The difference lies in emphasis and scope: formal analysis concentrates on illuminating the structures and relates them to meaning, intention, or effect. Interpretation concentrates on meaning. In scope, formal analysis considers primarily the object itself and provides mostly structural evidence for its assertions of meaning. By contrast, interpretation may consider many kinds of contexts (biography, social or political history, psychology, myth, feminist theory) to derive meaning from a work.

The forms that critics analyze differ from one art medium to another. A painting has arrangements of shapes and lines on canvas, brush strokes, color, light and dark, light sources, and point of view. Often these are rendered in a distinctive manner called a style. Music may employ modes and genres, melody, motives, key signatures and areas, meter, harmony, and instrumentation. Dance has the body and its parts in movement and stasis, one or many dancers and their relations, space, modes such as ballet or folk, pace, direction, and, generally, music. Literature has plot, character, dialog, chronological or nonchronological order, logical or some other kind of structure for advancing its ideas, figurative and literal language, and rhythm. Furthermore, each art medium has various types of forms. For example, a poem has metric, propositional, imagistic, rhetorical, and generic forms. Therefore, your first task will be to select the text or piece you want to analyze and start asking which of its forms most invites analysis.

Most important, a critical or formal analysis does not waver from a careful, close examination of the work of art itself. In other words, the focus will always be on the work of art, not on the context (historical, biographical, or social) in which it first appeared or on a person's responses and associations. Indeed, early formalist critics condemned as fallacious any artistic analysis sustained by reference to an artist's intent or a work's effect. They reasoned that the work had to accomplish its ends on its own, providing whatever resources readers or spectators needed.

For the purposes of this writing assignment, you need to stress *how* a work of art conveys meaning and creates its effects. However, few readers, not even experts, find mere description of structures interesting. They want to know, "So what?" Therefore, you will want to bring in ideas of meaning, effect, and intention when you say how the parts and elements function to make the work what it is. The balance between careful description and the "so what" makes good analysis rewarding — and tricky, especially in light of the fact that art is often as much *about* its materials and forms as about subject matter or ideas. That is, we can consider a painting to be about how to render a plate of fruit as much as about the fruit; a tragic drama to be about how to write tragedy, given the conventions and traditions available; a Bach fugue to be about how a fugue should be composed; a dance to be about how to choreograph and perform a particular type of dance; and a novel to be as much about language as about love or war-torn London, or about story more than certain characters overcoming obstacles between them, or about literary character more than life.

Note on Musical Analysis

Music offers an opportunity to see the relation between pure description and interpretation because it is not generally a representational medium. That is, whereas words have meanings that are hard to separate out of analysis, the sounds that comprise music are merely sounds, until they are arranged in a structure by a composer. Music therefore lends itself especially well to formal analysis. Even in music, however, few critics simply describe structures. Rather, they describe the structures because they have noticed something meaningful in them.

The question, "What does one analyze when one analyzes music?" has often cropped up. R. A. Sharpe observes: "In current writing about musical analysis, we find an assortment of philosophical presuppositions; we also find an assortment of philosophical errors that stem largely from muddle about the nature of analysis" (63). After reviewing a number of positions and errors, Sharpe observes:

> Analysis does not describe facts about music because there are no facts to match its "discoveries"; it does not formulate inferences because inferences cannot occur in music; and it does not describe listener competence because, by general acknowledgment, listener competence is pre-analytic and there is no reason at all to suppose that it describes how composers compose. What then, does it do?
>
> . . . Analysis is ultimately to do with interpretation, and the salient point about interpretation is that it is various. . . . What analysis does is to suggest, by implication, a way of hearing that requires us to foreground certain features of the music in such a way that they have a special prominence in our experience. We pay particular attention to them. Ideally, analysis enables us to experience the music in a richer way. It is an oblique invitation to interpretation by performer and listener. (71–72)

Although Clarke seems to confuse the structures in music for those facts, inferences, and responses that listeners formulate and experience (if the music in any way causes the latter types of thinking and feeling, then there is some type of correlation, and the structures that relate to the facts and inferences are what analysis wants to isolate), he leads us to three important points. First, just as people interpret the same artifact differently, they will produce different analyses. Second, the interpretation that leads to analysis and which, in turn, is made convincing by analysis, will create different "facts" and "inferences" within the artifact. Third, analysis rewards reading most when the interpretation and the structural details are both clear.

Two passages of musical criticism will illustrate the roles of analysis and interpretation. In the first, a music historian accounts for the lyricism (song-like quality) of Schubert's music:

> The structural features that give rise to the sense of lyricism continue throughout the movement. For instance, like many of Schubert's transition sections, the one seen in this movement seems to

point to the wrong key: though the secondary key is D major, the transition section ends on an apparent V of III. This softens the harmonic drive to the second key area. As many have pointed out, this harmonic strategy is similar to the one used by Beethoven in the first movement of his Piano Sonata op. 10, no. 2. In this sonata movement, the bridge section also seems to end on a V of III. But in the Beethoven, the second key enters abruptly, shoving aside the implied modulation. In contrast, Schubert's F-sharp chord at the end of the transition is not unceremoniously abandoned. Instead, it returns to be thoroughly absorbed within the key of D as a chromaticized III-sharp chord. In the Beethoven, the apparent V of III seems vanquished; in the Schubert, it seems reconciled. (Burstein 54)

Although this passage is meant for the musically educated reader, even without understanding the terms and symbols we can see a pattern in the ideas being put forward and the musical detail that supports the ideas. The paragraph starts out with an inference, a conclusion to which we can be led. It then provides details of the music, including a comparison to Beethoven, to demonstrate the inference.

In the next passage, a conductor draws attention to the strange, inconclusive nature of Mahler's Ninth Symphony:

This continuous lingering of isolated impulses from the immediate past—manifest by the timpani in m. [measure] 107, the tempo in mm. 108 and 109, and the B flat in mm. 111–114—is part of the first movement's broader preoccupation with giving a "presence" to the "past," whether it be the immediate past of each moment within the piece or the external, distant, even irretrievable worlds of music for which Mahler shows such a wistful affection. From the very beginning of the symphony there is a precarious avoidance of the affirmative statement, of unambiguous beginnings—as if, so to speak, nothing is to be expressed directly in the present tense. Even the theme of the second violins in mm. 6–16 is no less fragmentary than what preceded it; this theme joins a succession of one-measure fragments. (Its "expressivo" in m. 12 implies that until then it should be played in a more detached manner, with a mysterious absence of warmth. The "expressivo" is as momentary as the two-measure construction.) The precariousness of this opening is in part a result of the fact that the second violins extend an impulse from the first six measures rather than proceeding as if those bars were merely an introduction. In addition, the second violins' figures establish the movement's two most unsettling melodic features: the incessant upbeat orientation, and unresolved *mi–re*. (DeFotis 281)

Notice that the writer intersperses many interpretive statements with description of what happens in the music. We might even say that in this passage, the interpretation often fuses with the description. Can you see that both are present?

Purpose

Select a piece of music, a painting, a sculpture, a story, or other aesthetic product and take apart its forms and materials. Study it carefully until you begin to see it as a construct, deliberately carried out by the artist who arranged its materials in a certain fashion to achieve certain goals. Write an essay to share your insights, shaping the essay around a thesis and devoting the body of the essay to explaining how the materials and forms achieve what you see to be the artist's goals for the piece. In other words, don't just describe the elements; show how they make the work tick. Your thesis can state the "how." For example, your thesis might state, "Rembrandt's 'Self Portrait' creates playful tensions between the conventions of self-portraiture and those of allegory paintings, especially those depicting parables such as the prodigal son." Your essay will then describe the elements (the people depicted, their expression and posture, the setting) and then support your vision of how the parts contribute to the working of the whole.

Keep in mind that you do not need to write about every key element of a work. You will most likely zero in on a few, or even one, that you find most intriguing. But whatever you do, you must know what the different elements are and how they contribute to the whole.

Audience Considerations

Write to members of the class, your instructor, and a general audience of intelligent readers. Your audience will want you to elevate their appreciation of your subject matter as you increase their sophistication in understanding its interplay of structures. Provide both technical details and the ideas in relation to which the details gain significance.

Length and Scope

Because formal analysis involves close scrutiny, it is best to select one piece or a small number of related pieces by the same person.

Four pages, double-spaced.

Topic Suggestions

1. Select a building. Analyze it and relate its design and materials to its purpose and environment (downtown, campus, business park). What can we learn about the interplay of motive and design involved in its creation? "Interplay of motive and design" refers to the full range of factors that go into proposing, conceiving, and constructing a building. These include its purpose, size, location, relation to nearby buildings, institutional sponsorship, available budget (it's easy to bash a simple building, but it usually — though not always — takes many more real dollars to design and build a unique and pleasing structure), time of construction and the trends to be noted, materials available and used, as well as the attitudes and preferences of the architect. Don't forget to look at the building in both an aesthetic and technical frame of mind. With regard to the aesthetic and human, spend time

strolling through the building, looking from different angles, surveying the building's relation to surrounding buildings and locations. Get the feel of what the building says about the people who designed it and attitudes toward the people who spend time there. With regard to the technical, study the materials used, the spans, the junctions between parts, and the space allocation and space relations of parts of the building with different functions. Think about cost and materials and time available, the choice of materials with respect to both appearance and endurance. Was it built to last or to have a lifetime of thirty or forty years?

2. Select either a single graphics designer or a company that has a hallmark style to its promotional materials. Study the designs and convey what you see to the nonvisually-trained reader. Take time to inform the reader of the process by which a company or designer goes about creating graphic materials appropriate to the sponsor or client, the market, the times, and the media used. Talk about the designs themselves: What do they say about the product or service they promote? The designer? The use of available materials and media?

3. Photography students may wish to do something similar with a photographer. We have subtle reactions to the style typical of well known photographers when we leaf through a single artist's collection. By focusing on the photographs themselves, articulate what we are seeing and responding to. Select three or four photographs and discuss the use of the various parameters of photography and processing to convey the work of the artist chosen.

READING

An Insidious Reticence: The Sculptures of José Resende

Reynaldo Laddaga

FROM ART NEXUS, FEBRUARY–APRIL 1999

Years ago, at the family gatherings at Christmas or New Years, long after midnight, some children and adults, small imprecise beings, fiddled with the wire structures that covered the corks on the champagne bottles. I was immediately reminded of some of the finest works in a recent José Resende show at the Hélio Oiticica Art Center and in the Paulo Fernandes Gallery in Rio de Janeiro. The same, almost pathetic, grace of those animals of no species suddenly seemed to be inhabited by an object made of four iron sections, linked by rings, and supported upon a block of hay, which opened the show at the Oiticica Center; or a long "Z" made of metallic tubes wrapped with thin sheets of lead and tied with thin cables, which closed the show. This impression seems to have been shared by the Brazilian critic Ronaldo Brito, who wrote the text for the show's catalog, and who praises "the way in which

[Resende's works] appear in the world, quickly and fortuitously," in such a way that, in them, "the provisional is positively reevaluated."[1] Indeed, it seemed to me from the very beginning that there is something provisional in these pieces, something that is merely *for now*, and they propose themselves more as possible states of a body than as definitive and, therefore, in some way, necessary profiles.

But, who is José Resende? He is doubtless one of the central artists of the generation of Brazilian artists who, born between the late '40s and early '50s, perpetuated certain essential developments from the late '60s (developments especially associated with the names Lygia Clark and Hélio Oiticica). These artists include, for example, Cildo Meireles, Waltercio Caldas, Jac Leirner, and Tunga. Resende himself was born in São Paulo in 1945. He graduated with a degree in architecture in the same city and has shown his work primarily in São Paulo and Rio de Janeiro since 1964. His work was recently shown at the Robert Miller Gallery in New York and *Documenta 9* in Kassel.

Curiously, Resende's work is easy to describe. The description, however, gives a rather poor idea of his rare way of affecting the viewer. Let us consider a piece from 1994 which is particularly emblematic of his work: an object whose title in English would be *velvet, paraffin, copper, and steel cable*. It is a composition made of these materials placed in an unstable equilibrium. The piece is a sort of velvet sleeve spread out on the floor. Paraffin has been poured over the ends of the sleeve. The composition is pierced by a curved steel bar whose tips are joined by a tense metallic cable. The fragility of the construction (of the precipice) is extreme; it is obviously elegant, but at the same time there is something vaguely obscene about it, as if that elegance were to disappear from itself at the last moment; as if, upon presenting itself, instead of maintaining its composure, it were to lose it at the decisive moment.

It is quite suggestive that the majority of Resende's works have for their titles a list of materials used to make them, written in small letters—thus avoiding a title that refers to its contents or form, and avoiding the conventional use of *Untitled*. Resende's titles are minimums of denomination, denominations in their minimal form. However, minimal as they are, these titles never cease to indicate something: as far as the labeled objects are concerned, the titles indicate material rather than motive or form. Few artists adjust themselves better than Resende to what Roland Barthes wrote with respect to Cy Twombly's paintings (in a text from 1979 titled *Wisdom of Art*).

What is unique in Twombly's operation, according to Barthes, is that he "imposes material, not as something that is going to serve a purpose, but rather as an absolute material . . . that preexists the division of meaning." The power of the painter, says Barthes, is that *it makes material exist as material; even if one meaning rises from the canvas, the paintbrush and the color continue to be "things," obstinate substances from which nothing (no subsequent meaning) can*

---

[1] Ronaldo Brito, "Em forma de mundo," *José Resende* (Rio de Janeiro: Centro de Arte Hélio Oiticica, 1998) 17.

undo the obstinacy of "being there."[2] The title of this object is a discreet list of his materials, primarily because the program that Resende obeys as he works is that of presenting certain materials in their obstinacy.

However, this object, this scene, this unadorned theater not only finds its titles in the materials with which it is made, but its title is also in small letters: I believe that this is an indication of Resende's desire to avoid the melodrama of materials characteristic of certain art forms of the '50s, '60s, and '70s. The materials in Resende's works are deliberately exposed, but as something common and uncultivated: the banal materials with which everyone negotiates daily life, presented in their banality, with nothing especially "original" or "alchemical" (nothing in them, for example, of the felt and grease of a Joseph Beuys). There is nothing telluric or cosmic in the work of this artist (who has been realizing what I would call an art of *urbanity,* albeit a perturbed urbanity).

Resende's most auspicious pieces show or "impose" certain materials (and, more precisely, the *contact* between certain materials), but they also possess forms: even suggestive forms. Like the imaginary universe of a Lygia Clark, Resende's world is fundamentally animal: it is a universe of *imaginary animals,* of forms and attitudes that evoke imaginary animals that, nevertheless, have the virtue of perturbing the faculty of identification. In the face of those more — shall we say — , animal objects, we are not finished telling ourselves "that's an animal," when we begin to ask ourselves "what type?" These compositions make me think, in fact, of what the French philosopher Jean-Luc Marion calls, in a recent book, an "incident." According to Marion, an "incident" is "what arrives in such a way that it consists in nothing more than this first and final arrival, without preexisting in any way and without making itself visible before the incident." The "incident" consists entirely in the act of its own obstinate appearance, "with no background, no prevision or provision reduced to that act."[3] An *incident,* such as Marion defines it, is *something* that appears without allowing the person for whom it appears to identify it fully: *something* that begins by escaping its viewer, as if we had it on the *tip of our eyes* (as we say when words that escape us are "on the tip of our tongue"), and which arrives, which comes to occur, to present itself, at the same moment in which its identity is lost.

Resende's most intense compositions (which are generally the most squalid) recall the work of Clark (especially the Clark of the *Bichos* [*Animals* or *Beasts*] or Richard Tuttle, much more than certain *arte povera* sculptors like Giovanni Anselmo, with whom he shares some important propensities concerning matter and form. The same spirit of Tuttle's miserable constructions is found, for example, in a solid pouring of plaster, pierced by wires, that hung in the Paulo Fernandes Gallery, or a fragment of fabric that enclosed another fragment of leather in the Hélio Oiticica Center, or, finally, a small arabesque pendant of twisted lead that seemed to have been improvised (a work of quick pincers and hammers that is the three-dimensional equivalent of a sketch) bearing the scant title *plomo* (*lead*).

---

[2] Roland Barthes, *Oeuvres complétes,* vol 3 (Paris, Seuli, 1995) 1021.

[3] Jean-Luc Marion, *Etant donné. Essai d'une phénomenologie de la donation* (Paris: Presses Universitaires de France, 1997) 213.

Works like these make me think of a text in St. Augustine's *Confessions* (in which he deals with lost identities). The text is found in Book XII, and the context is a discussion on the notion of matter, which is, in the traditions referred to in the discussion, something that lacks form. St. Augustine explains the difficulty of imagining anything that completely lacks form, yet nevertheless exists. He writes: *For I could more readily imagine that what was deprived of all form simply did not exist than I could conceive of anything between form and nothing—something which was neither formed nor nothing, something that was unformed and nearly nothing* (XII, 6, 462). The stupor of not being able to propose to the imagination something that would be *almost nothing*, can only be overcome—says the saint—, by concentrating on one phenomenon: the mutability of bodies. Only by concentrating on the change of bodies can we imagine, momentarily and unstably, something formless. *And so I applied myself to the bodies themselves and looked more deeply into their mutability, by which they cease to be what they had been and begin to be what they were not. This transition from form to form I had regarded as involving something like a formless condition, though not actual nothingness.* But, what is that mutability between two forms? asks Augustine. Answer: "Could it be said, 'Nothing was something,' and 'That which is, is not'? If this were possible, I would say that this was it."

In my judgment, it would be the same to say that Resende fails at the exact moment in which his constructions acquire consistency, density, and the weight of the monument. This is the case with certain female silhouettes that he has realized in recent years which, unlike the great majority of the artist's work, have a big title (they are called *Venus*). It is also the case of a work from 1996 that recalls Giacometti. This composition is made of two large, curved steel sheets that evoke legs, installed in Rio de Janeiro's Largo de Carioca, bearing the title *Pasante (Passerby)*. The Brazilian artist finds himself at the polar opposite on the spectrum of sculptors, of a Richard Serra, whose effect is inseparable from the sensation of an overcome resistance and, in sum, a sensation of force. The impression of ease in the realization of his pieces is essential in Resende's sculptures: the impression that they were completed in a minute, almost without thinking, with no effort. And the impression that they are works (not so much works as operations) of leisure which issue from him, and which are directed towards him.

Why has Resende received less international exposure than other recent Brazilian artists, contemporaries of his who are at the same level? There is probably not an entirely good answer to that question. But it seems reasonable to think that one reason is that this work, unlike that of Cildo Meireles or Tunga, for example, is not made to impress, move, *enthuse*, but rather has another purpose. But what other purpose? Our critical vocabulary is so permeated by the idea that art is a basically *exciting* activity that it is difficult to pinpoint that purpose.

The virtue of these works does not reside in their ability to excite, but rather elsewhere. They do not appear except in the measure in which they are given time. The time that we are able to give them is directly proportional to the energy (we could say to the *weak* energy) of their unfolding. For the naturalness, which is one of his immediate characteristics, gestures, ways of appearing before us, is what these compositions lose in the measure in which we give them time. But, likewise, they are eminently able to give us time, a certain time, a certain quality of time: they give us a time not made taut, but rather one that expands. In a certain way, it is as if Resende's pieces disintegrated before the gaze and, in that insistence, that obstinacy of disintegrating, they distended the time they occupy (and, of course, their space).

It seems to me that these pieces are aimed more at moving, impressing, and dazzling, than tentatively making an *advance* (as we speak of "advances" in the vocabulary of seduction), leaving the viewer with the impression of a light touch. Is that what Ronaldo Brito refers to when he speaks of these pieces as "problematic evidences" that "insist on remaining there, throbbing, when they should be finished or undone"? I believe so. In reference to a string quartet by Paul Hindemith, the great Brazilian writer Clarice Lispector wrote that he "is before maturity," like a "root fallen asleep in its force" or a "smell that has no scent." This kind of entity (both reserved and insidious) constitute the greatest pieces of this artist: bodies without profiles? accumulations without character? volumes without body?

It is as if a *reticence to exist* were the passion that stimulates José Resende's finest works.

Interpretation Assignment

Meaning always invites discussion. Does a work only mean one thing? Does it always mean many things? How can such a meaning be separated from the phrase "means—to me"? How much meaning is *in* a work, how much in *us*? Given the fact that we all are engaged in interpreting, who gets to say which meaning—or which *kind* of meaning—will survive rigorous discussion?

Although many of us bristle at the idea that someone else has a greater right to pronounce on the meaning of a work, we all want to make meaning of things and are willing to listen to an interpretation that offers new understanding. But we don't listen to just anyone. We grant authority to interpret to those who show us that we can learn from them, and the best claim is simply the interpretation itself. This means that to give an interpretation is to enter a field of rhetoric where the goal is to gain and hold listeners by surprising insight, clear thinking, and persuasive expression.

Before tackling the writing assignment, study the "Interpretation" section in Problems in Aesthetic Discourse. It discusses in more detail than possible here the unavoidable nature of interpretation, as well as the types and challenges of interpretation.

Purpose

Interpret a work of art. Your instructor wants much more than a paraphrase of a poem, a summary of a story, or a description of a dance or sculpture. Go behind the surface; get between the lines. Take an unusual approach. Show that there is more to a work than meets the eye.

The instructor may direct you to do either an immediate or a contextual interpretation. For more information on these, consult the "Interpretation" section of Problems in Aesthetic Discourse.

Whatever approach you take, the success of your article will hinge large-ly on four things:

1. Detailed knowledge of the work, its times, and its maker
2. Clear identification of the type of context that will considered
3. Thoughtful statement of meanings and the connections between the work and its context
4. A thorough demonstration that the work reflects its context

This paper will probably involve some research, so with your instructor's permission, you might choose to write on something directly related to your research paper. Whenever you borrow information, be sure to acknowledge the source. To conceal such debts is a form of intellectual theft. And be true to the thought expressed in your sources. You may openly disagree, but don't distort someone's ideas to advance your own.

Audience Considerations

Write as if for a magazine or newspaper with highly educated readers. To give readers something to which they can relate, consider linking your discussion to an issue or event that will at first be more interesting to some readers than art. Perhaps you can find a social, religious, psychological, or political issue in which to anchor the work's meaning. Describe the issue and give it immedia-cy as you draw the reader into the work and show its perspectives on the problem. Also, consider the amount of background information readers may need on the artist, the work, or your approach.

Length and Scope

Interpretations of this sort can focus on extended periods of time and many works or on single episodes and works.

Consult your teacher on length and due dates. Contextual interpretations often require more length than the immediate type.

SAMPLE STUDENT ESSAY

SAMPLE: INTERPRETATION ESSAY

Li Po's Taoist Poetry
JULIE OTIS PATERSON

Throughout the centuries, artists have often used their art as a vehicle for expressing their beliefs, though only a few of the tens of thousands of such artists have enjoyed lasting fame. One of these few is the Chinese poet Li Po. Since the start of his career in 715 A.D. at the age of 14, Li Po has gained a continually growing audience of admirers as succeeding generations have fallen under the spell of his verse. Li Po's popularity lies within his poetic style and message. *The Encyclopedia Americana* describes Li Po's style as one that "is exhilarating, with sensuous description, elegant metaphors, and boldly juxtaposed images. With deft precision, time and space are made to expand and contract in [his] poems."

In Li Po's poetry are traces of his Taoist philosophical beliefs. Taoism was a well established philosophy when Li Po was born, and he began studying it early in his life. Li Yang-ping, a kinsman of Li Po's, stated that Li Po "would read nought but the books of the sages . . ." and that "his words resembled the speech of the heavenly genii."

Some of the Taoist concepts more commonly used by Li Po are the concepts of Te and Wu-Wei. These concepts are central to Taoist philosophy. Te, or the power, is often defined as that part of the Tao (the natural order of things) that defines anything as it really is. Taoists feel that everything should be true to its individual Te. Two examples of something following its Te are first, an animal that lives according to its instincts; and second, a flower seed that can only become a specific type of flower.

Li Po's poetry often illustrated this concept. One example in his poem "Fall River songs: #5":

Fall River's many white apes
hurry like flying snow
haul their children over the branches
lap at the moon in the water

In this poem the apes are an example of something following its Te. Li Po was a man that followed his Te; historians tell us that throughout this life he did what he wanted and was not bothered by societal norms. Innes Herdan states that Li Po "never sees to have set up his own home, did not sit the official examinations [something almost all educated men did at that time], and was not given any official appointment. . . . " Li Po is thus a good example of someone who was basically unfettered by the restraints of society.

Another example of Te in Li Po's poetry is his "Conversation in the Mountains":

If you were to ask me why
    I dwell among green mountains,
I shall laugh silently;
    my soul is serene.
The peach blossoms follows
    the moving water,
There is another heaven and earth
    beyond the world of men.

In this poem the subject lives among the green mountains because that is where he feels he should be at that time. Li Po himself traveled extensively and often retired to the mountains to meditate and to be free. The peach-blossom and the moving water are also examples of objects following their Te, for they do not struggle against their motion, but drift forward willingly.

Closely tied with Te is the concept of Wu-Wei, or active non-doing. Book thirty-seven of the *Tao Te Ching* explains Wu-Wei in this way:

> Tao abides in non-action,
> Yet nothing is left undone.
> If kings and lords observed this,
> The ten thousand things would develop naturally.
> If they still desired to act,
> They would return to the simplicity of
>   of formless substance.
> Without form there is no desire.
> Without desire there is tranquillity.
> And in this way all things would be at peace.

The first sentence is a key one. Wu-Wei is not a concept of non-movement, but rather an attitude of accepting things as they come. Jacob Needleman explains Wu-Wei as something involving "a state of openness or receptivity that is subtle, elusive and active." By accepting life as it comes and not trying to actively change a situation, one follows the concept of Wu-Wei. Li Po wrote many poems that touch on the theme of Wu-Wei, one being the above quoted "Fall River songs: #5." Another poem about Wu-Wei is Li Po's famous "In the Mountains on a Summer Day":

> Lazily I stir a white feather fan,
> Lying naked within the green wood.
> I hang my hat on a crag,
> And bare my head to the wind of the pines.

Here Li Po is expressing the contentment of simplicity. Implicitly in the line "I hang my hat on a crag" is a jibe intended for all the etiquette-conscious Confucian scholars of his time. The Confucian scholars "thrived" on Li, or proper roles, and wore a uniform which included a hat. By removing his hat Li Po is symbolically removing the stifling Confucian rules of behavior and putting on the simplicity of Taoist life. Another poem with Wu-Wei as its theme is "Taking Leave of a Friend":

> Blue hills rearing over the north wall;
>   white water swirling to the east of the city:
> This is where you must leave me —
> A lone puff of thistledown
>   on a thousand mile journey.
> Ah the drifting clouds
>   and the thoughts of the wanderer!
> The setting sun
>   and emotions of old friends.
> A wave of the hand now
>   and you are gone.
> Our horses whinnied to each other at parting.

This poem shows the acceptance of life as it comes. Although two friends are parting, there is no over-riding sense of sadness evident in the poem. The parting is simply an element of life that should be accepted.

Acceptance of life as it comes (Wu-Wei) and living according to our innate pattern (Te) are Taoist principles that guided Li Po's life. But these two concepts not only guided Li Po's life, they are also instilled in his poetry. The audience of today is captivated by Li Po's poetry, his artistic style and the message of personal freedom found in Taoist themes. Li Po's poetry has lasted throughout thirteen generations, and I predict it will continue to find succeeding generations in its ever-expanding audience.

Works Cited

Herdan, Innes. *300 T'ang Poems.* Taipei: Far East, 1984.

Lao Tsu. *Tao Te Ching.* Trans. Gia-Fu Feng and Jane English. New York: Vintage, 1989.

Needleman, Jacob. Intro. *Tao Te Ching* by Lao Tsu. Trans. Gia-Fu Feng and Jane English. New York: Vintage, 1989.

Obata, Shigeyoshi. *The Works of Li Po the Chinese Poet.* New York: Paragon, 1965.

Seaton, J. P. and James Cryer. *Bright Moon, Perching Bird: Poems by Li Po and Tu Fu.* Middletown: Wesleyan UP, 1987.

Yohannan, John D., ed. *A Treasury of Asian Literature.* New York: New American Library, 1984.

Note for discussion: the above paper has a list of works cited, but does the paper give in-text citations?

(USED BY PERMISSION)

READING

Who Killed King Kong?

X. J. Kennedy

FROM DISSENT: A QUARTERLY OF SOCIALIST OPINION, SPRING 1960.

The ordeal and spectacular death of King Kong, the giant ape, undoubtedly have been witnessed by more Americans than have ever seen a performance of *Hamlet, Iphigenia at Aulis,* or even *Tobacco Road.* Since RKO-Radio Pictures first released *King Kong,* a quarter-century has gone by; yet year after year, from prints that grow more rain-beaten, from sound tracks that grow more tinny, ticket-buyers by thousands still pursue Kong's luckless fight against the forces of technology, tabloid journalism, and the DAR. They see him chloroformed to sleep, see him whisked from his jungle isle to New York, and placed on show, see him burst his chains to roam the city (lugging a frightened blonde), at last to plunge from the spire of the Empire State Building, machine-gunned by model airplanes.

Though Kong may die, one begins to think his legend unkillable. No clearer proof of his hold upon the popular imagination may be seen than what emerged one catastrophic week in March 1955, when New York WOR-TV programmed *Kong* for seven evenings in a row (a total of sixteen showings). Many a rival network vice-president must have scowled when surveys showed that Kong — the 1933 B-picture — had lured away fat segments of the viewing populace from such powerful competitors as Ed Sullivan, Groucho Marx and Bishop Sheen.

But even television has failed to run King Kong into oblivion. Coffee-in-the-lobby cinemas still show the old hunk of hokum, with the apology that in its use of composite shots and animated models the film remains technically interesting. And no other monster in movie history has won so devoted a popular audience. None of the plodding mummies, the stultified draculas, the white-coated Lugosis with their shiny pinball-machine laboratories, none of the invisible stranglers, berserk robots, or menaces from Mars has ever enjoyed so many resurrections.

Why does the American public refuse to let King Kong rest in peace? It is true, I'll admit, that *Kong* outdid every monster movie before or since in sheer carnage. Producers Cooper and Schoedsack crammed into it dinosaurs, head-hunters, riots, aerial battles, bullets, bombs, bloodletting. Heroine Fay Wray, whose function is mainly to scream, shuts her mouth for hardly one uninterrupted minute from first reel to last. It is also true that *Kong* is larded with good healthy sadism, for those whose joy it is to see the frantic girl dangled from cliffs and harried by pterodactyls. But it seems to me that the abiding appeal of the giant ape rests on other foundations.

Kong has, first of all, the attraction of being manlike. His simian nature gives him one huge advantage over giant ants and walking vegetables in that an audience may conceivably identify with him. Kong's appeal has the quality that established the Tarzan series as American myth — for what man doesn't secretly image himself a huge hairy howler against whom no other monster has a chance? If Tarzan recalls the ape in us, then Kong may well appeal to that great-grand-daddy primordial brute from whose tribe we have all deteriorated.

Intentionally or not, the producers of *King Kong* encourage this identification by etching the character of Kong with keen sympathy. For the ape is a figure in a tradition familiar to moviegoers: the tradition of the pitiable monster. We think of Lon Chaney in the role of Quasimodo, of Karloff in the original Frankenstein. As we watch the Frankenstein monster's fumbling and disastrous attempts to befriend a flower-picking child, our sympathies are enlisted with the monster in his impenetrable loneliness. And so with Kong. As he roars in his chains, while barkers sell tickets to boobs who gape at him, we perhaps feel something more deep than pathos. We begin to sense something of the problem that engaged Eugene O'Neill in *The Hairy Ape*: the dilemma of a displaced animal spirit forced to live in a jungle built by machines.

King Kong, it is true, had special relevance in 1933. Landscapes of the depression are glimpsed early in the film when an impresario, seeking some desperate pretty girl to play the lead in a jungle movie, visits soup lines and a Woman's Home Mission. In Fay Wray—she's been caught snitching an apple from a fruit stand—his search is ended. When he gives her a big feed and a movie contract, the girl is magic-carpeted out of the world of the National Recovery Act. And when, in the film's climax, Kong smashes that very Third Avenue landscape in which Fay had wandered hungry, audiences of 1933 may well have felt a personal satisfaction.

What is curious is that audiences of 1960 remain hooked. For in the heart of urban man, one suspects, lurks the impulse to fling a bomb. Though machines speed him to the scene of his daily grind, though IBM comptometers ("freeing the human mind from drudgery") enable him to drudge more efficiently once he arrives, there comes a moment when he wishes to turn upon his machines and kick hell out of them. He wants to hurl his combination radio-alarm clock out the bedroom window and listen to its smash. What subway commuter wouldn't love—just for once—to see the downtown express smack head-on into the uptown local? Such a wish is gratified in that memorable scene in *Kong* that opens with a wide-angle shot: interior of a railway car on the Third Avenue El. Straphangers are nodding, the literate refold their newspapers. Unknown to them, Kong has torn away a section of trestle toward which the train now speeds. The motorman spies Kong up ahead, jams on the brakes. Passengers hurtle together like so many peas in a pail. In a window of the car appear Kong's bloodshot eyes. Women shriek. Kong picks up the railway car as if it were a rat, flips it to the street and ties knots in it, or something. To any commuter the scene must appear one of the most satisfactory pieces of celluloid ever exposed.

Yet however violent his acts, Kong remains a gentleman. Remarkable is his sense of chivalry. Whenever a fresh boa constrictor threatens Fay, Kong first sees that the lady is safely parked, then manfully thrashes her attacker. (And she, the ingrate, runs away every time his back is turned.) Atop the Empire State Building, ignoring his pursuers, Kong places Fay on a ledge as tenderly as if she were a dozen eggs. He fondles her, then turns to face the Army Air Force. And Kong is perhaps the most disinterested lover since Cyrano: his attentions to the lady are utterly without hope of reward. After all, between a five-foot blonde and a fifty-foot ape, love can hardly be more than an intellectual flirtation. In his simian way King Kong is the hopelessly yearning lover of Petrarchan convention. His forced exit from his jungle, in chains, results directly from his single-minded pursuit of Fay. He smashes a Broadway theater when the notion enters his dull brain that the flashbulbs of photographers somehow endanger the lady. His perilous shinnying up a skyscraper to pluck Fay from her boudoir is an act of the kindliest of hearts. He's impossible to discourage even though the love of his life can't lay eyes on him without shrieking murder.

The tragedy of King Kong then, is to be the beast who at the end of the fable fails to turn into the handsome prince. This is the conviction that the script-writers would leave with us in the film's closing line. As Kong's corpse lies blocking traffic in the street, the entrepreneur who brought Kong to New York turns to the assembled reporters and proclaims: "That's your story, boys—it was Beauty killed the Beast!" But greater forces than those of the screaming Lady have combined to lay Kong low, if you ask me. Kong lives for a time as one of those persecuted near-animal souls bewildered in the middle of an industrial order, whose simple desires are thwarted at every turn. He climbs the Empire State Building because in all New York it's the closest thing he can find to the cliff top of his jungle isle. He dies, a pitiful dolt, and the army brass and publicity men cackle over him. His death is the only possible outcome to as neat a tragic dilemma as you can ask for. The machine-guns do him in, while the manicured human hero (a nice clean Dartmouth boy) carries away Kong's sweetheart to the altar. O, the misery of it all. There's far more truth about upper-middle-class American life in *King Kong* than in the last seven dozen novels of John P. Marquand.

* * * *

Every day in a week on a screen somewhere in the world, King Kong relives his agony. Again and again he expires on the Empire State Building, as audiences of the devout assist his sacrifice. We watch him die, and by extension kill the ape within our bones, but these little deaths of ours occur in prosaic surroundings. We do not die on a tower, New York before our feet, nor do we give our lives to smash a few flying machines. It is not for us to bring to a momentary standstill the civilization in which we move. King Kong does this for us. And so we kill him again and again, in much-spliced celluloid while the ape in us expires from day to day, obscure, in desperation.

State of the Art Assignment

Suppose you were hired as the director of an art institution and had to choose what to perform or display for the next three years. Or suppose you were asked to give a workshop on contemporary abstract sculpture or poetry or South American folk music. Unless you were already up-to-date, how would you find out what was current and what other institutions were doing? You would probably talk to colleagues who knew today's arts. You would pore over arts periodicals and reviews. If you were lucky, you would run across a few articles that summed up today's trends and players. Such articles perform a much needed and appreciated service.

Purpose

Define where an art form is going. What is happening in the world of abstract painting, musical theater, poetry, the novel, cast sculpture, regional folk music, ballet, architecture, illustration, or other art form.

Summarizing the state of an art is a great challenge. It requires a grasp of many artists and their work, as well as of social and political trends that affect the arts. And it also requires taste and judgment to separate artists of quality from those who merely parrot the fashions.

If defining the current state of an art seems too difficult, define an art at a past moment. Even this task is not easy. You must first of all be aware of the variety in a particular medium or genre and decipher patterns in the variety. Suppose, for example, you choose to write about British dramatic comedy ten years after Charles II reopened the theaters (they were closed in 1642 because of the English Civil War and reopened at the Restoration of the monarchy in 1660). You would have to know the variety of plays being produced, their shared traits and differences, audience preferences, rising playwrights, theatrical fads and trends, pressure from competing forms such as musical theater, and developments in theatrical technology. And to produce the most meaningful insights, you would yet need to perceive the constitutive patterns, that is, those patterns that would anticipate the future and influence theater in the next decade.

As you prepare for this assignment, remember that there is no final word. Offer your best perspective. See the assignment as an opportunity to become better acquainted with what is happening in your field.

Audience Considerations

This kind of essay has an immediate appeal to those already interested in the arts; but to those not usually interested, it can still convey the pulse of the times. Few people have time to stay informed of important people and friends in more than one field. Your essay promises readers a catch-up course in what leading artists deem relevant; so survey the field, recognize the main players, and discern the trends. In writing your views, you may want to convey both the disparate variety and the unifying patterns that show where an art is going. To show you know what is going on, pack your essay with references to artists, their works, their ideas, and the writings about them.

Length and Scope

Consider building your paper around several major figures, around a chronology showing change over time, around a classification of several main schools or movements, or around some other scheme.

Consult your teacher on length and due dates.

READINGS

Who Killed Poetry?

Joseph Epstein

FROM COMMENTARY, AUGUST 1988: 13–20.

> "There are certain things in which mediocrity is intolerable: poetry, music, painting, public eloquence."
>
> —La Bruyere

I am not about to say of poetry, as Marianne Moore once did, that "I, too, dislike it," for not only has reading poetry brought me instruction and delight but I was taught to exalt it. Or, more precisely, I was taught that poetry was itself an exalted thing. No literary genre was closer to the divine than poetry; in no other craft could a writer soar as he could in a poem. When a novelist or a dramatist wrote with the flame of the highest inspiration, his work was said to be "touched by poetry"—as in the phrase "touched by God." "The right reader of a good poem," said Robert Frost, "can tell the moment it strikes him that he has taken an immortal wound—that he will never get over it." Such quasi-religious language to describe poetry was not unusual; not so long ago, it was fairly common. "The function of poetry," wrote Robert Graves, "is religious invocation of the Muse; its use is the experience of mixed exaltation and horror that her presence excites."

Both these quotations and several others in the same spirit are to be found at the back of Oscar Williams's *A Little Treasury of Modern Poetry* (revised edition), a small stout volume that has something of the look and heft of a missal or other religious tome. Even Delmore Schwarz, not a man noted for heightened rhetoric or empty ecstasy, referred to the poet as "a kind of priest." To those for whom literature, and culture generally, came increasingly to stand in as a substitute for religion, poetry—and modern poetry specifically—was High Church.

The copyright date on my edition of Oscar Williams's anthology is 1950, and it was during the 1950's that poetry last had this religious aura. Many of the high priests of the cult—T. S. Eliot and Wallace Stevens, Robert Frost and William Carlos Williams, e. e. cummings and W. H. Auden—were still alive and still writing, even if the best of their work was already behind them. The audience for poetry was then less than vast; it had diminished greatly since the age of Browning and Tennyson. In part this was owing to the increased difficulty of poetry, of which T. S. Eliot, in 1921, had remarked: "It appears likely that poets in our civilization, as it exists, at present, must be difficult." Eliot's justification for this difficulty—and it has never seemed quite persuasive—is that poetry must be as complex as the civilization it describes, with the modern poet becoming "more comprehensive, more allusive, more indirect." All this served to make the modern poet more exclusive as well, which for those us who adored (a word chosen with care) modern poetry, was quite all right. Modern poetry, with the advance of modernism, had become an art for the happy few, and the happy few, it must be said, are rarely happier than when they are even fewer.

But such snobbish considerations aside, the generations of poets between W. B. Yeats (1865–1939) and W. H. Auden (1907–1973) produced an impressive body of poetry—of the kind that, in Frosts's phrase, really does make "an immortal wound"; once read, it never is quite forgotten. Nor were all of these poets imposingly difficult: Yeats isn't, nor is Robert Frost. The most difficult poems of all, the *Cantos* of Ezra Pound, seem over the years to have slipped outside the canon of great modern poetry and to be thought instead the interesting fragments of a great cultural impresario—the Diaghilev of modernist poetry—who finally flipped, betraying both his country and himself. These poets did not, except occasionally, teach. Occupationally, they ranged from physician (William Carlos Williams) to editor (Marianne Moore) to insurance executive (Wallace Stevens); in personal style, from traditionally formal (T. S. Eliot) to bohemian (e. e. cummings) to suicidally desperate (Hart Crane). But for all their variety, no one would ever think to describe them as academic.

They were, however, the first living poets to be given the full academic treatment. Their works were dissected in classrooms, the intellectual quarterlies ran solemn essays about them even while continuing to run their poems, book-length critical studies about them began to be written and continue to be written even now. Their fame was neither of the general nor of the wealth-producing kind that Ernest Hemingway and William Faulkner knew—though

T. S. Eliot was an international celebrity—but within the circumambience of the university they were revered. No body of critical writing produced during this period was more efficacious than that of T. S. Eliot, whose essays could affect the reputation—"the place in the canon," as academics now put it—of writers born three hundred years earlier. In the view of F. R. Leavis, Eliot, along with Samuel Johnson, Coleridge, and Matthew Arnold, is one of the four great English literary critics, yet without the authority lent his criticism by his poetry, it is plain that Eliot's critical power would have been nowhere near so great.

But the clearest evidence of the reverence in which these poets were held is found in the way they were worshiped by the generation of poets, or at least those in America, who followed them. Randall Jarrell, Robert Lowell, John Berryman, Delmore Schwartz not only wrote some of the most brilliant essays on their immediate poetic forebears, but in their lives they tended to be obsessed with them. The young Robert Lowell set up a tent on the lawn of the home of Allen Tate, to learn at the feet of one of his masters. Delmore Schwartz viewed T. S. Eliot as a culture hero, pure though not so simple, and his letters and conversation were filled with references to Eliot. Randall Jarrell, after writing about Wallace Stevens's latter-day weaknesses, capped his criticism with the thought that Stevens was "one of the true poets of our century, someone whom the world will keep on reading just as it keeps on listening to Vivaldi or Scarlatti, looking at Tiepolo or Poussin."

Jarrell, Lowell, Berryman, Schwartz, as anyone who has read much about them cannot mistake, were all immensely ambitious men. Had their ambitions been applied to business or politics or perhaps anything other than careers in poetry—and all four were the most careful caretakers of their careers—they might not have ended as sadly as they did: in repeated mental breakdown, alcoholism, early death, and suicide. I believe poetry was implicated in their disastrous lives in that they had set out to forge brilliant careers like those of their predecessors and knew that, for a complex of reasons, they could not make it. Jarrell wrote an essay entitled "The Obscurity of the Poet," which he claimed had to be surmounted if civilization were to carry on, and another entitled "The Taste of the Age," which he found trashy. Delmore Schwartz wrote essays on "The Isolation of Modern Poetry," "The Vocation of the Poet," "Views of a Second Violinist, Some Answers to Questions about Writing Poetry," and "The Present State of Poetry," a state that he thought, to put it gently, uninspiring. The main modernist poets had written with assurance in their bones, as if they knew their worth and knew that posterity would one day know it, too. But the poets who came after them were less sure; they knew something had gone wrong. And they were right. It had.

Before I attempt to get at what I believe has happened, perhaps I ought to describe what I think is the situation of contemporary poetry. Pressed to formulate this situation in a single sentence, I should write: contemporary poetry in the United States flourishes in a vacuum. Today there are more than 250 universities with creative-writing programs, and all of these have a poetry component, which means that they not only train aspiring poets but hire men and women who have published poetry to teach them. Many of these men and women go from being students in one writing program to being teachers in another—without, you might say, their feet, metrical or anatomical, having touched the floor. Many colleges and universities that do not have formal writing programs nonetheless hire poets to teach a creative-writing course or two; and the course in writing poetry has also become a staple of the community-college and adult-education menu. None of this puts poets up there with the Helmsleys and the Trumps, but it has made it possible for a large number of poets—and more than 6,300 poets and other writers are listed in the most recent edition of the *Directory of American Poets and Fiction Writers*—to earn their living in work closely connected with their craft. Such work, thirty or so years ago, was available only to a small handful of poets, and these of the highest stature.

Robert Frost, when in his eighties and a great draw on the poetry-reading circuit, thought it a good thing that poets had become teachers "in a thousand, two thousand colleges," and added that colleges and universities gave poets "the best audiences poetry ever had in this world." Writing in 1985, in an essay entitled "The Poetry Reading: Public Performance\Private Act," the poet Donald Hall noted: "in the past thirty years, the poetry reading, which used to be rare, has become the chief form of publication for American poets. Annually, hundreds of thousands of listeners hear tens or thousands of readings." The great majority of these take place on college campuses, but many others are given at such cultural centers as the 92nd Street Y in New York, the Poetry Center at the Art Institute in Chicago, the International Poetry Forum in Pittsburgh, not to mention various churches, synagogues, bars, art galleries, bookstores, and other public forums, Donald Hall reminds us that such poets as Rachel Lindsay, Carl Sandburg, and Robert Frost were giving readings in the 20's and 30's, but it was Dylan Thomas, in the late 40's and early 50's, who by providing quite beautiful performances and the added attraction of outrageous behavior really put poetry reading on the cultural map.

Poetry readings can draw anywhere from a pathetic handful of bedraggled students to a tony audience of several hundred. The fame of the poet is decisive. Fame, too, determines fees. Donald Hall, in 1985, claimed that a standard good fee for a reading was $1,000, though most poets, I suspect, accept a good deal less, while others—Allen Ginsberg, Adrienne Rich, John Ashbery—can command more. James Dickey claimed to have received as much as $4,500 for a reading. Sometimes two or three nearby colleges will invite a poet to read at each of their institutions, and the poet will pick up two or three fees while the colleges share the cost of a single airplane ticket. Intramurally, there are arguments about whether readings are corrupting to poets. Some claim that reading too frequently can make a poet tend to compose simpler, jokier poems that can be readily understood by an audience, whereas complex poems—imagine hearing Wallace Stevens's "Le Monocle de Mon Oncle" without ever having read it—do not, so to say, play well at readings. Yet readings have helped many poets who do not have, or want, teaching jobs to keep going financially. Readings, too, are often the only payment in the coin of the realm of the ego that they ever receive, for the printed work of poets, sometimes including poets who have been at it a long while, often gets hardly any response at all in the way of reviews or even letters from readers.

No one keeps very precise records on such matters, but the general sense is that more poetry is currently being published than ever before. Poets are not being all that widely published by the major trade houses of New York and Boston, though almost all of them do publish some contemporary poets. Many university presses have begun to issue books of poetry, and some have been doing so for years. (Howard Nemerov, our new poet laureate, has been published by the University of Chicago Press for as long as I can remember.) What have come to be called the "small presses" also publish a fairly large amount of poetry. Some of these—David R. Godine of Boston, for example, or North Point Press of Berkeley—aren't as small as all that, but others, which carry such names as Dragon Gate or Aralia Press, truly are. The best general answer to the question of how well these books of poetry sell is probably "not very." It used to be said that the only serious poet in America who was ever able to live off the sale of his work was Robert Frost, but according to Donald Hall, even Frost was able to do so only at the end of his life.

Yet there is no shortage of outlets for poetry. The *New Yorker* publishes it, most of the literary monthlies and quarterlies do; *Poetry*, founded by Harriet Monroe in 1912, rolls along. And beyond such publications are the many little magazines that print vast quantities of poetry. The circulation of these magazines is often not in the thousands but in the hundreds. Almost all of them would go under without subsidization. So numerous are the little magazines that there exists an organization—an "umbrella organization," in the bureaucratic phrase—called The Coordinating Council for Literary Magazines. It, too, is heavily subsidized, in good part by the National Endowment for the Arts. Sometimes it seems as if there isn't a poem written in this nation that isn't subsidized or underwritten by a grant either from a foundation or the government or a teaching salary or a fellowship of one kind or another.

And so, as the disc jockeys say, the beat goes on. The pretense is that nothing is wrong, that business is proceeding pretty much as usual. There are today, for example, prizes galore: Pulitzers and Lamonts and National Book Critics Circle and Yale Younger Poets and Rome Fellowships of the American Academy and Institute of Arts & Letters and Guggenheims and National Endowment for the Arts Fellowships and Library of Congress Consultantships and the Lilly Prize and now a national poet laureate and even—how he, most ambitious of poets, would have wryly smiled at the news—a Delmore Schwartz Memorial Award. Poets regularly parade as spokesmen and women for their ethnic group or race or political tendency. Some few poets—Robert Penn Warren, perhaps Richard Wilbur is soon to arrive at this position—have more medals than Baron von Richthofen.

No shortage, then, of honors, emoluments, publication possibilities, opportunities to garner public adulation. In such ways may contemporary poetry be said to be flourishing.

But what of the vacuum? I should say that it consists generally of this: that however much contemporary poetry may be honored, it is, outside a very small circle, scarcely read. Contemporary poetry is no longer a part of the regular intellectual diet. People of general intellectual interests who feel that they ought to read or at least know about works on modern society or recent history or novels that attempt to convey something about the way we live now, no longer feel the same compunction about contemporary poetry. The crowds in London once stood on their toes to see Tennyson pass; today a figure like Tennyson probably would not write poetry and might not even read it. Poetry has been shifted—has shifted itself?—off center stage. Literarily, poetry no longer seems in any way where the action is. It begins to seem, in fact, a sideline activity, a little as chiropractic or acupuncture is to mainstream medicine—odd, strange, but with a small cult of followers who swear by it.

One might counter that poetry was in a similar state when the modernist poets set out on their ambitious artistic adventure. They published their work in magazines read only by hundreds; their names were not known by most members of the educated classes; their following, such as it was, had a cultish character. But beyond this nothing else seems comparable. Propelling the modernist poets was a vision, and among some of them a program—a belief that the nature of life had changed fundamentally and that artists now had to change accordingly. Free verse, fragmented syntax, radical dysjunctions, slangy diction, the use of subjects before then thought poetically impossible— these were among the techniques and methods employed by the modernist poets. New, too, was their attitude toward the reader, whom they, perhaps first among any writers in history, chose in a radical way to disregard. They weren't out to *épater*. If what they wrote was uncompromisingly difficult, they did not see this as their problem. They wrote as they wrote; as for their difficulty, the question was whether or not, in Henry James's phrase, theirs was "the difficulty that inspired." By that phrase I take James to have meant difficulty of a kind that inspires one to surmount it because one senses the reward to be eminently worthy of the struggle. Somehow, through the quality of their writing, the authority of the sacrifices they made for their art, the aura of adult seriousness conveyed in both work and life, the modernist poets won through. Theirs was the difficulty, ours the inspiration.

Whereas one tended to think of the modernist poet as an artist—even if he worked in a bank in London, or at an insurance company in Hartford, or in a physician's office in Rutherford, New Jersey—one tends to think of the contemporary poet as a professional: a poetry professional. Like a true professional, he is rather insulated within the world of his fellow-professionals. The great majority of poets today live in an atmosphere almost entirely academic, but it is academic with a difference: not the world of science and scholarship but that of the creative-writing program and the writing workshop. (Everything that has gone wrong with the world since World War II, Kingsley Amis once noted, can be summed up in the word "workshop.") The poets who have come out of this atmosphere are oddly positioned both in academic life and in the world at large; they are neither wholly academics nor wholly artists. They publish chiefly in journals sheltered by universities, they fly around the country giving readings and workshops at other colleges and universities. They live in jeans yet carry a curriculum vitae. I have seen scores of such curricula, and they tend to run along the following lines:

> James Silken [a name I have made up] published his first book of poems, *Stoned Jupiter*, with the University Presses of Florida. His

second book, *The Parched Garden*, will be published early next year by Black Bear Press. A chapbook, *Apaches and Parsley*, was brought out by Wainscoting Books in 1983. His poems and reviews have appeared in such journals as *Poetry Northwest, New Letters, The Arizona Review, TriQuarterly*, and *Worcester Review*. He has given readings at Iowa State University, the University of Michigan, Drake University, and Bread Loaf. Next summer he will be a fellow at the Oregon Center for the Creative Arts. A native of Tennessee, he now lives in Tempe, where he directs the writing program at Arizona State University.

Well, it's a living.

In 1941 Delmore Schwartz, in an essay originally published in *Kenyon Review* and entitled "The Isolation of Modern Poetry," wrote that "It is not a simple matter of the poet lacking an audience, for that is an effect, rather than a cause, of the character of modern poetry." The character that Schwartz then had in mind was its difficulty (in the Henry James sense). In *Partisan Review*, in 1949, Schwartz added, "Anyone who wants to understand modern poetry can do so by working about half as hard as he must to learn a language, or acquire any new skill, or learn to play bridge well." But in fact, with an occasional exception (the obscurity of much of the poetry of John Ashbery comes to mind), contemporary poetry has not grown more but less difficult, and the audience still isn't there.

If Delmore Schwartz blamed the obscurity of modern poetry on its difficulty, Randall Jarrell, in a lecture at Harvard called "The Obscurity of the Poet," blamed the national culture. "The poet," said Jarrell, "lives in a world whose newspapers and magazines and books and motion pictures and radio stations and television stations have destroyed, in a great many people, even the capacity for understanding real poetry, real art of any kind." In more recent years, poets have taken this a step further to blame America for an anti-intellectual and anti-artistic strain in our national life. "Pushkin could count on railway workers to know his poems," John Berryman told Eileen Simpson, his first wife. "*Think of it!* Who reads poetry in America?" Poetry, it is elsewhere claimed, is ill-taught in grammar and high schools. The neglect of poetry by major trade publishers is sometimes blamed. Capitalism generally comes in for its share of lumps, sometimes for encouraging supermarket bookselling techniques, sometimes for holding up the wrong models: What kind of country is it in which Lee Iacocca is better known than A. R. Ammons? Everything, in short, is blamed but the drinking water.

Some poets, attempting to swallow the hand that feeds them, even blame the university, arguing that, through the emergence of so many creative-writing programs, poets have created their own, largely inbred audience that simultaneously requires a great deal in the way of care and feeding and asks little of them, the poets, in the way of literary ambition. ("Within five years," wrote Greg Kuzma, a poet and teacher of poetry, "there will be a creative-writing program available for anyone in America within safe driving distance of his home.") Creative-writing programs, this argument runs, are not only producing more people who think of themselves as poets than this or any other country needs, but, through the encouraging, the somewhat therapeutic, atmosphere of the workshop, are generally lowering the high standard of work which is poetry's only serious claim on anyone's attention.

From a higher, more historical point of view, there are those who claim that the game was up for poetry with the advent of romanticism, which retained great themes for poetry but saw them through a filter of the self—whereas now, this argument holds, the great themes are gone and all that remains to poetry is a pallid subjectivity. "With the development of romantic theory in the 18th, 19th, and 20th centuries," the eminent critic Yvor Winters wrote, "there has been an increasing tendency to suppress the rational in poetry and as far as it may be to isolate the emotional." A grave mistake this, at least for those who tended to view poetry as a vehicle for truth and a repository as useful as any ever invented for ideas and insights. Christopher Clausen, author of an excellent little book entitled *The Place of Poetry, Two Centuries of an Art in Crisis*, underscores this point when he writes: "Since the rise of science to intellectual preeminence, poets have been less able either to show equal claim with scientists to clarify the problems Western civilization has (perhaps wrongly) seen as most important, or to incorporate and epitomize the conclusions of their rivals."

Romanticism, science; even modernism itself has been put in the dock, for draining the joyousness out of poetry or, with the introduction of free verse, depriving poetry of the delights of meter and rhyme. Philip Larkin, for one, laid the blame for the broken connection between poets and readers on what he called "the aberration of modernism, that blighted all the arts." He meant in particular the modernist tendency to deify the artistic vocation, to separate it from any obligation on the part of a writer to instruct or entertain an audience. In a three-page essay entitled "The Pleasure Principle," Larkin wrote that "at bottom poetry, like all art, is inextricably bound up with giving pleasure, and if a poet loses his pleasure-seeking audience he has lost the only audience worth having, for which the dutiful mob that signs on every September is no substitute."

To screw things yet one notch higher, there are those who believe that the decline of poetry in our day is an inevitable accompaniment of the disintegration of language generally. Wendell Berry, a poet and essayist, writes: "My impression is that we have seen, for perhaps 150 years, a gradual increase in language that is either meaningless or destructive of meaning. And I believe that this increasing unreliability of language parallels the increasing disintegration, over the same period, of persons and communities"—and, one gathers, by extension, of the power of poetry to recover much of value from the wreckage. At a slightly lower level of generality, others believe that the use poetry has traditionally made of rhythm and meter, of image and metaphor, to bring its readers to a condition of susceptibility to the emotion and thought it wishes to convey simply no longer finds an adequate response in any but a minuscule handful of trained readers. It is as if an old human skill, like following a trail or scenting game, had atrophied and died. Still others appeal to the mysteries of history. Might we not just be going through a bad patch in the history of poetry, as the country did between, say, 1870, when Emily Dickinson and Walt Whitman were still at the height of their powers, and 1910, when the modernist poets exploded upon the scene?

No doubt romanticism, modernism, and other literary ideas and ideological movements have all had their effect in landing poetry in the position it finds itself in toward the close of the 20th century. Institutional, linguistic, historical factors have also doubtless exerted their influence in pushing poetry into the dark corner it now inhabits. Yet nearly every explanation of the situation of poetry in our time — attempting to account for its isolation, its seeming irrelevance to the general culture, the depressing sense that this once most elevated of human activities is now rather second-rate — seems to let the poets themselves off the hook. There may be something to Walt Whitman's remark that "to have great poets, there must be great audiences too," but, as Delmore Schwartz once rejoined, "To have great poetry it is necessary to have great poets. . . ."

Not that anyone has been claiming that ours is a great age of poetry. Literary forms, or genres, after all, have their own, odd, often indecipherable rises and falls. English drama never again reached the heights attained in the Elizabethan Age. Who could have predicted the great burgeoning brilliance of the novel in mid-19th-century Russia? It may well be that sixty or seventy years ago, in our Eliots and Yeatses and Stevenses and Hardys and Frosts, we had our Donnes and Marvells and are now living through our Wallaces and Lovelaces. Another view, one straightforwardly formulated by Karl Shapiro, holds that there is precious little poetic talent around even at the best of times. As Shapiro notes:

> I have for a long time come to the conclusion that at any one time the production of true works of art is even rarer than we think. I even devised a rule-of-thumb dogma which I call the B-S-K theory of poetry: Byron, Shelley, and Keats. According to this dogma, there can only be three poets at any one time. In periods of resplendent renaissance, the number increases slightly but not much, perhaps up to half a dozen. Around the points of these stars, there are a certain number of satellites, and so on. Actually, this is a historically realistic way of looking at art.

But even if there were any B's or S's or K's about nowadays, it is not certain we would know who they were. Poetry is published in such plenitude that last year the Los Angeles *Times* announced it would no longer review books of poems, on the grounds that it was impossible to tell which were important. The same, by extension, applies to poets. There is nothing resembling a consensus on who might be the important poets of our day. The most lauded must be Robert Penn Warren, but one does not hear him often spoken of, or see him written about, as the kind of poet whose work is central to the lives of his readers. Richard Wilbur, the past poet laureate, is everywhere taken for eminent, and everyone for whom poetry matters reveres him for his craftsmanship, yet Wilbur does not seem to stir passionate advocacy in his readers, except when held up as a model of the literary decorum that has been lost to poetry in its confessional, sexier, Visigothic aspects. Seamus Heaney, the Irish poet who currently teaches at Harvard, is generally written about as if he were a major figure, yet his poetry, too, has failed to break out of the tight, claustral little circle of professionals. Doubtless the most famous poet in

America is Allen Ginsberg, but poetry isn't really what he is famous for: politics and homosexuality and a talent for the outrageous and a small genius for publicity are the four cornerstones on which his fame rests. John Ashbery is also publicly honored and written about with critical reverence; yet, though he is not himself an academic, his poetry—about which he has said, "Poetry does not have subject matter because it is the subject. We are the subject matter of poetry, not vice versa"—is perfect for academic treatment, being allusive, desultory, and nicely self-deconstructive, which also means that it is most unlikely to hold any interest outside the academy.

Other names of equal weight are on the scene. Of the senior generation, there are Stanley Kunitz, Karl Shapiro, David Ignatow, and (in England) Stephen Spender. Of the generation of poets now in or almost in its sixties, there are Howard Nemerov, James Merrill, John Hollander, Anthony Hecht, Donald Davie, Hayden Carruth, Donald Hall, W.S. Merwin, Galway Kinnell, Richard Howard, Mona Van Duyn, Philip Levine, Maxine Kumin, Derek Walcott, Adrienne Rich, William Meredith. "When I find myself among those who don't know my name," said Virgil Thomson, "I know I'm in the real world." But the poets mentioned in this paragraph, though large names in the small world in which they operate, are again for the most part unknown outside universities or the pages of *Poetry, American Poetry Review,* and *Parnassus.*

I not long ago had occasion to hear two poets read and talk about their craft. Both were men, both in their thirties, both had regular teaching jobs at large universities, both had published two books and had their share of grants and awards. One of the two was a Hawaiian of Japanese ancestry, the other was middle-class Jewish. Both were zealous about poetry, which they took to be insufficiently appreciated in an essentially philistine country. The first poet viewed himself as a spokesman for his people, the truth of whose past he saw it as his task to keep alive in his own poetry. The second poet did not announce himself as a spokesman for the Jews, but he came across in the style one thinks of as tough but sensitive, the champion of a beleaguered art. His father, he disclosed, is a salesman, and it had been no easy thing to get him to understand his son's need to be a poet. (A salesman, evidently, can die deaths unknown even to Arthur Miller.) In their discussions after they read, both poets were full of quotations from Pound and Eliot and Kant and Rilke, giving off a strong whiff of the classroom.

As for the works themselves, the first read a lengthy poem about a visit to a strip of land in Hawaii that had once been the site of the cemetery where his grandfather was buried but which had since been plowed up by a developer. His was a poem, in short, about victimization, with a bit of anti-capitalism thrown in at no extra charge. The second read a poem entitled "Proustian" about the brief happy moments when, as a child, his grandmother fed him cookies and milk and he had no knowledge of time, and another poem about a visit to his former high-school football coach, who had always preached the powers of the body, but was now sadly powerless in a body racked by cancer. A poem, the New Critics held, cannot be paraphrased, but in paraphrasing—summarizing, really—these poems I do not think I am doing them a grave injustice. I bring them up only because they seemed so characteristic, so much like a great deal of contemporary poetry: slightly political, heavily preening, and not distinguished enough in language or subtlety of thought to be memorable.

Is it all up with poetry, then? As early as the 1940's, Edmund Wilson wrote an essay carrying the questioning title, "Is Verse a Dying Technique?" Wilson's answer was, essentially, yes, it is. Prose, in Wilson's view, had overwhelmed poetry. By Flaubert's time, he notes, "the Dantes present their vision in terms of prose dramas or fiction rather than epics in verse." Wilson mentions Flaubert because he is the first novelist to lavish the kind of care on his prose that poets did on their verse; James Joyce would be another. Yeats was the last great poet to write convincingly in iambic pentameters, which, Wilson noted, "no longer [have] any relation whatever to the tempo and language of our lives." Antiquated forms can only render an antiquated point of view, and "you cannot deal with contemporary events in an idiom which was already growing trite in Tennyson's and Arnold's day. . . ."

Wilson does allow that our lyric poets may be compared with any who have ever written, but he adds: "We have had no imaginations of the stature of Shakespeare or Dante who have done their major work in verse." Edgar Allan Poe had anticipated much of this a century earlier. In"The Poetic Principle," his essay of 1848, Poe wrote: "if, at any time, any very long poems *were* popular in reality — which I doubt — it is at least clear that no very long poem will ever be popular again." We shall continue to read Homer, Dante, Shakespeare, Milton, perhaps Byron and Browning, to cherish and derive great pleasure from them, but with the understanding that what they did — specifically telling magnificent stories in poetic form — can never be done again.

Not that writers haven't tried. Philip Toynbee published a novel in verse in the 1960's. Clive James has written lengthy travesties of contemporary London literary life in heroic couplets. The most recent effort, a 307-page novel entitled *The Golden Gate,* composed in a Pushkinian rhyme scheme by a young writer named Vikram Seth, appeared in 1986 to much acclaim. But it was a claim of the odd kind that Samuel Johnson felt was owed to women preachers and dogs walking on their hind legs: "You are surprised to find it done at all." So swept away were readers by the sheer freakiness of Vikram Seth's accomplishment that they overlooked its rather clichéd Berkeleyan (California not Bishop) message about making love not war.

Poets have not altogether given up on telling stories. Some of Robert Frost's best poems are narratives. Although fragmented and disjunctive, even "The Waste Land" tells a story; so, too, in a very different way, does Wallace Stevens's "Sunday Morning." In *Life Studies* (1957), Robert Lowell conveyed portions of his autobiography in verse. Among contemporary poets, Herbert Morris, in finely controlled blank verse, has written dramatic monologues and accounts of his childhood that are essentially narrative in character and quite successfully so. But for the vast most part contemporary poetry has gone off in the direction of the lyric. In practice, this means a shortish poem, usually fewer than forty lines, generally describing an incident or event or phenomenon of nature or work of art or relationship or emotion, in more or less distinguished language, the description often, though not always, yielding a slightly oblique insight.

Samuel Johnson, who said of *Paradise Lost* that "None ever wished it longer than it is," said in the same essay on Milton that "All that short compositions can commonly attain is neatness and elegance." There are various reasons why so many contemporary poems are, in Johnson's phrase, "short compositions," and not the least among them is that most magazines do not provide space for long poems. They choose not to do so on the assumption, probably correct, that few even quite serious readers wish to read a poem that runs ten or more pages. (Let us not speak of the talent that it takes to sustain an extended poetic performance.) But in taking up the lyric as its chief form, contemporary poetry has seriously delimited itself. It thereby gives away much that has always made literature an activity of primary significance; it gives away the power to tell stories, to report on how people live and have lived, to struggle for those larger truths about life the discovery of which is the final justification for reading. Thus has poetry in our day become, in the words of the intelligent young poet and critic Brad Leithauser, "a sadly peripheral art form."

Even here on the periphery, though, it would help to be able to make a few distinctions. Although it hardly guarantees the production of great poets, a start might be made by deciding who are the greatly overrated ones. This, however, is not likely to happen soon. Contemporary poetry, in the cumbersome new usage of the academic literary criticism of the moment, has been "privileged" — that is, in our day it has been given a special dispensation, set apart, released from the burden of undergoing tough criticism. Helen Vendler, the most talented critic of contemporary poetry now at work, almost exclusively writes elucidary appreciations; one can only infer which poets Professor Vendler doesn't care for by her neglecting to write about them. Randall Jarrell, the most talented critic of contemporary poetry in his day, felt no such compunction; he kissed and slapped with equal exuberance. But then poetry in Jarrell's time may not have seemed as sickly as it does now. Now, for so many poets, critics, editors, small-press publishers, creative-writing programs, the chief thing seems to be keeping the patient alive.

Yet if survival is genuinely at stake, it won't do to ignore symptoms. For an account of symptoms, of what is wrong with so much contemporary poetry, one does well to consider an extraordinary essay by Witold Gombrowicz, the Polish novelist who died in Paris in exile in 1969. The essay is entitled, straight out, "Against Poets." In his second paragraph Gombrowicz states, if not his case against contemporary poetry, his condition when reading it:

> The thesis of the following essay, that almost no one likes poems and that the world of verse is a fiction and a falsehood, will seem, I assume, as bold as it is frivolous. Yet here I stand before you and declare that I don't like poems at all and that they even bore me. Maybe you will say I am an impoverished ignoramus. Yet I have labored in art for a long time and its language is not completely alien to me. Nor can you use your favorite argument against me, claiming that I do not possess a poetic sensibility, because I do possess it and to a great degree. When poetry appears to me not in poems but mixed with other, more prosaic, elements, for example, in Shakespeare's dramas, in the prose of Pascal and Dostoevsky, or simply as

a very ordinary sunset, I tremble as do other mortals. Why does rhythm and rhyme put me to sleep, why does the language of poets seem to me to be the least interesting language conceivable, why is this Beauty so unattractive to me and why is it that I don't know anything worse as style, anything more ridiculous than the manner in which poets speak about themselves and their poetry?

When Gombrowicz gets down in his bill of particular complaint, it turns out that he is put off by the professionalization of poetry — "today one is a poet, the way one is an engineer or a doctor" — which has robbed poetry of its spontaneity, made poetry itself seem artificial, and rendered the poet a less than complete human being. Poetry has been surrounded by altogether too much piety, so that poets have begun to think themselves priestly in their exclusivity. Poets tend to keep the company of other poets, which not only fortifies them in "their ostrich politics in relation to reality," but protects them from seeing their own weaknesses. Poets create chiefly for other poets — for people like themselves, which, in Gombrowicz's view, is another weakness. Here, he notes, "I am not demanding that they write 'in a way comprehensible to everyone.'" He merely wishes that they would not so insistently pose as artists and neglect the fact that beyond their enclosed private world exist other, quite as interesting worlds. He mentions the way poets honor and praise and generally suck up to one another, writing about their fellow poets in a "bombastic gibberish so naive and childish that it is difficult to believe that the people wielding the pen did not feel the ridiculousness of this publicism." But enough.

If Gombrowicz's condition seems slightly self-exacerbated, his case more than slightly exaggerated, nevertheless anyone who has followed contemporary poetry will have shared some of his irritation with it and will recognize a general truth to his charges. No world I have ever peered in upon can seem simultaneously so smug and so hopeless as that of the world of contemporary poets, especially in its creative-writing program phase. All too often contemporary poets comport themselves as if they were self-appointed to E. M. Forster's little aristocracy of the sensitive, the considerate, and the plucky. ("When what they really are," a wag I know has said, "is the insensate, the outrageous, and the lucky.") The last thing they wish to hear is that they are producing something not many people outside the classroom want; and instead they act as if those who do not appreciate what they do are, on the face of it, spiritually crippled.

But among serious poets, and people serious about poetry, there is a stabbing recognition that something has happened. It is as if poetry has lost its weight, and hence its reality, and hence its value. Speaking for myself, there have been contemporary poets I have much admired — to mention only the recently dead, Elizabeth Bishop, L. E. Sissman, Philip Larkin — but none has been able to plant language in my head the way that poets of an earlier generation could: "The salmon-falls, the mackerel-crowded seas"; "Complacencies of the peignoir, and late/Coffee and oranges in a sunny chair"; "But I have promises to keep/And miles to go before I sleep"; "In the room the women come and go/Talking of Michelangelo"; "All in green went my love riding"; "a low dishonest decade"; "Something there is that doesn't love a wall"; "imaginary gardens with real toads in them."

Where did all that elegant, potent, lovely language go; or, more precisely, where went the power to create such language? Perhaps, like W. B. Yeats in Auden's poem, it "disappeared in the dead of winter."

To return to Marianne Moore, whence we set out:

I, too, dislike it.

Reading it, however, with a perfect contempt

for it, one discovers in

it, after all, a place for the genuine.

And more than the genuine, I should say, though just now the entire enterprise of poetic creation seems threatened by having been taken out of the world, chilled in the classroom, and vastly overproduced by men and women who are licensed to write it by degree if not necessarily by talent or spirit. It was Wallace Stevens who once described poetry as "a pheasant disappearing in the brush." One gets a darting glint of it every once in a while in the work of the better contemporary poets, but to pretend that that meaty and delectable bird freely walks the land isn't going to get him out of hiding, not soon, and maybe not ever.

The Wrong Stuff

John Michael Vlach

FROM NEW ART EXAMINER, SEP. 1991

The 1924 exhibition "Early American Art" held at the Whitney Studio Club ranks in most histories of American folk art as pivotal. Put on display were some 45 works (most of them discovered in New England antique shops) owned by artists active in the New York avant-garde, men like Charles Sheeler, Yasuo Kuniyoshi, William Zorach, and Robert Laurent.[1] While the popularity of folk things had been building steadily at least since the celebration of the American Centennial in Philadelphia in 1876, at the Whitney show folk objects were presented finally as works of art rather than relics of history. This apparent honor was ironically the first misstep of several along the twisting path of folk art appreciation.

The new sanction expressed in the Whitney show conferred greater prestige on these artifacts even as it fostered a serious misunderstanding of folk art, one that has persisted into the present. The Whitney show concentrated on folk art's formal aesthetic qualities and moved deliberately away from the original social contexts to which these objects had once been so causitively linked. Thus, folk works were, and have since been, misunderstood according to the values of Modernist fine art. The avant-garde dogma of the 1920's

---

[1] See Beatrix T. Rumford, "Uncommon Art of the Common People: A Review of Trends in the Collecting and Exhibiting of American Folk Art," in Ian M. G. Quimby and Scott T. Swank, *Perspectives on American Folk Art* (New York: W. W. Norton, 1980), pp. 16–19.

involved, in part, an attempt to emulate the art of exotic peoples—African masks and Oceanic woodcarvings. And, by a wild leap, the artist-discoverers of American folk works considered their new finds home-grown primitives, the equivalent of tribal arts. Folk art was judged desirable because it seemed to bear a formal resemblance to so-called primitive art.

The new enthusiasm for folk art—what was at the time called "folk art fever"—proved so contagious that soon noted patrons of the arts, particularly collectors who were eager to associate themselves with the Modern movement, were off in search of shop figures, weather vanes, theorem drawings, and limner portraits. The social caliber of this patronage, which included wealthy art collectors like Abby Aldrich Rockefeller and Electra Havermeyer Webb, served to boost the popularity of folk art even higher. While crowds flocked to folk art exhibitions in the 1920s and 1930s, the attraction had more to do with the fame and prestige of its early discoverers and collectors than it did with traditional art or artists. Who collected folk art was more important than the art that was collected.

In fact, the folk attributes of this art mattered so little that early collectors and curators would continue to establish folk art's significance expressly by linking it formally to Modern art. In order for Jean Lipman, the reigning grand dame of the folk art world, to claim repeatedly since 1942 that folk art had "a power and originality and beauty . . . not surpassed by the greatest of the academic painters," she has focused solely on features of form and the fortuitous presence of similar features in works by contemporary fine artists. In support of her claim, she has presented what she calls "provocative parallels" between folk expression and works by Jim Dine, Andy Warhol, Modigliani, Marisol, Alexander Calder, and many others. She compares, for example, Warhol's prints of soup cans to quilts because they share an underlying grid design.[2] Other commentators following Lipman's lead have so emphasized formal aesthetic attributes that the human dimension of folk art, its social history, has been consigned to the distant background.

As the history of folk artists and their clients was obscured, another misstep was taken. Indeed, it was only a simple move to replace the actual experiences of folk artists with a false consciousness. According to art historian Kenneth L. Ames, American folk art has, almost from its moment of discovery, been wrapped up in a redemptive myth, a narrative that supports a heroic image of the folk artist as a fiercely independent handicrafter who, in spite of his or her poverty, was happy to be living in a democratic country.[3] This patriotic fantasy, a far cry from lived experience, satisfied popular desire for a congratulatory version of American history, a need that was particularly acute during the era of the great Depression and again during the so-called Eisenhower years. The rosy propaganda of this myth is indicative of the

---

[2] Jean Lipman, from the preface to Jean Lipman and Alice Winchester, eds., *The Flowering of American Folk Art (1776–1876)* (New York: Viking Press, 1974), p. 7; Jean Lipman, *Provocative Parallels* (New York: E. P. Dutton, 1975).

[3] Kenneth L. Ames, *Beyond Necessity: Art in the Folk Tradition* (New York: W. W. Norton, 1977), p. 21.

wrong-headed, if well-intentioned, interpretations of folk art that continue to be widely accepted.

Not only have most commentators of folk art had a simplistic view of history, they have also failed in their attempts to read the art they claim to celebrate. Since the 1924 show at the Whitney, the prevailing standards for evaluation have been derived principally from the traditions of western fine art. Almost three-fourths of the works displayed at he Whitney show were paintings and drawings, revealing a fine-art bias. The appropriateness of using studio-based standards was rarely questioned: these standards were simply imposed. In other words, if art was assumed to consist mainly of paintings and sculpture, folk art was also assumed to consist mainly of paintings and sculpture. Further, if paintings were considered superior to sculpture, then the so-called folk paintings that ranked highest in the canon of prime folk objects should be sought with more enthusiasm than three-dimensional objects. Because this rationale is so deeply ingrained—and because folk art was simply presumed to echo the academic tradition—half to three quarters of the objects displayed in even the most recent exhibitions are paintings and drawings.[4]

To see pictorial works (especially the nineteenth-century portraits so often lauded as "five-star" folk art) as representative of American folk tradition ignores the very social and formal considerations that in fact distinguish folk from academic art. Such portraits were seldom produced within American folk societies, particularly during the first half of the nineteenth century (the era considered to be the golden age of American folk art), nor did the common men and women commission many paintings of any kind. The images that are so frequently suggested as representative of the common folk were actually painted for the upper-middle class segment of society, a group whose numbers accounted for less than ten percent of the total population. Moreover, they were an arriviste group committed to improving their social position by aggressively surrounding themselves with material signs of improvement. High on their list of prestige-conferring or -enhancing goods were paintings, particularly portraits. Ownership of a portrait, even one that failed to provide an anatomically correct likeness, proved that an individual possessed the sufficient discretionary wealth to engage in a fashionable ritual of success. By commissioning a portrait, an individual could appear to belong to the class of prominent social elites even if he or she was never admitted into their company.

Likewise these so-called folk paintings, while they were often flawed with respect to resemblance (and it is the mistakes that have legitimized these works as folk art), represented not a folk tradition but a deliberate and

---

[4] See for examples Jean Lipman, Elizabeth V. Warren, and Robert Bishop, *Young America: A Folk Art History* (New York: Hudson Hills, 1986); Beatrix T. Rumford and Carolyn J. Weekly, *Treasures of American Folk Art from the Abby Aldrich Rockefeller Folk Art Center* (Boston: Little Brown and Co., 1989); Jean Lipman, Robert Bishop, Elizabeth V. Warren, and Sharon L. Eisenstat, *Five-Star Folk Art: One Hundred American Masterpieces* (New York: H. M. Abrams, 1990).

conscious effort to participate in the taste culture of studio art.[5] A close look at he life histories of any of the painters whose canvases are presented as emblematic works of folk art reveal that those artists clearly had fine-art ideals in mind. The career of Joseph Whiting Stock (1815–1855) of Springfield, Massachusetts, an artist whose works have routinely been included in exhibitions of American folk art since the 1930s, provides telling proof that the so-called folk painters were doing their best to emulate the style and technique of fashionable studio idioms. First, Stock received his initial training, albeit indirectly, form Chester Harding, the most celebrated social portraitist of the day. Whatever Stock failed to learn from direct instruction he would pick up later from various instruction manuals like Charles Davie's *A Treatise on Shades and Shadows and Linear Perspective* (1832) and John G. Chapman's *American Drawing-Book* (1847). Indeed, at the time of his death, more than half the books in his 60-volume library were art titles. There can be no question that he was well acquainted with the academic requirements of illusionistic easel painting. Over the course of his 20-year career Stock was able to transform himself from an awkward amateur into a competent and knowledgeable professional. After an initial apprenticeship period during which he was only capable of producing stiff, rather two-dimensional images, he eventually developed a professional control over brush and palette and was able finally to satisfy the needs of the more discerning sitter.[6] Wherever sufficient biographical information is available for so-called folk painters, such a pattern of gradual improvement is noticeable. To identify these artists as folk is to miss both what they were trying to do and what they were able to accomplish. Put most simply, Stock's paintings and other works by painters of his ilk were the wrong stuff to claim as folk art. Rather than advancing the genres of folk societies, artists like Stock aspire to the aesthetic and status of nineteenth-century academic art.

Beyond the lack of a clear definition—a problem arising from repeated attempts to certify that imperfect attempts at fine art should be accepted as important folk creations—the field of folk art suffers from a contradictory discourse. The seeming terms of endearment that one frequently hears offered in praise of folk art—that it is said to be bold, vigorous, clever, witty, sincere, etc.—are actually expressions of mild contempt. At their best, or so runs the prevailing logic, folk artists can only hope to approximate the fine art ideal. Folk art is cast, then, as second rate art, good perhaps but not great, charming but never profound, entertaining but never important. The adjectives most often used to describe folk art generally carry negative, if not pejorative, connotations: naive, primitive, innocent, country, provincial, outsider, nonacademic. Collectively these words form a dialect of derogation, a vocabulary good mainly for offering back-handed compliments; for example, an artist might be said to possess a "sophistication . . . lacking in most folk art" or to manifest a

---

[5] John Michael Vlach, *Plain Painters: Making Sense of American Folk Art* (Washington, D.C.: Smithsonian Institution Press, 1988), Chapter 3.

[6] Juliette Tomlinson, ed., *The Paintings and Journal of Joseph Whiting Stock* (Middletown, Connecticut: Wesleyan University Press, 1976), p. 20.

"pleasant stability . . . very different from the obsession and striving that mark the work of so many other folk artists."[7] While such evaluations are offered as sympathetic praise, there is evidently plenty of snickering in the background.

For most of the twentieth century, a confusing aesthetic game has been played at the expense of American folk art. Common sense and better judgement have been suspended so that works of arrested talent could be celebrated as masterpieces. Gradually, misstep by misstep, the term has become one of negation so that according to noted gallery director Jane Kallir, the label is now seen as "a catchall category for misfits—wallflowers at the dance of Western civilization."[8] If this is so, it is because misfits have been deliberately sought out. In place of works that might express the sentiments of tradition bearing groups—communities formed on the basis of shared ethnicity, region, religion, occupation, or other social experience—what collectors have most frequently sought is a foil for fine art. In the process, they have represented folk art as the rough-hewn, country cousin always prone to laughable social errors. A general failure to connect works of folk art to the lived experience of folk groups has thus given rise to a folk art that ironically has no folk attached to it other than those imagined to justify less-than-flattering stereotypes. Thus, regardless of their professed respect for folk art, many collectors, and curators, too, have persistently reinforced the well-entrenched hegemony of high culture categories that necessarily confines folk artist to an inferior position.[9]

A different approach to folk art is needed, one that empowers artists as competent creators who choose to work in ways that do not require the sanction of academies, galleries, and other official institutions. This is the only way to get beyond the stereotypes regarding class, creativity, and value that have for so long hidden folk art behind a veil of demeaning assumptions. What has been missed for so long is the essential fact that every day all over the United States thousands of people who do not necessarily consider themselves artists use their imagination to create things of value, things of beauty. Just think of the millions of quilts that are stitched each year: the magnitude of this creativity becomes overwhelming. While these bedcovers might be seen more as crafted items than as works of art, there can be no question that they warm the body, or that their colors, textures, and designs go far beyond the requirements of pragmatic need. The same could be said for countless other "tools for living" that are produced as the part of a thousand daily routines. These objects can properly be considered art that is made in the context of work. Sanctioned usually by decades if not centuries of local custom, these domestic objects express collectively held views about what is decent, beautiful,

---

[7] Jay Johnson and William C. Ketchum, American Folk Art of the Twentieth Century (New York: Rizzoli, 1983), pp. 274, 54.

[8] The Folk Art Tradition: Naive Painting in Europe and the United States (New York: Viking Press, 1981), p. 8.

[9] Daniel Robbins, "Folk Art Without Folk," In Folk Sculpture, U.S.A., ed. by Herbery Waide Hemphill, Jr. (New York: Brooklyn Museum, 1976), p.20.

helpful.[10] Not every item made, of course, is perfect: only a select few are held up as proud examples of excellence. And here, the usual judgments offered or implied about folk art — that it is somehow flawed, botched, or inept — do not fit. These works are the equal of fine art, not its weak and imperfect echo. They are the right stuff, and they are the works that have been missing from gallery walls and from the usual commentary about American folk art.

---

[10] For examples see John Michael Vlach, *Charleston Blacksmith: The Work of Philip Simmons* (Athens: University of Georgia Press, 1981); John A. Burrison, *Brothers in Clay: The Story of Georgia Folk Pottery* (Athens: University of Georgia Press, 1983); Geraldine N. Johnson, *Weaving Rag Rugs: A Woman's Craft in Western Maryland* (Knoxville: University of Tennessee Press, 1985); Simon J. Branner, *Chain Carvers: Old Men Crafting Meaning* (Lexington: University Press of Kentucky, 1989); Dale Rosengarten, *Row Upon Row: Sea Grass Baskets of the South Carolina Low Country* (Columbia, SC: McKissick Museum, 1986); Eli Leon, *Who'd a Thought It: Improvisation in African-American Quiltmaking* (San Francisco: San Francisco Craft and Folk Art Museum, 1987); Michael Owen Jones, *Craftsman of the Cumberlands: Tradition and Creativity* (Lexington: University Press of Kentucky, 1989); Rosemary O. Joyce, *A Bearer of Tradition: Dwight Stump, Basketmaker* (Athens: University of Georgia Press, 1989).

Nature and Function of Art Assignment

Up to now, you've mostly been writing about individual artists and single works of art. Now broaden your focus to the art form, medium, style, abstract problem, or concept of art itself. Since your focus will move from concrete works to more abstract issues, you may want to guard against becoming too detached from the world. Remember your audience, and use specific illustrations whenever possible. Study the section "Defining Art" in Problems in Aesthetic Discourse.

Purpose

Write an article for nonacademic, nonexpert readers, in which you explain your views on an issue like:

- What is art?
- Can we define art generally without subtly favoring one medium over another?
- What processes determine what we consider high and low art or who gets discovered and who doesn't?
- What makes good or bad art?
- Are there necessary links between the moral or political and the aesthetic qualities of art? Do some works, though excellent in structure and technique, promote bad moral ideas, political principles, or social prejudices?
- Are artists free to produce whatever they want? If so, to what standards may we reasonably hold them as they use that freedom?
- How does art serve (or not serve) the needs of the individual and society? Given your ideas on this, what kinds of art do we really need, and what do we do with the other kinds?
- What principles inform a certain art, style, medium, or movement?

You will probably discover that every issue of art's nature and function is contested. Some critics take one position, some take another, and others undermine everyone else. In response to this apparent lack of unity, you may stake out your own position in relation to what others think, address the issue of uncertainty itself and explain why it exists, or take a knowingly contested position and argue for it. Reading may help you formulate ideas about your own position. Use quotes where the ideas of others help clinch your own reasoning, but remember that this assignment focuses primarily on revealing your own "truths" regarding the nature of art.

Audience Considerations

Abstract speculation makes some people reckless and others conservative and cautious. Remember that readers like new opinions, especially when they sense a real voice with commitment behind it. Don't be afraid to speak from out on a limb and to open up new areas of reflection for readers. The history of art and art criticism is one of new limbs. Just take care to pick a strong branch, and don't saw it off behind you. Readers also like careful thinking that rigorously defines known problems and sorts through available theories to reach conclusions that are, if not daring and innovative, sound and insightful.

The least successful writers mistake strong prejudice for deep thought. They announce their truth, dust their hands off, and walk away before the questions crop up, as if to say, "I am Sir Oracle, and when I open my lips let no dog bark" (*Merchant of Venice* I.i). Provide ample support for your views and show awareness of possible arguments against them. Also, show an awareness that each issue connects with others. You can hardly argue for the special value of art without already making assumptions about art's nature and the way it achieves its effects.

And the very least successful writers simply substitute clichés (e.g., "beauty is in the eye of the beholder" or "one man's junk is another man's treasure"), dictionary definitions for "art," or excuses (such as beginning by saying that for hundreds of years others have tried to define art and no one has come to any conclusions) for careful reasoning.

Length and Scope

Consult your teacher on length and due dates.

WORKSHOP EVALUATION SHEET: NATURE AND FUNCTION OF ART

Author _____ Reviewer _____

Part I. Ideas

1. Is the main idea clear, focused, and stated near the beginning? State in one or two sentences what the writer believes the nature and function of art to be. If you can't do this, tell the writer.

2. From reading this essay, can you summarize orally for the writer *why* he or she takes the position stated in question #1? That is, what reasoning and evidence does the writer provide for the thesis? Does the writer agree that you have understood the reasoning or evidence?

3. What other points of view are expressed or referred to? Are they fairly represented? Does the essay acknowledge the possibility of many points of view on art? If not, would the essay be better if it did?

4. Rate the essay on its complexity and depth (scale of 4, with 4 the highest).

5. Has the writer persuaded you? If not, can you suggest ways to strengthen the essay?

Part II. Writing Technique

1. Can you state how the essay is organized? Can you find transitions or other types of signals to its organization?

2. Do you see specific examples and details in support of its main ideas?

3. In two paragraphs from the body of the essay, find what you see to be the topic sentences (main idea of the paragraph). Where do these come in the paragraphs? Could they be more effectively placed?

4. Does the writer use precise words and phrases (rather than "awesome," "wonderful," "really")?

SAMPLE STUDENT ESSAYS

SAMPLE 1: NATURE AND FUNCTION OF ART

Mocha Orchid Wafer Fluff

SIMEEN BROWN HANNIG

When asked "What is art?" Andy Warhol replied coyly, "Art is a boy's name." And so it is. But the overactive human brain is not satisfied with such an obvious answer. Every action must have a reason. There must be a purpose for hanging a toilet on the wall, stuffing a corner full of lard, strapping yourself to the front of a car, draping miles of landscape with pink plastic, or gyrating to the beat of the bongo drum.

After categorizing human behavior into appropriate reasons for actions such as survival, power, popularity, the incapable brain tosses the remaining fat into the left-over barrel category of art. We now smirk smugly knowing we have defined all things. This brings me back to Timpview High School, oddly enough. I remember the athletes or "jocks" were the ones who sat on stud wall; the social student government people stuffed themselves endlessly into the yearbook; F dudes took coach Kauo's class; and new wavers bleached their long bangs and smoked cloves. Everyone had a category. Everyone fit somewhere. It's in all of us since grade school, since we were old enough to distinguish between Gilligan's Island and Pat Schumaker's Spotlight 5. Since Mrs. Goodman taught in the first grade about the Russians and Americans, the white people and the black people, the cowboys and the Indians, the boys and the girls.

But that was only the beginning. Last year I sat in my nineteenth-century painting class and learned about the impressionists and the realists, the Germans and the Spanish, the Dark Ages and the Renaissance. Then it came time to discuss Manet. Mrs. Palmer warned that the critics could not agree which group he really belonged to. Was he a new wave or a jock? At that moment I remembered the many conversations I'd had with high school graduates and the surprising number who always say "You know I didn't really belong to a particular clique in high school. I was friends with people in all different groups." There goes that human nature again which, with great ease, packs Starlee Hanen, Biff Watters and Edouard Manet into individually wrapped processed ready-to-serve slices and considers itself the omniscient big cheese.

The conflict between these two human tendencies — the practice of "classing" and the struggle for individuality — is a plaguing problem in art. I believe this fight between the artists and their critics has poisoned the art world of today. There sits that woman with a doctor's degree from the ivy league, acclaims from her peers, and free tickets to the Mets. This person keeps attempting to shove a size ten foot into Cinderella's glass slipper. "I am not a new wave!" exclaims the artist. Sometimes the artist's sole purpose is to shock and confuse the poor critic who is continually attempting to organize people and ideas into rows like the shoes in her closet.

Sometimes it's a battle between the artist and the logician with the public as victims. The public must accept the critic's conclusion about which art is "good." They're the ones whose taxes support a man who photographs homosexuals engaged in intercourse. If they object, the art world laughs and pronounces them stupid. Both critic and artist are too rich, self centered, and bored, a problem that came with technology, free enterprise, and the new attitude of "every man for himself." Art has not always been so gluttonous.

Art at one time had a reason or a purpose for its creation aside from the self-serving attitude of some today. Leonardo Da Vinci drew the figure to practice where all the muscles go. Ancient drawings carved women with huge bosoms to encourage fertility. The medieval Byzantine architects included gold mosaic scenes from the Bible to teach the common people. The native Americans sang and chanted to bring long-awaited rain. Michelangelo painted the Sistine Chapel because the Pope made him do it. There was an outside consequence or result which encouraged the artist. He acted in harmony with society instead of against it.

The question of the purpose art should serve involved me very personally as an artist. Art to me should be more than simply a reaction to a voyeuristic critic, although I understand this motive. I don't wish to puzzle the critic while laughing under my breath "Hee, hee hee, They think that kitchen chair from the 70's framed in glass is art." Instead, I prefer creating for a purpose even as simple as Michelangelo's. I wish to serve society instead of use it.

I do not discard the black five-foot-by-eight-foot-square hanging in the MOMA, or dislike the four story clothespin. I love them as well as whirling multi-colored kinetic sculptures with flashing lights and bizarre performance art. These things make me giggle. But I am an ancient woman at heart, the one who fashioned her fertility talisman, who painted her history on cave walls, who decorated her dinner plate. I am the minstrel who sang legends to the queen; who played the lute. I am the man in the Dark Ages who built cathedrals and golden plated icons to his God. If I could paint something which would hang on the wall over Aunt Clara's sofa or design a pair of beautiful and unusual shoes, then I would feel my worth as an artist. The opinion of the critics interests me little since they themselves do not personally create. If they could, they would discover how much more exciting it is to sculpt a pot, sing in an opera, or write poetry than to discuss someone else and their reasons for doing such. They would also discover how little they truly understand about the artist. The ballet dancer is practicing from breakfast until dinner, the weaver is busy at the loom, the painter is in her studio covered with paint stains on her clothes. The talk about art is left to those unqualified, unwilling, and incapable of participating. It is like the difference between eating Mocha Orchid Wafer Fluff and just talking about it. I'd rather live life than discuss it.

Perhaps my work will be of interest to these art talkers. They might write papers about my reasons for making art, my feelings as I did it, and its inherent worth. They will be happy only when I have found a place either as a new wave or an F dude. Analysis and great research will be involved. In the meantime, if they need to contact me, I'll be out dancing to bongo drums, weaving necklaces for the homeless, or in some cafe eating Mocha Orchid Wafer Fluff on my date with Art.

(USED BY PERMISSION)

SAMPLE 2: NATURE AND FUNCTION OF ART

I Heard Nietzsche in the Clerestory

TIFFANY LUNDEEN FROST

Plato called it a kind of play or sport, a copy of an image of virtue three times removed from reality. Perhaps all subsequent philosophies of art have been merely footnotes. In my study of aesthetics and the great defining minds of Western civilization, I had been confined by four blank walls, buried by books that seduced me into thinking that with only my eyes I might see the truth or fallacy of Plato's and other behemoths' philosophies of art. From my perch, however, one particular German caught my attention in his response to Plato.

Friedrich Wilhelm Nietzsche was critical of the major schools of aesthetics and explained that most immediately art causes the gulfs between self and the Other to give way to an overwhelming feeling of unity. Not only is the union between these two reaffirmed, but Nature, "which has become estranged . . . celebrates once more her reconciliation with [the prodigal]." With art we console ourselves, we who are "so singularly constituted for the most sensitive and grievous suffering." Art saves us. Art does not give a "reflection," but "true knowledge and insight into the terrible truth." We see everywhere only the terror or the absurdity of existence. But at this juncture, when the will is most imperiled, art approaches, "as a redeeming and healing enchantress."[1] We feel godlike: we have become a work of art. The role of art is to create this metaphysical supplement absolutely necessary to make life livable—even bearable—and sometimes beautiful.

Still, I never took any of these dead philosophers to heart; in my age of gestural expressionism and kinetic sculpture their academic treatises seemed to contribute little to understanding twentieth-century chaos. It was not until I set out on my pilgrimage that I could devote all my mind and strength to the consideration of their words and the formation of my own. With the intention of uncovering art and its nature, I made the arduous journey to my own Mecca: Western Europe.

From Italy I made my way north through southern France, resting occasionally under the heavy canopies of vines that quilted the countryside. Watching the people as if behind a glass pane, I saw that their lives are still rooted in the dark soil and determined by the harvest. Their sunburnt lips drink the world's sweetest wine, but still speak of the difficult manual existence they plow into deep furrows each winter. When I finally walked into the Musée d'Orsay, it seemed to me a great temple where I would find Apollo and

---

[1] Friedrich Nietzsche, *The Birth of Tragedy and the Genealogy of Morals,* trans. Francis Golffing (NY: Doubleday, 1956).

Aphrodite. Instead I found my friends from the Provence in *The Gleaners* of 1857 by Jean-Francois Millet. Here were three gleaners in heroic monumentality, noble laborers who strain to satisfy their hunger and who call up religious associations—any one of them might have been Ruth. In their rhythmic motion, these figures give beauty and nobility. This is the painting that orders and places universal significance on their lives; it sings of their common experiences, anxieties, and frustrations, and makes their labor glorious. I wondered how many had been to Paris to see themselves, and how many had reveled in the beauty of their calling.

From Paris I tumbled to Vienna, where it seemed that the statuettes on the bus were carrying some secret grief. Perhaps it was only the culture, but I wondered if each frigid face concealed the violent horrors and the quiet despairs of our shared mortality, of daily disappointments and lifelong hunger. One unusually warm night, I slipped into a concert hall where Beethoven's ninth symphony was being performed in its entirety, his masterpiece that charts his final journey from darkness into light. After one hour, the opening chords of the final movement exploded through the hall. Soon the chorus joined the orchestra with Beethoven's own text, crying, "Brethren, let us no longer sing of such dark things. Let us sing of more joyous things." I saw that I still did not understand the music. The Austrians around me were translucent—still unsmiling, but unspeakably moved. To them, the music was revelation, an intoxication that brought them together, and they consoled one another without words. The shouts from stage-right were strains of reconciliation, of hope, of renewal, of healing.

Many miles later, I found myself cloudless in Barcelona at the tremendous park built by the architect Gaudí. At the bottom of great ceramic steps, four women from three generations danced around one another, gently and rhythmically lifting and falling into one another. They were performing some strange ritual, a familiar dance—patterns of reliance and friendship, birth and death, failure and triumph. Their movements were liquid but charged, and people sat hypnotized, without sound, and listened to the dancers' labored breathing. Theirs was the story of life, of the struggle of men and women to find meaning, of relationships of loyalty and relief. The women invited the observers around them to join in the dance, to share their common passions, to give order and significance to the random events of their lives. I was breathless on the brilliant concrete, absorbed into collective arms and legs.

I left Europe. I found angels in train stations, temples downtown, and poetry in torn posters. But I found true art in all places where the individual and the world were reconciled, where Nature welcomed back the prodigal, where the individual's relationship with the human family was healed. Where the slave was freed, where the stubborn, hostile barriers between us were broken down, where we expressed ourselves as a part of a higher community—there I found art. I need not have gone to Europe to find it; once I knew what I was looking for, art was crying to me from the pages of Sophoclean tragedy and the furniture of Frank Lloyd Wright. Months later I thought back on the nave of Notre Dame and recognized Nietzsche's voice as that song I heard echoing in the clerestory. It was Nietzsche who had articulated this before me, who had declared that art revealed the common experience of humankind. And so I scotch-tape my addition to Nietzsche's footnote to Plato, and can affirm only what I lived: art relieves each of us of our individual burdens, too immense to carry alone, and reassures us that we are part of something greater. Art places meaning and order on human existence by uncovering our fundamental relationships to nature and to one another and offers us some metaphysical power to survive.

(USED BY PERMISSION)

READING

The Cultural Importance of Art

Susanne K. Langer

FROM PHILOSOPHICAL SKETCHES (BALTIMORE: JOHNS HOPKINS UP, 1962).

Every culture develops some kind of art as surely as it develops language. Some primitive cultures have no real mythology or religion, but all have some art-dance, song, design (sometimes only on tools or on the human body). Dance, above all, seems to be the oldest elaborated art.

The ancient ubiquitous character of art contrasts sharply with the prevalent idea that art is a luxury product of civilization, a cultural frill, a piece of social veneer.

It fits better with the conviction held by most artists, that art is the epitome of human life, the truest record of insight and feeling, and that the strongest military or economic society without art is poor in comparison with the most primitive tribe of savage painters, dancers, or idol carvers. Wherever a society has really achieved culture (in the ethnological sense, not the popular sense of "social form") it has begotten art, not late in its career, but at the very inception of it.

Art is, indeed, the spearhead of human development, social and individual. The vulgarization of art is the surest symptom of ethical decline. The growth of a new art of even a great and radically new style always bespeaks a young and vigorous mind, whether collective or single.

What sort of thing is art, that it should play such a leading role in human development? It is not an intellectual pursuit, but is necessary to intellectual life; it is not religion, but grows up with religion, serves it, and in large measure determines it.

We cannot enter here on a long discussion of what has been claimed as the essence of art, the true nature of art, or its defining function; in a single lecture dealing with one aspect of art, namely its cultural influence, I can only give you by way of preamble my own definition of art, with categorical brevity. This does not mean that I set up this definition in a categorical spirit, but only that we have no time to debate it; so you are asked to accept it as an assumption underlying these reflections.

Art, in the sense here intended — that is, the generic term subsuming painting, sculpture, architecture, music, dance, literature, drama, and film — may be defined as the practice of creating perceptible forms expressive of human feeling. I say "perceptible" rather than "sensuous" forms because some works of art are given to imagination rather than to the outward senses. A novel, for instance, usually is read silently with the eye, but is not made for vision, as a painting is; and though sound plays a vital part in poetry, words even in poetry are not essentially sonorous structures like music. Dance requires to be seen, but its appeal is to deeper centers of sensation. The difference between dance and mobile sculpture makes this immediately apparent. But all works of art are purely perceptible forms that seem to embody some sort of feeling.

"Feeling" as I am using it here covers much more than it does in the technical vocabulary of psychology, where it denotes only pleasure and displeasure, or even in the shifting limits of ordinary discourse, where it sometimes means sensation (as when one says a paralyzed limb has no feeling in it,) sometimes sensibility (as we speak of hurting someone's feelings), sometimes emotion (e.g., as a situation is said to harrow your feelings, or to evoke tender feeling), or a directed emotional attitude (we say we feel strongly *about* something), or even our general mental or physical condition, feeling well or ill, blue, or a bit above ourselves. As I use the word, in defining art as the creation of perceptible forms expressive of human feeling, it takes in all those meanings; it applies to everything that may be felt.

Another word in the definition that might be questioned is "creation." I think it is justified, not pretentious, as perhaps it sounds, but that issue is slightly beside the point here; so let us shelve it. If anyone prefers to speak of the "making" or "construction" of expressive forms, that will do here just as well.

What does have to be understood is the meaning of "form," and more particularly "expressive form"; for that involves the very nature of art and therefore the question of its cultural importance.

The word "form" has several current uses; most of them have some relation to the sense in which I am using it here, though a few, such as "a form to be filled in for tax purposes" or "a mere matter of form," are fairly remote, being quite specialized. Since we are speaking of art, it might be good to point out that the meaning of stylistic pattern — "the sonata form," "the sonnet form" — is not the one I am assuming here.

I am using the word in a simpler sense, which it has when you say, on a foggy night, that you see dimly moving forms in the mist; one of them emerges clearly, and is the form of a man. The trees are gigantic forms; the rills of rain trace sinuous forms on the windowpane. The rills are not fixed things; they are forms of motion. When you watch gnats weaving in the air, or flocks of birds wheeling overhead, you see dynamic forms — forms made by motion.

It is in this sense of an apparition given to our perception that a work of art is a form. It may be a permanent form like a building or a vase or a picture, or a transient, dynamic form like a melody or a dance, or even a form given to imagination, like the passage of purely imaginary, apparent events that constitute a literary work. But it is always a perceptible, self-identical whole; like a natural being, it has a character of organic unity, self-sufficiency, individual reality. And it is thus, as an appearance, that a work of art is good or bad or perhaps only rather poor—as an appearance, not as a comment on things beyond it in the world, or as a reminder of them.

This, then, is what I mean by "form"; but what is meant by calling such forms "expressive of human feeling"? How do apparitions "express" anything—feeling or anything else? First of all, let us ask just what is meant here by "express," what sort of "expression" we are talking about.

The word "expression" has two principal meanings. In one sense it means self-expression —giving vent to our feelings. In this sense it refers to a symptom of what we feel. Self-expression is a spontaneous reaction to an actual, present situation, an event, the company we are in, things people say, or what the weather does to us; it bespeaks the physical and mental state we are in and the emotions that stir us.

In another sense, however, "expression" means the presentation of an idea, usually by the proper and apt use of words. But a device for presenting an idea is what we call a symbol, not a symptom. Thus a word is a symbol, and so is a meaningful combination of words.

A sentence, which is a special combination of words, expresses the idea of some state of affairs, real or imagined. Sentences are complicated symbols. Language will formulate new ideas as well as communicate old ones, so that all people know a lot of things that they have merely heard or read about. Symbolic expression, therefore, extends our knowledge beyond the scope of our actual experience.

If an idea is clearly conveyed by means of symbols we say it is well expressed. A person may work for a long time to give his statement the best possible form, to find the exact words for what he means to say, and to carry his account or his argument most directly from one point to another. But a discourse so worked out is certainly not a spontaneous reaction. Giving expression to an idea is obviously a different thing from giving expression to feelings. You do not say of a man in a rage that his anger is well expressed. The symptoms just are what they are; there is no critical standard for symptoms. If, on the other hand, the angry man tries to tell you what he is fuming about, he will have to collect himself, curtail his emotional expression, and find words to express his ideas. For to tell a story coherently involves "expression" in quite a different sense: this sort of expression is not "self-expression," but may be called "conceptual expression."

Language, of course, is our prime instrument of conceptual expression. The things we can say are in effect the things we can think. Words are the terms of our thinking as well as the terms in which we present our thoughts, because they present the objects of thought to the thinker himself. Before language communicates ideas, it gives them form, makes them clear, and in fact makes them what they are. Whatever has a name is an object for thought. Without words, sense experience is only a flower of impressions, as subjective as our feelings; words make it objective, and carve it up into *things* and *facts* that we can note, remember, and think about. Language gives outward experience its form, and makes it definite and clear.

There is, however, an important part of reality that is quite inaccessible to the formative influence of language: that is the realm of so-called "inner experience," the life of feeling and emotion. The reason why language is so powerless here is not, as many people suppose, that feeling and emotion are irrational; on the contrary, they seem irrational because language does not help to make them conceivable, and most people cannot conceive anything without the logical scaffolding of words. The unfitness of language to convey subjective experience is a somewhat technical subject, easier for logicians to understand than for artists; but the gist of it is that the form of language does not reflect the natural form of feeling, so that we cannot shape any extensive concepts of feelings with the help of ordinary, discursive language. Therefore the words whereby we refer to feeling only name very general kinds of inner experience — excitement, calm, joy, sorrow, love, hate, and so on. But there is no language to describe just how one joy differs, sometimes radically, from another. The real nature of feeling is something language as such — as discursive symbolism — cannot render.

For this reason, the phenomena of feeling and emotion are usually treated by philosophers as irrational. The only pattern discursive thought can find in them is the pattern of outward events that occasion them. There are different degrees of fear, but they are thought of as so many degrees of the same simple feeling.

But human feeling is a fabric, not a vague mass. It has an intricate dynamic pattern, possible combinations and new emergent phenomena. It is a pattern of organically interdependent and interdetermined tensions and resolutions, a pattern of almost infinitely complex activation and cadence. To it belongs the whole gamut of our sensibility — the sense of straining thought, all mental attitude and motor set. Those are the deeper reaches that underlie the surface waves of our emotion, and make human life a life of feeling instead of an unconscious and metabolic existence interrupted by feelings.

It is, I think, this dynamic pattern that finds its formal expression in the arts. The expressiveness of art is like that of a symbol, not that of an emotional symptom; it is as a formulation of feeling for our conception that a work of art is properly said to be expressive. It may serve somebody's need of self-expression besides, but that is not what makes it good or bad art. In a special sense one may call a work of art a symbol of feeling, for, like a symbol, it formulates our ideas of inward experience, as discourse formulates our ideas of things and facts in the outside world. A work of art differs from a genuine symbol — that is, a symbol in the full and usual sense — in that it does not point beyond itself to something else. Its relation to feeling is a rather special one that we cannot undertake to analyze here; in effect, the feeling it expresses appears to be directly given with it — as the sense of a true metaphor, or the value of a religious myth — and is not separable from its expression. We speak of the feeling of, or the feeling in, a work of art, not the feeling it means. And we speak truly; a work of art presents something like a direct vision of vitality, emotion, subjective reality.

The primary function of art is to objectify feeling so that we can contemplate and understand it. It is the formulation of so-called "inward experience," the "inner life," that is impossible to achieve by discursive thought, because its forms are incommensurable with the forms of language and all its derivatives (e.g., mathematics, symbolic logic). Art objectifies the sentience and desire, self-consciousness and world-consciousness, emotions and moods, that are generally regarded as irrational because words cannot give us clear ideas of them. But the premise tacitly assumed in such a judgment—namely, that anything language cannot express is formless and irrational—seems to me to be an error. I believe the life of feeling is not irrational; its logical forms are merely very different from the structures of discourse. But they are so much like the dynamic forms of art that art is their natural symbol. Through plastic works, music, fiction, dance, or dramatic forms we can conceive what vitality and emotion feel like.

This brings us, at last, to the question of the cultural importance of the arts. Why is art so apt to be the vanguard of cultural advance, as it was in Egypt, in Greece, in Christian Europe (think of Gregorian music and Gothic architecture), in Renaissance Italy—not to speculate about ancient cavemen, whose art is all that we know of them? One thinks of culture as economic increase, social organization, the gradual ascendancy of rational thinking and scientific control of nature over superstitious imagination and magical practices. But art is not practical; it is neither philosophy nor science; it is not religion, morality, or even social comment (as many drama critics take comedy to be). What does it contribute to culture that could be of major importance?

It merely presents forms—sometimes intangible forms—to imagination. Its direct appeal is to that faculty, or function, that Lord Bacon considered the chief stumbling block in the way of reason, and that enlightened writers like Stuart Chase never tire of condemning as the source of all nonsense and bizarre erroneous beliefs. And so it is; but it is also the source of all insight and true beliefs. Imagination is probably the oldest mental trait that is typically human—older than discursive reason; it is probably the common source of dream, reason, religion, and all true general observation. It is this primitive human power—imagination—that engenders the arts and is in turn directly affected by their products.

Somewhere at the animalian starting line of human evolution lie the beginnings of that supreme instrument of the mind—language. We think of it as a device for communication among the members of a society. But communication is only one, and perhaps not even the first, of its functions. The first thing it does is to break up what William James called the "blooming, buzzing confusion" of sense perception into units and groups, events and chains of events—things and relations, causes and effects. All these patterns are imposed on our experience by language. We think, as we speak, in terms of objects and their relations.

But the process of breaking up our sense experience in this way, making reality conceivable, memorable, sometimes even predictable, is a process of imagination. Primitive conception is imagination. Language and imagination grow up together in a reciprocal tutelage.

What discursive symbolism—language in its literal use—does for our awareness of things about us and our own relation to them, the arts do for our awareness of subjective reality, feeling and emotion; they give form to inward experiences and thus make them conceivable. The only way we can really envisage vital movement, the stirring and growth and passage of emotion, and ultimately the whole direct sense of human life, is in artistic terms. A musical person thinks of emotions musically. They cannot be discursively talked about above a very general level. But they may nonetheless be known—objectively set forth, publicly known—and there is nothing necessarily confused or formless about emotions.

As soon as the natural forms of subjective experience are abstracted to the point of symbolic presentation, we can use those forms to imagine feeling and understand its nature. Self-knowledge, insight into all phases of life and mind, springs from artistic imagination. That is the cognitive value of the arts.

But their influence on human life goes deeper than the intellectual level. As language actually gives form to our sense experience, grouping our impressions around those things which have names, and fitting sensations to the qualities that have adjectival names, and so on, the arts we live with—our pictures books and stories and the music we hear—actually form our emotive experience. Every generation has its styles of feeling. One age shudders and blushes and faints, another swaggers, still another is godlike in a universal indifference. These styles in actual emotion are not insincere. They are largely unconscious—determined by many social causes, but *shaped* by artists, usually popular artists of the screen, the jukebox, the shop-window, and the picture magazine. (That, rather than incitement to crime, is my objection to the comics.) Irwin Edman remarks in one of his books that our emotions are largely Shakespeare's poetry.

This influence of art on life gives us an indication of why a period of efflorescence in the arts is apt to lead a cultural advance: it formulates a new way of feeling, and that is the beginning of a cultural age. It suggests another matter for reflection, too—that a wide neglect of artistic education is a neglect in the education of feeling. Most people are so imbued with the idea that feeling is a formless, total organic excitement in men as in animals that the idea of educating feeling, developing its scope and quality, seems odd to them, if not absurd. It is really, I think, at the very heart of personal education.

There is one other function of the arts that benefits not so much the advance of culture as its stabilization—an influence on individual lives. This function is the converse and complement of the objectification of feeling, the driving force of creation in art: it is the education of vision that we receive in seeing, hearing, reading works of art—the development of the artist's eye, that assimilates ordinary sights (or sounds, motions, or events) to inward vision, and lends expressiveness and emotional import to the world. Wherever art takes a motif from actuality—a flowering branch, a bit of landscape, a historic event, or a personal memory, any model or theme from life—it transforms it into a piece of imagination, and imbues its image with artistic vitality. The result is an impregnation of ordinary reality with the significance of created form. This is the subjectification of nature that makes reality itself a symbol of life and feeling.

The arts objectify subjective reality, and subjectify outward experience of nature. Art education is the education of feeling, and a society that neglects it gives itself up to formless emotion. Bad art is corruption of feeling. This is a large factor in the irrationalism which dictators and demagogues exploit.

Review Assignment

The reviewer has a great and occasionally abused responsibility. He or she acts as an intermediary between the public and the work of art. On the one hand, the reviewer is only one individual among many, a person whose views may carry no more intrinsic authority than anyone else's. On the other hand, we require reviewers who can help us sift through the many books, films, art shows, music, dance, and plays that appear daily.

Reviewers differ in their opinions, so we might ask what elevates them to their privileged position. Depth and breadth of knowledge, sensitive judgment, awareness of the state of an art form, informed assessment of general culture, and effective verbal style earn it. Together, they demonstrate cultural competence. Regardless of critics' differences, these factors may keep readers from simply brushing aside their judgments.

The role of the reviewer, then, is an excellent example of how keen thought and the skilled use of language can earn one a place of respect. They grant authority in a field in which each person's experience — not the critic's commandment — is the final test. Yet this statement immediately opens up issues we will need to address in class discussion: Is it true that one person's views of art are as equally valid as another's? Are aesthetic judgments rationally grounded? Does good writing create the illusion of deeper perception, or does deeper perception create good writing, or both? Are there timeless and natural aesthetic standards, or do these change? If standards change and highly informed critics differ even over how a work meets today's expectations, why do reviewers often sound so dang sure of themselves?

Before writing, read and discuss "Critical Evaluation" in the Problems in Aesthetic Discourse section. Also, read reviews in your discipline to learn the conventions and the customary approaches to purpose, audience, scope, and tone.

Purpose

Write a review of an individual art work, performance, show, or collection.

Audience Considerations

Prepare the review as if you were going to submit it to a specific publication such as a theater arts or film magazine, a weekly or monthly magazine with arts coverage, or a newspaper. To help your instructor understand who your audience is, photocopy a review out of the publication you selected and include it with your paper. Include, also, a brief (one paragraph) audience analysis.

Length and Scope

Your first task will be to select the topic of your review. Check to see what plays, films, concerts, and art shows are currently playing or think of the things you've recently read or viewed that you've strongly liked or disliked.

A typical review addresses a number of topics relating to the subject's background, quality, and reception. Below is a list of such topics. Writers pick from these according to the occasion for reviewing, the type of work, the publication, and the audience:

- What the work depicts.
- Why the author/artist created it.
- How it fits into the artist's previous works.
- How it fits into the current traditions.
- What techniques the artist used in its creation—especially if these are unusual.
- What it means. This can be seen in terms of timeless or time-bound issues of human value, perception, creation, politics, etc.
- What will or will not appeal to readers/spectators.
- How excellent it is.

Again, you needn't cover all these points, but you should select from these to make your review coherent and informative.

WORKSHOP EVALUATION SHEET: REVIEW

Author _____ Date _____

Reviewer _____

Examine the review you read in class and answer the following questions (use the back if necessary):

1. Does the title catch your attention and also give some hint about the substance of the review?

2. How does the first paragraph function? Do you immediately sense the purpose? Do you have to wait until the end of the review to find out how the reviewer feels about the performance?

3. What details about the performance or work are presented? Does the reviewer provide enough—but not too much—detail to support the context of the review?

4. What kind of person does the writer seem to be? Do you trust his or her authority? Does the author reveal an awareness of other artists and works of this type?

5. Who is the reviewer writing for? and for what purpose?

6. What type of publication would the review appear in? How does the review fit into the publication's purpose? In other words, what rhetorical situation produces the review?

SAMPLE STUDENT ESSAYS

SAMPLE 1: REVIEW

A Breath of Fresh Air

AWADAGIN PRATT. A LONG WAY FROM NORMAL, *EMI CLASSICS*
AMANDA CLEERE

Awadagin Pratt's debut recording, *A Long Way From Normal*, is aptly named. The title refers to the young pianist's long journey from his hometown in Normal, Illinois to first prize at the Naumburg International Piano Competition, a grand concert tour, and even appearances at the White House. It could also refer to Pratt's unique appearance on the concert stage. An African-American with a thick, long head of dreadlocks and a full beard, he is far from the stereotypical white European male concert pianist. When he plays he does not sit on a normal piano bench but a small stool that is only a foot or two off the ground.

Perhaps the title most relevantly applies unique musical abilities. Unlike many young competition winners who have astounding technical ability but lack original interpretation and personal expression, Pratt has impressive technique and rare musical character and integrity. Rather than playing it safe by rendering works according to traditional (and predictable) performances, Pratt listens to his own muse. The results are distinctive and intensely involving performances that electrify audiences.

In this collection each work either departs into a new style for the composer or varies an established genre. The first selection, Franz Liszt's *Funerailles (Harmonies poetiques et religieuses*, N. VII), is a heroic lament for those killed in the 1848–9 Hungarian Revolution. Somber and thoughtful, it is a far cry from Liszt's usual glitz and glitter pieces. Pratt performs it with great power and an instinctual awareness of its poetical nature. Cesar Franck's *Prelude, Chorale and Fugue* follows. Although a composer of the Romantic era, Franck resurrects these austere forms of the Baroque era which his contemporaries had rejected and fuses them with the rich Romantic harmonies and sentiments. Pratt effectively brings out the dual nature of these pieces with intellectual understanding of their form and their emotional content. He also overcomes its great technical difficulties with apparent ease. The *Four Ballades* (op. 10) by Johannes Brahms which follow are more restrained and intimate than other ballades written in Brahms's time. Pratt's rendition brings out their intense emotion and often capricious nature. The final piece, Ferruccio Busoni's transcription for piano of the *Chaconne* from J. S. Bach's *Second Partita* for solo violin, is a unique glance at the nineteenth century's perspective of the eighteenth century. The romantic Busoni, while remaining quite faithful to the original score, transforms the Baroque composer's simple variations on a theme into a work of the grandest virtuosity and majesty. As in Franck's *Prelude, Chorale and*

Fugue, Pratt successfully brings out both the complex Baroque structure and counterpoint and the Romantic emotional content and virtuosity.

Awadagin Pratt has already made a start on his career, and his future should be equally impressive. In an era in which it seems that every upcoming pianist sounds the same, Pratt is definitely a breath of fresh air. Thank goodness!

(USED BY PERMISSION)

SAMPLE 2: REVIEW

Aboard the H. M. S. Miramar

TIFFANY SALLENBACH

The genius of Naguib Mahfouz's *Miramar* appears not in the love story we've all seen and heard before, but in how the characters and their environment interact together. In a situation reminiscent of "The Love Boat," very different people meet while staying at a pension in Alexandria. Mahfouz's characters interact because they have the pension in common, but they share as well in the effects of the recent Egyptian socialist revolution. As do many light-hearted sitcoms, the novel deals with love as three young tenants fall in love with the young peasant Zohra who works at the pension. Unlike "The Love Boat," however, we don't get to see everything work out in the kind of happy ending we're so used to. Mahfouz's characters must struggle through the storms of the revolution, and some don't make it to their destination. With keen insight Mahfouz presents this stream-of-consciousness novel which throws the reader in the midst of the storm brewing at the Pension Miramar.

Aboard Mahfouz's Love Boat we meet Sarhan, Hosni, and Mansour, three men from different classes searching for their own place in the new social structure of post-revolution Egypt. Sarhan represents the lower-class peasant taking advantage of the new socialist regime, ambitiously climbing up the economic ladder and stepping on anyone who gets in his way. As he falls for Zohra because of her remarkable beauty, he struggles within himself because he knows she will be of no use to him in his quest for financial security. Hosni represents the upper-class snob whose land has been sequestered by the state, desperately trying to maintain the lifestyle he has known all his life. His regard for Zohra stems from his conceited nature and his view of women as pleasure objects. Mansour represents the learned middle class, a vivacious student who supports the revolution but must betray his friends because of family and political ties. His love for Zohra doesn't become apparent until he realizes that she is the only one he knows who has any hope for a better life in the new world they live in. The love that all three share for Zohra eventually causes their fall. The Miramar traps them as the storm rages on.

The weather plays an important role on this voyage through personal struggle and revolution. The bleakness of the world in which Sarhan, Hosni, Mansour, and Zohra live manifests itself in the constant rain that both drenches and cleanses everything it touches. The Miramar is subject to the elements, something beyond the control of the people it carries. Mahfouz uses the weather to parallel the changing nature of each character's mind, "the elements mixing their warring natures to grapple and heave as if a new world were about to be born" (84). The Miramar becomes a plaything to the warring elements, and Zohra is the only one anchored in, and full of hope for, the new world. The others get lost at sea, groping all the way for a means of escape.

Mahfouz makes a dry story line come to life by presenting the story through the minds of the characters. The plot is revealed, piece by piece, as we experience life inside the skin of each person. We become personally involved in each decision, each perception, and each problem. We understand each character because we see how each sees the world. Mahfouz also uses intense images associated with the elements of the shifting and changing weather to correlate the struggles of the characters, making them more real for the reader. Aboard Mahfouz's Love Boat we are not greeted by Gopher or Captain Stubing. We are greeted by four people seeking to find answers for themselves in the aftermath of the Egyptian revolution. We are greeted by the storms amidst the furor of life. All ashore who's going ashore.   (USED BY PERMISSION)

READINGS

Object of Rage: The Satanic Verses of Salman Rushdie

Andrew Welsh-Huggins

FROM THE PROGRESSIVE, MAY 1989

"Fantasy can be stronger than fact," says a minor character early in Salman Rushdie's novel *The Satanic Verses*, and in the wake of the bizarre international uproar over the book it's hard to disagree. The riots, book burnings, and death threats which Rushdie's novel has incited resemble certain events in the novel itself. Oscar Wilde said it was life that imitated art, and not the other way around: One wonders what that Englishman, condemned for his sexual opinions, would have to say about this latter-day compatriot, condemned for a set of artistic opinions which prefigured reality much more closely than anyone could have predicted.

Yet as the Ayatollah Khomeini's execution order made headlines around the world and publishers and writers debate the issue of free speech, no one bothered to say much about the biggest irony of all; that Rushdie, whose novel contains several scathing attacks on the British treatment of Asian immigrants, is now in hiding, protected by the very same police he previously excoriated.

Because the focus of the controversy has been on the book's allegedly blasphemous passages, anathema to the Muslim world, Rushdie's true intent, to wipe out the old images of England in favor of post-colonial realities, is completely overshadowed. For the author, an English citizen born in Bombay, England is no longer "warm beer, mince pie, common-sense" (if it ever was). As the stuttering film producer character, Sisodia, puts it, what the English really like are "cow corpses in bubloodbaths, mad barbers, etc. . . . Their pay papers full of kinky sex and death."

Those pundits who feel the novel's true intent has been ignored would do well to recall last summer's controversy over Martin Scorsese's film *The Last Temptation of Christ.* Over several weeks, Scorsese's critics proved conclusively — at least to themselves — that familiarity with a disputed work of art is not necessarily a requirement for opposing it. More important, like the townspeople flimflammed by the Duke and Dauphin in *The Adventures of Huckleberry Finn,* people who actually saw the movie were impressed not so much by its controversial approach to the subject as its lack of cinematic interest. In short, many found it dull.

People who take time to read Rushdie's novel will not find it dull, but they may find it confusing, recondite, and at times excessive. They will find it to be a complicated work of art which, though it may not deserve the consideration which a bounty on the author's life has afforded it, is nevertheless a fine addition to what the author himself has termed the "psychological realist" style.

What has enraged members of the Muslim world are passages in the novel which they say portray Mohammed as having written the Koran instead of merely dictating God's word, and in which the prophet's twelve wives are depicted as prostitutes. Both allegations, neither of which is true, occur in one chapter, "Return to Jahilia," one of two dream sequences in the book in which a modern-day Indian actor named Gibreel Farishta dreams he is the archangel Gabriel in the days of the birth of a religion named Submission (the English translation of Islam).

Just as Rushdie's 1983 novel *Shame* was set in a country that is "not Pakistan, or not quite," however, the religion which Gibreel dreams into "existence" is not literally Islam. The name of Submission's prophet, "Mahound," is actually a term for the Devil. The book's title refers to passages dictated to Mohammed by the Devil which the prophet later repudiated. In Rushdie's book Mahound — like Mohammed — is a businessman turned prophet; the scribe he chooses to dictate the holy word to is a man named Salman; "some sort of bum from Persia."

One day, suspicious of the truly divine nature of Mahound's revelations, Salman "decided to test him. . . . If Mahound recited a verse in which God was described as *all-hearing, all knowing,* I would write, *all knowing, all wise.* Here's the point: Mahound did not notice the alterations." Minor leads to major: soon Salman is substituting *Jew* for *Christian,* then composing entire lines on his own. Eventually, Salman realizes the prophet is on to him. He flees, fearing for his life, knowing that the prophet's "power has grown too great for me to unmake him now." That the real-life Salman has now been forced to flee an equally powerful prophet is an irony that should not be lost on anyone.

These are the hard passages—real-seeming dreams draped in allegory and especially difficult for Western readers not familiar with the history of Islam. The sheer opaqueness of such scenes makes it obvious that Rushdie is offering an alternative, skeptical version of the founding of Islam, a view meant not so much to injure as to question, though this is probably small comfort to the Ayatollah. The mistaken belief that Mohammed's wives are portrayed as prostitutes is another example of skepticism, not blasphemy. In actuality, twelve prostitutes in a brothel decide to take on the names and demeanors of the prophet's twelve wives in order to boost business. (It works.)

Like a single flash of genitals in an otherwise chaste film, however, these brief passages are the ones causing so much trouble. Unfortunately, the rest of the book—in many ways written in defense of expatriated Asians, Moslems among them—goes largely unnoticed.

Rushdie's premise for the novel is a fantastic one, and at least superficially it places him squarely in the tradition of Gunter Grass and Gabriel Garcia Marquez. Two Indian actors, Gibreel Farishta and Saladin Chamcha, are returning to London from India when their plane is hijacked and later blown up over the English channel. As the book opens, Farishta and Chamcha are plummeting earthward from 30,000 feet—singing the entire way. They land, apparently unharmed, on an English beach.

Unharmed but not unaltered. Soon after an Englishwoman takes them into her home, Gibreel is transformed: "And around the edges of Gibreel Farishta's head, as he stood with his back to the dawn, it seemed to Rosa Diamond that she discerned a faint, but distinctly golden, *glow*." Meanwhile, out of Chamcha's temples,"growing longer by the moment, and sharp enough to draw blood, were two new, goaty, unarguable horns."

Through it all, however, Rushdie reserves his sharpest barbs not for Islam but for Margaret Thatcher's England. The Prime Minister's goal is simple: "literally to invent a whole . . . new middle class in this country . . . people who really *want*, and who know that with her, they can bloody well *get*." In London, Gibreel and Chamcha are taunted by a white gang. As the gang's leader hurls obscenities at the two men, Gibreel "was wearing an expression that said, loud and clear: so this is what the British, that great nation of conquerors, have become in the end."

The official explanation for the death in prison of Dr. Uhuru Sirnba, a black activist arrested for a series of Jack the Ripper-style murders, leads people to wonder whether "a nightmare was by no means the only possible explanation for the screams of a black man in the hands of the custodial authorities." The capture of the real murderer by a group of Sikh youths sparks a fierce riot not unlike those waged in protest against Rushdie's book.

Scathing stuff—but enough to vault Rushdie from "mere" literary fame to several days running on NBC News? Not really. *The Satanic Verses* lacks the seamless weave of such books as Garcia Marquez's *One Hundred Years of Solitude*, and its multitude of characters, settings, and language shifts, all of which evoke some kind of strange Dickens-Warhol hybrid, is hard going in spots. Short of settling for a constricting label—colonial epic—it's difficult to tell what Rushdie hopes to accomplish in leading us through a thicket of verbiage at times hilarious, at times moving, at times downright confusing.

What was clear in the days following the first riots over the book is that ultimately it's power, not blasphemy, that's at stake. The Ayatollah Khomeini, unnerved by the end of the war in the Persian Gulf and the prospect of freer relations with the West, found in *The Satanic Verses* an opportunity to revive, if only briefly, the flames of his Islamic revolution. The Western world's continued suspicion toward Moslems, coupled with a shameful lack of knowledge about their religion and culture, has only increased the rage of zealots who believe they still have excellent reasons to regard America as the Great Satan.

Understanding this rage, which is as political as it is religious, may be the most important issue of all, even beyond that of free speech. Otherwise, those who read *The Satanic Verses* may miss the frightening resonance of one of the novel's most recurrent themes: "To be born again, first you must die."

Tom Stoppard's Mystery and Metaphysics

Robert E. Lauder

FROM AMERICA PRESS, MAY 11, 1985.

In *The Real Thing* Tom Stoppard rephrases the questions he raised in *Rosencrantz and Guildenstern Are Dead*, *Travesties*, and *Jumpers*. The answers remain elusive.

In the winter of 1983, Tom Stoppard's *The Real Thing* opened to just about unanimous raves. Some critics seemed to suggest that this play about love revealed a radically new Stoppard. Not quite. Rather, *The Real Thing* does mark a significant development in the vision of one of the most stimulating and thought-provoking of our contemporary playwrights. Stoppard can be described as a metaphysical playwright: His latest work forms a continuous line with his previous plays, though it does reveal a kind of giant step to a new level of being.

A distinctive aspect of Stoppard's more important plays has been the author's preoccupation with comparisons between reality and art that often are articulated in dazzling language and dramatized in striking theatrical fashion. An oft-quoted statement of Stoppard's is his response to a question about why he writes: "I write plays because dialogue is the most respectable way of contradicting myself." Though not quite true, the statement does speak to a viewer's experience of attending a Stoppard play: Ideas rapidly race by in language that seems to dance over reality. In *The Real Thing* playwright Henry Boot describes the experience of writing a play: "What we're trying to do is to write cricket bats, so that when we throw up an idea and give it a little knock, it might . . . travel."

In *Rosencrantz and Guildenstern Are Dead* (1966), Stoppard depicts two minor characters from Shakespeare's *Hamlet* waiting to go on stage. Since other characters from *Hamlet* stroll in and out of the play and since speeches from Shakespeare's masterpiece are occasionally spoken, this play highlights Stoppard's preoccupation with the world of art. However, the primary referent in *Rosencrantz and Guildenstern Are Dead* is not Shakespeare's *Hamlet* but Samuel Beckett's *Waiting for Godot*. In Shakespeare's tragedy Rosencrantz and Guildenstern had small parts to play; in Stoppard's play they are offstage waiting to become part of the action, which is largely unintelligible to them. Like Beckett's Vladimir and Estragon waiting for Godot, Rosencrantz and Guildenstern are waiting for some meaningful event. It never happens. That Rosencrantz and Guildenstern are adrift in a sea of meaninglessness is vividly illustrated near the end of Act II. Claudius, before leaving the stage, has just told Rosencrantz and Guildenstern that Polonius has been slain by Hamlet and that they should seek Hamlet out. After commenting that this advice "is a step in the right direction," the two men spend a considerable amount of time discussing in which direction they should go and whether they should go together or separately, while making a number of false starts on their journey to look for Hamlet. After much misunderstanding and much movement that ends with the two men having made no progress, one says "Well, at last we're getting somewhere."

I do not know of any play in which there is more academically philosophical dialogue, much of it about God, than *Jumpers* (1972). The play's action centers around an aging professor of moral philosophy, George Moore, who in his study is trying to compose a lecture on "Man — Good, Bad or Indifferent." In the room next to the professor's study is a corpse. Down the hall the professor's wife, Dotty, an ex-musical comedy star, is seductively entertaining the professor's university boss, Sir Archibald Jumpers. A group of gymnasts called Jumpers appear from time to time to announce philosophical ideas. In her book *Tom Stoppard*, Felicia Landre summarizes the play as well as can be done: "The intellectual argument in *Jumpers* pits moral philosophy against logical positivism. The moral view of the universe (upheld by the play's protagonist George Moore) is based upon absolute standards of what constitutes good and evil. . . . The logical positivists outnumber George, objectifying Stoppard's view that most of modern society tends to rationalize human behavior through pragmatic considerations. The mental acrobatics needed to justify this relativistic philosophy are cunningly externalized in the theatrical image of the team of university professors-cum-gymnasts."

In *Travesties*, the theatrical link is to Oscar Wilde's *The Importance of Being Earnest*. In an introduction to the published text of *Travesties*, Stoppard explains that James Joyce was the business manager of The English Players, a group of both professional and amateur English-speaking actors who were residents of Zurich during World War I. In casting their first production, *The Importance of Being Earnest*, Joyce decided to cast as Algernon a minor official named Henry Carr whom Joyce had seen working in the British consulate.

Eventually Joyce and Carr had a falling out that led to a court case. In his play Stoppard has Joyce and Carr interact with two other historical characters, Lenin and Tristan Tzara, the leader of the Dada revolution in art. *Travesties* is a memory play—a random selection of moments filtered through the memory of Henry Carr. Within the play there are travesties of *Ulysses* and *The Importance of Being Earnest*. At the end of the play, we discover that Carr's memory is faulty, and so the play itself has been a travesty. What has been staged as real is the dream world of the senile Carr.

In *The Real Thing*, while not forsaking either his preoccupation with art and reality or his dazzling dialogue, Stoppard does take a significant step forward. Kenneth Tynan criticized *Travesties* as having no narrative thrust. No such barb could be directed at *The Real Thing*, which opens with a marital dispute between an exceptionally elegant Englishman and his wife, who supposedly has returned from a business trip. Even as the husband confronts the wife with evidence that she has had an adulterous affair, the sophisticated snappy repartee *a la* Noel Coward belies the seriousness of the situation. The scene is anything but true to life. Of course it is not supposed to be. We've been watching not the real thing but a play-within-a-play entitled "House of Cards." In this play-within-a-play the wife is Charlotte, who offstage is the wife of the playwright, Henry Boot. The husband in "House of Cards" is played by Max, whose offstage wife is Annie. The behind-the-scenes drama is that Annie is having an affair with Henry. When Annie tells Max about her affair, his reaction is about as different from the one he portrayed in the drawing room farce as possible: In "House of Cards" we watched a self-composed character trivialize his wife's infidelity; in *The Real Thing* we watch Max disintegrate. We have moved from art to reality!

After Annie's confession, Stoppard's play focuses on the new marriage between Annie and Henry, and Stoppard's prime interest is clearly Henry. Though there are subplots that also dramatize the play's theme, Henry is the center of Stoppard's vision. Like his creator, Henry is a playwright who is a master of words. While discussing writing with Annie, Henry says "I don't think writers are sacred but words are."

While they are experiencing the bliss of their new marriage, there is an especially important conversation between Annie and Henry that foreshadows the climax of the play. Annie wishes to articulate an emotion she is experiencing. Remarking that there is no literature that expresses her present emotion, Annie tries to come up with the right word but cannot. Each time she fails, Henry suggests a word but Annie finds it inadequate. Henry has yet to learn that there are dimensions to reality that he cannot master with words.

Henry describes "House of Cards" as a play about a man who achieves "self-knowledge through pain." Though we have doubts that "House of Cards" successfully depicts that theme, we have no doubts that *The Real Thing* does. Much of Henry's pain comes from his discovery that Annie, though she loves him, is having an adulterous affair. Though Henry has been able to talk glibly about love as an idea, the real thing flattens him. When Annie leaves for her adulterous rendezvous, Henry is spiritually stripped of all his supports. Henry, alone on stage with words failing him, is close to being spastic as he pleads almost prayerfully "Please, please, please, don't." We sense that though in terrible pain, Henry has found his best self. He has encountered the real thing and, as all people in love are, Henry is called to surrender, to enter more deeply into a mystery that words cannot capture.

Because the three plays depict people who do not seem to be able to plant their roots on any level of reality that is permanent or substantial, "exile" seems a fit image for *Rosencrantz and Guildenstern Are Dead, Jumpers,* and *Travesties.* However, it does not fit *The Real Thing.* Though he has had to surrender his verbal mastery of reality, Henry has traveled from exile to home. Through his love commitment, Henry Boot has journeyed more deeply into the mystery of being. With his brilliant play about love, Tom Stoppard seems to have made the same journey.

Editorial / Issue Essay Assignment

What university, local, or national problem with the arts or the humanities has concerned you? This problem could be connected with the lack of support for artistic endeavors, unbalanced support, the public's indifference to specific areas of the humanities, the promotion or suppression of various kinds of art, and similar public matters.

Purpose

Write an editorial essay that makes clear that there is a problem involving the arts or humanities. Take a stand and recommend how the problem should be solved.

Audience Considerations

Write to readers of a campus or local newspaper.

Length and Scope

Consult your teacher on length and due dates.

The editorial should contain clear, incisive thinking without playing to prejudice. However, it generally doesn't include lengthy, minute reasoning as would a longer essay.

READINGS

The two following editorials express viewpoints on issues in graphic design.

Status and Academe

Elizabeth Resnick

FROM AIGA JOURNAL OF GRAPHIC DESIGN, *1998*

> "There's something about categorizing things, about putting things in their place. Maybe it's about a kind of comfort. Maybe it's about setting things straight, putting first things first. Whatever it is, it surely has a hold on us. We seem intent on labeling and ordering. It's how we get on with our lives, how we proceed."
>
> —Barbara Kruger[1]

I am sitting in my backyard on a fine summer's day reading Barbara Kruger's essay "Arts and Leisures" (which was originally written for the *New York Times*). Kruger uses the "Arts and Leisure" section of the Sunday *New York Times* to challenge her readers "to figure out which is art and which is leisure." Or, in other words, what is "high" and what is "low." These two terms are hot buttons for me, as they trigger another set of similar questions: what is "fine arts"and what is "popular culture?" Popular culture? Funny, a few years ago, I would have said "applied arts" or maybe even "commercial arts." But this is the '90s, and graphic design has found its shelter in popular culture.

This was not always the case. Growing up in the New York City area, I remember being exposed to the visual and performing arts at an early age. Museums and galleries, theater and dance, books, magazines, television and the movies; they were considered "the arts," each uniquely distinctive yet sharing creative expression as a commonality. My youth was spent drawing, painting, acting, and dreaming of becoming an artist. I attended one of the public art high schools and after graduation continued to learn at an art college in New England. For someone coming of age in the 1960s, the possibilities were limitless. The need to identify what kind of visual artist I wanted to become seemed less important somehow, until my sophomore year, when I was required to choose a major. The decision was difficult, as I had many interests. But after much thought, I settled on graphic design mainly because I loved to draw. It never occurred to me that I might be categorizing myself into second-class status within the arts hierarchy.

Now, with more than twenty years experience in teaching and practicing graphic design, I have noticed these decisions become far more complicated for those entering the arts. Attitudes are surfacing that perpetuate the conventional gap between the fine arts and the applied arts in our universities

---

[1] "Arts and Leisures," *Remote Control: Power, Cultures, and the World of Appearances* (Cambridge, MA: MIT Press. 1993), p. 2.

and colleges of art. It can't help but spill over into the consciousness of contemporary society. As practitioners and educators, we need to question the sanctity of these categories themselves.

But this is old news, you think. Many designers who have taught graphic design in a fine arts program can attest to perceiving subtle undertones of second-class-ness emanating from fine arts colleagues. It is also no secret that many university fine arts departments offer graphic design classes as "cash cows" to keep the departments financially viable in a time of dwindling enrollments. Too often these graphic design classes are taught by the full-time fine arts faculty in order to keep them employed. Given their predispositions, I wonder what they are teaching their students.

In the art colleges, fine arts departments squabble over slices of the funding pie with the design departments. It is not uncommon for fine arts departments to get more money per student (i.e., a lower faculty-student ratio) than design departments, which often struggle with oversubscribed classes and not enough faculty to staff them. I know of many art colleges where almost 40 percent of the matriculated upper-class students major in design programs. Does this mean that these programs get 40 percent of the funding? I don't think so.

Exhibition programs at many of these colleges follow a similar bias. In committees with ten to fifteen members culled from faculty and administration, usually only one member teaches design or has a design background. Is it any wonder that 90 percent or more of the exhibitions voted in are fine arts? As exhibitions budgets are usually funded by student fees, do these committees take into account that 40 percent of their budgets come from students studying design? When interest in design exhibitions is growing, why is there so little support to organize them? The answer clearly lies in the interests of the voters who sit on these committees.

Rather than working together to close the gap between the visual arts, the opposite seems to be happening. Categories are being maintained and strengthened, identities fiercely protected. Last semester, several of my tenured design faculty colleagues proposed to an incoming college president that an ad hoc committee be established to review adding "and Design" to the college name. Considering the large design community, this formal acknowledgment seemed appropriate, timely, and a long-awaited gesture of validation. A committee was formed composed of a representational cross-section of our college community. After months of research, polling faculty, students, and alumni, the unanimous recommendation of the ad hoc committee was to retain the original name of the college. They also recommended that the college logo be redesigned and that all program offerings be listed in promotional materials. Many disappointed design faculty interpreted this message as: "Sorry, we cannot formally acknowledge that you exist, but we will redesign the logo." How could the committee have missed the point?

I do not advocate handicapping existing fine arts programming with less funding, or sacrificing valuable institutional name recognition. But if we continue to view art through existing rigid categorizations, it will surely mean business as usual. In a time when advancements in digital imaging technologies could democratize the visual arts, exposing our commonality, why is the status quo holding so firmly to its sacred ground? I have to ask, to what end, and for what purpose?

What can be done? I would advocate for a balance brought on by genuine mutual respect and goodwill on all fronts. After all, we share a language. Isn't it this common language that we strive to teach freshman in their first-year programs?

> "Running in place at the speed of light, we defensively cling to our unexamined notion of categories, our dilapidated signposts in a bleak landscape. They make things simple again . . . . they are easy systems. Use them but doubt them. They are the rules of the game, but perhaps no longer the one being played."
>
> —Barbara Kruger

Style and Its Abuses

Lisa Rosowsky

FROM AIGA JOURNAL OF GRAPHIC DESIGN, 1999

The longer I teach graphic design, the more my patience with the persistently surface aspects of the study of design wears perilously thin. I am tired, I realize, of style: of the primacy of the formal, of concern with what things look like rather than what they are. Design students are at serious risk of what I call "style abuse" for a number of reasons. For many, learning involves copying the published work they see around them, which tends to look hip but is stubbornly inbred, the result of a market that rewards style for its safe sameness. The ubiquity of high-quality color output devices means that student work is more polished, more seductively about appearance than ever before. Even the job market conspires to reward style. Though we faculty give lip service to the importance of the Good Idea, it is no longer deemed acceptable for a graduating student's design portfolio to contain multi-layered comps, with the result that students spend many hundreds of dollars producing slick, but often empty-headed, work. This costly obsession with single-surface output—the so-called "professionalism" demanded of portfolios—demonstrates the market's concern with style over content.

What can we do about this? As the old joke goes, I've got good news and bad news. The bad news is that style abuse is here to stay. Students will continue to try on others' work, output technology will get better and cheaper, and the market will keep upping the ante of what's expected of design portfolios. But the good news is that there are ways in which design educators can move students away from the cult of the design object, toward an understanding of design in which style is secondary—or even forgotten. Following are a few of the ways in which I try to combat style abuse in my curriculum:

Develop the conceptual with the formal.   One of the first discussions I have with beginning design students focuses on the difference between concept and idea, and the necessity of developing the former before the latter. Students at all levels will say that I drill them in this notion of concept until they want to scream, but I am merciless. If thinking about concept becomes second nature for my students—before they choose typefaces, before they start pushing a mouse around—they are less at risk of style abuse later on. Insisting that students understand and develop a concept for each project is equivalent to insisting that they have something to say.

The seductiveness of form over content is the reason why I don't give projects that rely on the use of dummy type. Working with a good text rich in possibility gives students practice in extracting meaning, which is the first step toward generating a concept. When form and content merge with concept, you get good design—and when this happens, style becomes of no importance to the student. No endless waffling between PhotoShop filters, thumbing through design annuals, trying on and then discarding typefaces like jeans at the Gap. Once form is understood as emerging from the problem to be solved—just the opposite of style—the design process feels effortless, and the work is true.

Trust breeds failure; failure is success.   One of the things I insist upon is that students respect one another and are careful with their criticism. Having been on the receiving end of harsh and even derisive crits several times, I vowed long ago that respect would define the atmosphere of my own classroom. Respect fosters trust. Trust allows students to take risks with their work, for in a trusting classroom failure is supported along with success. And a willingness to fail, because it means there is a concept or idea at stake, leaves little room for safe but meaningless style.

Give personal projects.   In every syllabus, I try to include projects designed to encourage students to bring their own life experience into their work, projects such as an installation about students' experiences with racism or a multimedia piece based on family myths and stories. Students often tell me in their course evaluations that such projects were their favorites, but were also the most difficult of the semester. I have had students whose projects centered around physical abuse, rape, and the death of a family member—how to tread delicately in such terrain while at the same time offering constructive design criticism? But it seems to me important that design students experience what it feels like to bring something highly personal to their work. So many of their assignments are corporate or commercial in nature, as befits the nature of the career for which they are preparing. In the so-called real world, frenetic schedules and conservative clients will make it all too easy to choose surface over substance. Personal projects make relying on a native facility with style nearly impossible.

The well-rounded student.   Although I teach at a four-year college of art and design, I'll admit to a liberal arts bias. One of the things a liberal arts approach to education does best is to teach students how to learn. Learning yields content, and content, after all, is the ultimate antidote to style. The best designers I know of are Renaissance people who read avidly on a wide range of subjects, express themselves well in writing, are fascinated by history, and have interests that lie far outside the field of graphic design. Students of design need to experience what it's like to be such a Renaissance person, and this means that we design faculty must include reading and analytical writing as an integral part of their design education. When we require students within our design courses to think historically, read, and be knowledgeable about the world, we are telling them that we prize information above appearance, and that we expect professional designers to enrich the content they work with—not just decorate it.

Among the greatest challenges I face as a working graphic designer are the diminished expectations of uninitiated clients, who think they're engaging the services of a stylist. With a missionary zeal that, admittedly, has dimmed a bit with time, I talk with the unenlightened about the breadth of knowledge a designer can bring to a project. If I'm lucky, the results of our collaboration mean one more informed advocate out there in the world of commerce. If we want to redeem the profession from its reputation (not entirely undeserved) as a purveyor of style, we've got to look to our own back-yard. Our design education programs need to stop being in breathless thrall to style, and commit to valuing and rewarding work of meaning.

LISA ROSOWSKY is an assistant professor of graphic design at Massachusetts College of Art.

WORKSHOP EVALUATION SHEET: SHORT PAPERS/ESSAYS

Author _____

Title of Paper _____

Implied Audiences for Paper _____

Evaluator's Name _____

1. How well does the title of this paper describe the purpose of the paper?

2. What is the purpose of this paper? Is the thesis stated clearly?

3. Does the paper support the thesis throughout? Is the paper well focused? If not, how could the focus be better maintained?

4. Are the assertions made in this paper clear? Are they well supported? Does the writer provide ample evidence in the way of explanations, examples, and quotes or paraphrases? If the evidence seems weak at any point, what kinds of information could make it stronger?

5. Is the paper organized well according to ideas? Do the arguments proceed in a logical fashion? Are there places where better transitions could be used to promote the flow of the ideas?

6. What elements of effective writing are present? Is the language clear, concise, and concrete? Does the author show concern for effective word choice and sentence construction? Does the writer use concrete, descriptive (precise) nouns and strong, vigorous verbs? Has the author avoided grammar, spelling, and punctuation mistakes?

7. Are the opening and closing paragraphs well crafted? Comment on this.

8. Overall, is the paper interesting to you as a reader? Does the writer have "something to say" to you?

WORKSHOP EVALUATION SHEET: SHORT PAPERS/ESSAYS

Author _____

Title of Paper _____

Implied Audiences for Paper _____

Evaluator's Name _____

1. How well does the title of this paper describe the purpose of the paper?

2. What is the purpose of this paper? Is the thesis stated clearly?

3. Does the paper support the thesis throughout? Is the paper well focused? If not, how could the focus be better maintained?

4. Are the assertions made in this paper clear? Are they well supported? Does the writer provide ample evidence in the way of explanations, examples, and quotes or paraphrases? If the evidence seems weak at any point, what kinds of information could make it stronger?

5. Is the paper organized well according to ideas? Do the arguments proceed in a logical fashion? Are there places where better transitions could be used to promote the flow of the ideas?

6. What elements of effective writing are present? Is the language clear, concise, and concrete? Does the author show concern for effective word choice and sentence construction? Does the writer use concrete, descriptive (precise) nouns and strong, vigorous verbs? Has the author avoided grammar, spelling, and punctuation mistakes?

7. Are the opening and closing paragraphs well crafted? Comment on this.

8. Overall, is the paper interesting to you as a reader? Does the writer have "something to say" to you?

Workshop Sheet: Short Papers/Essays

Author _____ Reviewer _____

Please circle only *one* answer for each question				Points
Is the draft complete?	Yes	About Half	No	
Did you find a well-defined *purpose*?	Yes	Somewhat	No	
Were there enough details to fully support the *purpose*?	Yes	Somewhat	No	
Were ideas organized effectively to carry out the *purpose*?	Yes	Somewhat	No	
Does author meet the needs of the specified *audience*?	Yes	Partially	No	
Has the author focused topic properly for this assignment?	Yes	Partially	No	
Does the draft read smoothly (is its style pleasing)?	Yes	Somewhat	No	
Are there errors in spelling, punctuation, or grammar?	No	A Few	Yes	
Comments:				

-------------------------------- *Cut Along This Line* -------------------------------------

Workshop Sheet: Short Papers/Essays

Author _____ Reviewer _____

Please circle only *one* answer for each question				Points
Is the draft complete?	Yes	About Half	No	
Did you find a well-defined *purpose*?	Yes	Somewhat	No	
Were there enough details to fully support *purpose*?	Yes	Somewhat	No	
Were ideas organized effectively to carry out the *purpose*?	Yes	Somewhat	No	
Does author meet the needs of the specified *audience*?	Yes	Partially	No	
Has the author focused topic properly for this assignment?	Yes	Partially	No	
Does the draft read smoothly (is its style pleasing)?	Yes	Somewhat	No	
Are there errors in spelling, punctuation, or grammar?	No	A Few	Yes	
Comments:				

PART 4

The Research Paper

Writing Research Papers

Jeanette Harris and Donald H. Cunningham put the reason for research very simply: "Research begins with the need to find answers to questions" (400). Finding these answers is, in many ways, like trying to solve a mystery. In college or university settings, research is a commonly required task. But why be concerned about such "mysteries" after you graduate? Perhaps part of the answer lies in this: "The humanist," says Christine A. Hult, "deals in significance, insight, imagination, and the meaning of human experience" (6) — all mysteries. Hult goes on to write that "there is no absolute proof that leads unerringly to a particular interpretation or theory. Rather, the humanist will make a claim and argue for that claim" (9). Significance, insight, imagination, meaning, and the ability to make solid, reasoned claims generally come from searching for knowledge in many ways. One way is to engage in formal research projects.

For many of you, then, doing research and writing reports based on that research may become — at various times and in various situations — one focus of your working life. Think of situations where professionals in your own field would need to do some type of research. What might an art curator need to know (or find out) in a given instance? An illustrator or graphic designer? A linguist? A performing artist? An art teacher? Could the quality of their research have an impact on their careers? Their businesses? And, ultimately, their success?

The myriad of skills that you learn while completing this assignment (library and original research techniques, documenting, audience recognition, analytical approaches, stylistic considerations, formatting concerns, and so forth) can form an integral part of your "portfolio" as you move from the educational to the professional world. Hult conveys the importance of having these skills when she writes,

> Researching, that is, exploring a problem systematically, is a crucial skill for an educated person. . . . Learning to research promotes careful, critical, systematic thinking. Learning to write promotes the effective communication of the ideas and insights gained in the research. Researching and research writing necessarily go together, with each building on and promoting the other. (1)

Harris and Cunningham provide some practical questions to help you begin developing your skills. They begin by saying that

> Your chances of succeeding in research depend on how well you understand your research project. With a clear and guiding idea about what you are seeking to learn, why you want to learn it, how you might learn it, and to whom you plan to communicate your findings, you will set yourself up to be successful. (401)

They go on to suggest that you consider these questions regarding the research topic you have chosen:

- Is this a question that needs answering?
- Does the question merit research?
- Is this a question you can answer?
  Can you handle the level of information required?
  Are sufficient sources of information available?
  Do you have enough time to complete the research project?
- Can you develop a hypothesis? (401–406)

While these suggestions will give you a feel for the status of your own research process and project, you should realize that not all questions can be answered definitively. In such cases, what you must do is to supply enough evidence to convince your readers that you have something — perhaps a step toward a final answer — worth careful consideration. To supply this evidence, learn to select material from credible authorities and from reputable publications. (This is especially important when you take material from the Internet.) Such sources are instrumental in supporting your own claims or in rebutting the claims of other authorities. In addition, Leonard J. Rosen maintains that "draw[ing] on the work of others [on related ideas]" allows you to help your readers understand your own point. He suggests that good sources enhance your research in four ways:

- sources can provide you with facts,
- sources can provide you with examples,
- sources can provide you with authoritative opinions, and
- sources can help situate [your own idea] . . . in a broader context. (58–61)

All of the information above is geared toward helping you succeed in the research projects you undertake both in college and in the professional world. Again, before you begin your research project, carefully assess your research question. Then determine what might be helpful to you in searching out new information related to your question and in understanding what you find. Once you have thoroughly reviewed your sources, how will you analyze the information? What strategies can you use to organize your material and to communicate your findings and insights to your audience? Look back at the two excerpts found in the "Review of Literature" section of the Guide for Proposal Assignment and look at the sample research paper at the end of this section. Can you re-create the steps these students went through in completing their projects?

RESEARCH PAPER ASSIGNMENT

Purpose

Write an academic paper based on research from other sources and your interpretation of the information from those sources. Think broadly about the requirement for research. Although you will need to spend time in the library, don't restrict yourself solely to the library when other sources can be useful to you—sources such as interviews with practicing artists and critics, your own reading or viewing of primary works, documentaries, videos, and the Internet (make *sure* that your sources are *reliable* here).

As you move through the process of gathering information from sources, be sure to critically read for an author's meaning and then faithfully report that material in your own work. Take care not to distort the original material in order to support your own hypothesis.

Your first and most crucial step in writing this paper will be to select a topic. The quality of your thesis (or research question) will affect the quality of your entire paper, so think carefully about it. Refine your purpose as you gain more depth of understanding. One way to establish a purpose for this paper is to find a number of articles that take conflicting positions on an individual work, artist, or tradition and then to take a position and present support for it. For example, one student researched the published literature on whether Shakespeare's works were, in reality, written by Christopher Marlowe, and then analyzed passages in the works of both authors to support his own view. Another way could be to apply a particular method of interpretation (perhaps a particular *-ism*) to a work (something like "Dada in Eliot's *Wasteland*"). If you know a specific art work very well and have a good background in another field, you may be able to combine the two into something rewarding and interesting (mathematical laws in Beethoven's 9th symphony or "The Three Phases of Rites of Passage in *Moby Dick*"). Or, you may choose a subject that allows you to apply what has been done to something you wish to do ("Conceptualizing and Directing Anouilh's *Antigone*").

The following brief list of the titles of student papers will, perhaps, help you as you think about your own topic:

- Revolutionizing Sculpture: How Rodin Injected Fragmentation into the Art World
- Independent Reading Texts for Second-language Vocabulary Acquisition: A Comparison of *Le Petit Prince* and *Astérix Gladiateur*
- The French Language in Québec: A Distinctive Regional Appellation?
- How the Ancient Art of Chinese Calligraphy Influenced Three Modern Chinese and Three Modern American Artists
- Akira Toriyama's *Dragonball* and its Roots in Wu Cheng'en's *Hsi Yu Chi*

Remember: your research paper is more than a collection of other people's views (this should *not* be a summary paper). The most important part of this assignment is to show your audience the connections *you* have made between the data you have gathered and *your own* insights. In other words, you must interpret the evidence for your audience.

Audience

While this is pretty much a standard term-paper assignment, take care to translate your knowledge into terms that educated but nonexpert readers (such as the members of your class) can understand. It should have all the content, analysis, and research of an academic term paper, but the same kind of clarity and movement as an article written for a periodical. Remember your audience's interests, knowledge of technical terms, and boredom levels. Keep your readers hooked.

Scope

Length: 10 to 12 pages, double spaced. Choose a topic that can be focused sufficiently for the space allotted but still allows for proper exploration.

Schedule

Consult your syllabus.

Format

Double space your text. If you wish, use relevant graphic aids to enhance reader understanding. Use MLA format and documentation style unless you prefer to follow the style accepted in your field. If you choose to do the latter, please obtain permission from your instructor and provide the instructor with a sample of that style from a journal in your field.

Some instructors will require that you alter your format slightly so that you can include a cover page, an outline for the research paper, and an abstract. If so, your instructor will give you specific instructions on the structure and format of the paper and on how to create the outline and abstract.

COMMON QUESTIONS ABOUT CITING AND DOCUMENTING IN MLA STYLE

(1) How do I introduce and smoothly integrate quotations (IQ) into my own text?

One important thing you must do before quoting or paraphrasing sources in your own text is to read your source material carefully for meaning and context; and when you do use passages from other works in your own documents, you must not distort the meaning of the original works to suit your own purposes. You must also consider *how* you place borrowed material in your own paper. Work to integrate these passages into your paper in a way that "organizes" *your* points. Remember, too, that you must provide citations for all borrowed work. The following excerpts have been taken from student samples.

Original:

"We cannot obey the command to sympathize because we are imprisoned within a circle of our own egotism . . . my experience falls within my own circle, a circle closed on the outside; and with all its elements alike, every sphere is opaque to the others which surround it." (Abrams 2195) Eliot's philosophy relates to the . . .

Not integrated into paragraph. Confusion about who said this. Punctuation should come after citation. Citation not correct.

Revision:

T. S. Eliot notes that "we cannot obey the command to sympathize because we are imprisoned within a circle of our own egotism . . . my experience falls within my own circle, a circle closed on the outside; and with all its elements alike, every sphere is opaque to the others which surround it" (qtd. in Abrams 2195). His philosophy . . .

Integrated into paragraph. Punctuation correct.

Citation correct.

Both Joseph Conrad and Francis Ford Coppola seem to be very much against imperialism. "It is well known," Conrad once claimed, "that curious men go prying into all sorts of places . . . and come out with all kinds of spoil" (qtd. in Jean-Aubrey 18).

First sentence directs reader. Quote split, but integrated into paragraph. Citation correct.

Jesus Christ exemplified "standing faithfully to one's moral principles" (Delattre 4), when he refused to lie about and deny his identity . . .

Integrated, with quote and correct citation in the middle.

Original:

The sea is constantly changing and it is only through observing the ocean that a marine artist is able to capture the changing motions.

Introduction doesn't lead reader directly into quote.

> Concerning the picture *Rock and Surf,* reproduced in full color, I must have painted this subject twenty times right on the spot. I know the place very well, yet each time the effect is different. The sea is ever changing so the design must change too and this makes it always interesting. — John Chetcuti (Kent, 66).

Citation not correct.

Revision:

Only through observing the ocean can a marine artist capture its changing motions. John Chetcuti confirms this when he says of his *Rock and Surf,*

> . . . I must have painted this subject twenty times right on the spot. I know the place very well, yet each time the effect is different. The sea is ever changing so the design must change too and this makes it always interesting. (qtd. in Kent 66)

Good introduction to quote. Naming the source and the title of the work of art in the introduction eliminates the problem above with the citation. Citation correct.

(2) How do I properly insert long quotes (blocked quotes; four lines or more) into my text?

In MLA style, the body of your blocked quote should be indented ten spaces from the left margin and run to the right margin. Blocked quotes should be **double spaced** like the rest of your text.

The sample research paper, the long quote on the previous page, the material below, and the general introductions to each section in this book provide examples of how to smoothly **introduce** a long quote. These examples also show proper in-text **citation** (MLA) for the blocked quotes. Note how the citation differs from the citation used when shorter quotes (1 to 4 lines) are incorporated directly into your paragraphs.

Notice, too, that **quotation marks** are *not* used at the beginning and at the end of blocked quotes unless the quote you borrow contains quotes within it or you quote dialog.

If you wish to quote only a **part of a paragraph**, you may do so by indicating with brackets and ellipses that you have left some of the original material out.

> These towers were frequently named after the archangels Michael and Gabriel. Such architectural nomenclature derived from [. . .] Germany's pagan past: it was from the west, where the sun sets, that the demons of darkness come, and the *Westwerk*, conceived and built as a protective bulwark against such evil spirits, acquired extra strength if it was dedicated to the archangel who carries a sword and slays dragons. (Pothorn 53)

To indicate a cut, use brackets to enclose ellipses. If an ellipsis appears in the original material, do not use brackets.

Be sure that the dots end up on the same line.

You can see that part of the original text within the quote itself has been elided (cut out) already by a student, as indicated by the brackets and ellipsis. You may also leave out part of the beginning or part of the end. Introduce the quote, then put something like this:

> [. . .] it was from the west, where the sun sets, that the demons of darkness come, and the *Westwerk*, conceived and built as a protective bulwark against such evil spirits, acquired extra strength if it was dedicated to the archangel who carries a sword and slays dragons. (Pothorn 53)

Or this:

> These towers were frequently named after the archangels Michael and Gabriel. Such architectural nomenclature derived from [. . .] Germany's pagan past: it was from the west, where the sun sets, that the demons of darkness come, [. . .] (Pothorn 53)

You may stop without completing a sentence, retain the original punctuation, then add the ellipsis.

The lead-in sentence to your long quote can end with no punctuation or with various punctuation marks (comma, period, colon, dash; but rarely a semi-colon). Use whatever makes the sentence mechanically sound and completes your thought best.

See the general introductions to the sections of this text, the sample research paper, and the material on the previous page for examples.

(3) How do I refer repeatedly to one particular text?

If you decide to analyze one particular work, you will probably refer repeatedly to that work in your own writing. If, in *one paragraph* of your own text, you use more than one quote from *the same page* of the source document, you may withhold the parenthetical citation until after the last quote.

> "Had Elizabeth's opinion been drawn from her own family," writes Jane Austen in *Pride and Prejudice,* "she could not have formed a very pleasing picture of conjugal felicity or domestic comfort." Mr. Bennet, "captivated by youth and beauty, [. . .] had married a woman [of] weak understanding and illiberal mind" and had soon taken refuge in his library. Although disposed to excuse her father, Elizabeth "could not overlook" her father's "continual breach of conjugal obligation and decorum [. . .]" (243; vol. 2, ch 19). A closer analysis of Mr. Bennet's behavior reveals [. . .]

Note that when many editions of an important work exist, you can help the reader (who may have another edition of the work) find the information quickly by listing chapter, part, or volume numbers, as shown above.

If you quote from *multiple pages* from a work within one of your own paragraphs, you need to provide page citations where appropriate throughout the paragraph. For example:

> Quite appropriately, the orphaned Ishmael chooses the Pequod as "the whaler best fitted to carry [him and Queequeg] and [their] fortunes securely" (Melville 103). Ahab, who commands this whaling ship, is a man "nominally included in the census of Christendom, [but] still alien to it" (156); his crew of castaways—Tashtego, "an unmixed Indian from Gay Head," Daggoo, "a gigantic, coal-black negro-savage" (238), Fedallah, "a muffled mystery to the last" (237)—like Queequeg, are pagans, "old idolator[s] at heart [. . .] yet [living] among these Christians, [wearing] their clothes, and [trying] to talk their gibberish" (58). Estranged from their own community, these men board the whaling ship [. . .], haul the anchor up, and set sail to forge another communal state.
>
> (USED BY PERMISSION OF KODY PARTRIDGE)

For citing important poems or plays that are printed in many different editions, give act, scene, line, canto, book, or part numbers, *not* page numbers. For instance, if you wanted to quote some lines from *King Lear* from Act I, Scene I, you might set it up as follows:

> When Lear asks his daughters, "Which of you shall we say doth love us most," (*King Lear* 1.1.51), Cordelia replies that "[. . .] I cannot heave / My heart into my mouth. I love your Majesty / According to my bond, no more nor less" (1.1.91-93).

(4) How do I format graphics and provide citations for them?

If you use graphics to illustrate points you wish to make in your paper, provide a *label*, a *title*, and a *legend* for each graphic.

- *Label* = An indicator of sequence; e.g., Figure 1, Plate 1, Photo 3
- *Title* = The name of the graphic; e.g., The Mexican Hat in Southeastern Utah
- *Legend* = What the reader should notice; e.g., The evening shadows in the photograph provide . . .

In addition, when you borrow a graphic from a published source, you *must* provide a complete *citation* at the bottom of the graphic (see Figure 1).

While the general rule is to *put the graphic as close as possible to the text that refers to it,* the placement of graphics and of text around graphics can vary according to your purposes and the design of your paper. For tables the label, title, and legend are placed at the top of the graphic: for figures and examples, these are placed at the bottom, as shown in Figure 1. Whenever you use graphics, be sure that the graphics are carefully made or copied and that they enhance reader understanding or illustrate a point.

Figure 1. The Mexican Hat in Southeastern Utah. The evening shadows in the photograph provide depth and delineate features. (Black, Dianna M. *Photos of Southeastern Utah.*)

(5) How do I cite material "second hand"?

In as many cases as possible, you should rely on **primary sources**—that is, you should quote or paraphrase from the original (first) publication (to reduce error in content, meaning, or citing). Nevertheless, finding the primary source is not practical in some cases (and impossible in others). When this happens, you may quote material you find in a **secondary source**.

Suppose you are reading a book written by John Smith and you find that he quotes something you need for your own paper out of Plato's *The Republic* — a source that someone has already checked out of your library. Yet you need the quote to make your own point. You may use the quote as presented by Smith; but make sure you cite Smith as your source for the quote.

Your Text

Plato questions art as imitation, and focuses, at one point, on painters: "I would like to know whether he may be thought to imitate that which originally exists in nature, or only the creations of artists?" (qtd. in Smith 56).

Works Cited

Smith, John. *The Fine Art of Imitation*. New York: Doubleday, 1990.

(6) How do I cite from books that contain a collection of essays or chapters written by different authors?

At times you will use books containing essays or chapters by various authors that are collected into one volume by an editor. When you do, should you provide the editor's name or the author's name in your in-text citation and in the bibliographic entry for the Works Cited? Try in all cases to provide the name of the original author. See the examples below for citing material from just *one* essay or chapter from a particular book and for citing material from *three or more* articles. Note, specifically, the "shortcut" method MLA style provides to eliminate repetition. Notice also that even with the use of the shortcut method, the entries remain in alphabetical order.

Your Text, with Citation

*(MATERIAL FROM **ONLY ONE** ESSAY/ CHAPTER IN A BOOK)*

When Jean-Paul Sartre claims that existentialism "is the least scandalous, the most austere of doctrines [. . . and that] it is intended strictly for specialists and philosophers" (250), he distinguishes . . .

Your Works Cited, MLA Style

(NOTE THE USE OF THE HANGING INDENT)

Sartre, Jean-Paul. "Existentialism is a Humanism." *A Community of Voices: Reading and Writing in the Disciplines*. Eds. Toby Fulwiler and Arthur W. Biddle. New York: Macmillan, 1992.

Your Text, with Citation

(MATERIAL FROM **MULTIPLE** ESSAYS/CHAPTERS IN A BOOK)

When Jean-Paul Sartre claims that existentialism "is the least scandalous, the most austere of doctrines [. . . and that] it is intended strictly for specialists and philosophers" (250), he distinguishes . . .

Jeremy Bentham's Utilitarianism includes the notion that "the community is a fictitious *body*, composed of the individual persons who are considered as constituting as it were its *members*" (230).

Contrary to much of our modern conventional wisdom, Peter Singer maintains that "if it is in our power to prevent something bad from happening, without thereby sacrificing anything of comparable moral importance, we ought, morally, to do it" (269).

Your Works Cited, MLA Style

(NOTE THE SHORTCUT PROCEDURE)

Bentham, Jeremy. "Of the Principle of Utility." Fulwiler and Biddle 228–33.

Fulwiler, Toby, and Arthur W. Biddle, eds. *A Community of Voices: Reading and Writing in the Disciplines.* New York: Macmillan, 1992.

Sartre, Jean-Paul. "Existentialism is a Humanism." Fulwiler and Biddle 250–59.

Singer, Peter. "Famine, Affluence, and Morality." Fulwiler and Biddle 267–78.

If you have further questions about any of the MLA documentation problems given above, or if you have questions about other common types of citing, please consult the *MLA Handbook.* In the *Handbook* you will also find instructions for entering some types of online references on your Works Cited page.

(7) MLA Style Exercise

Part 1: In-text Citations

Write the in-text parenthetical citations in MLA format for the following:

1. Page thirty-six of Martin Russell's book, *Picasso's War: The Destruction of Guernica and the Masterpiece that Changed the World*, published in New York by Dutton in 2002.

2. Page sixty-seven of Russell's book when Russell is named within the sentence that introduces the quotation or paraphrase.

3. Page one hundred thirty-two of Bill D. Moyer's *The Language of Life: A Festival of Poets*, published in New York by Doubleday in 1995 — one of two Moyers books in a Works Cited list. (Moyers' other book on the list is *Healing and the Mind*, published in New York in 1995 by Doubleday.)

4. Page eighty-four of *Composition in Four Keys: Inquiring into the Field*, written by Mark Wiley, Barbara Gleason and Louise Wetherbee Phelps, published by Mayfield in London in 1996.

5. Page one hundred twenty-three of Stephen King's essay, "On Impact," pages one hundred twenty through one hundred thirty-one in a collection of essays titled *The Best American Essays of the Century*, edited by Kathleen Norris, published in 2001 in Boston by Houghton Mifflin.

6. Pages five hundred twenty through five hundred twenty-one of John S. Mebane's article, "Pluralism, Relativism, and the Question of Evidence in Shakespearean Studies," pages five hundred seventeen through five hundred forty in *College English*, volume 58, published in September of 1996.

7. A single-page (thirty-five) unsigned article titled "What's Love Got to Do With It?" from the May 7, 1990 *Time* magazine.

8. An article with no author cited, titled "Pierre Auguste Renoir" from the Internet site *http://hyperion.advanced.org/17142/celebrated-artists/renoir.htm*, dated 1998, published by Modern Masterworks, no page numbers provided.

Part 2: Works Cited

(Please remember that the entries on your *own* Works Cited page will be in alphabetical order.)

Prepare a Works Cited page for the in-text citations you did on the previous page:

1.

2.

3.

4.

5.

6.

7.

8.

SAMPLE RESEARCH PAPER

Jeffrey P. Thompson
English 311, Section 400
Dianna Black
March 24, 1998

Re-inventing the Mystery Novel:

Agatha Christie, Daphne du Maurier, and Helen MacInnes

Abstract: The mystery genre that began with Edgar Allen Poe and caught on with Arthur Conan Doyle's Sherlock Holmes, flourished during its Golden Age, which lasted roughly from after World War I through World War II. Dramatic changes occurred during these years. Agatha Christie took the mystery novel from low-society to the upper-middle class, bringing murder much closer to home. She broke the Holmes prototype by creating Miss Marple, an atypical, elderly female sleuth. She also came up with ingenious murder techniques. Daphne du Maurier made marriage and family central issues to her mysteries, an area that had previously been taboo. She set a trend by having her mystery novels turned into screenplays and is the only novelist to have had three of her books filmed by Hitchcock. Helen MacInnes used evocative language in describing real locales to heighten the realism of her novels. She also popularized the use of innocent people involved in espionage and included politics and World War II in her novels. The new elements created by these writers are still evident in mystery fiction today. Dick Francis's characters are of upper society; Mary Higgins Clark and P. D. James capitalize on family relationships; quality films are made of John Grisham and Tom Clancy novels; and Robert Ludlum and John Le Carré use real locales and politics in their novels.

W. H. Auden once said, "For me, as for many others, the reading of detective stories is an addiction like tobacco or alcohol . . . the story must conform to certain formulas (I find it very difficult, for example, to read one that is not set in rural England)" (qtd. in Hart 1). Auden defined the basic formula as follows: "a murder occurs: many are suspected; all but one suspect, who is the murderer, are eliminated; the murderer is arrested or dies" (qtd. in Symons 14). Such was the state of the mystery story during the Golden Age of crime fiction, an era that lasted roughly from World War I through World War II (Maida and Spornick 3). Though mystery novels were sometimes formulaic, the Golden Age was not static. During these years authors developed many literary innovations and changes that have had lasting effects on the genre. Three authors of note, namely Agatha Christie, Daphne du Maurier, and Helen MacInnes, each made considerable contributions that changed, refined, and ultimately re-invented the mystery genre. Christie transformed mysteries from stories of low-life criminals into thrillers of manners, showing that murderers can be "one of us." She also created a unique female sleuth and novel murder techniques. Du Maurier included marriage and family secrets in her works, three of which became the inspiration for films by Alfred Hitchcock. MacInnes made the spy thriller more realistic by adeptly describing her locales, by involving the innocent in espionage, and by including politics in her books.

To understand the contributions of these authors, one must be aware of the history of mystery fiction. The genesis of the mystery detective story began in 1841 with the publication of Edgar Allen Poe's short story "The Murders of the Rue Morgue" (Haycraft 4). The story differed from Poe's usual irrational and macabre fare in that it was rational and was logically solved by Auguste Dupin, the first literary sleuth (Haycraft 9). A few more Dupin stories followed; but when Poe's personal crises worsened, he returned to his earlier morbid imagination to find solace. During the following decades, the genre caught on mildly. The mystery detective motif would occasionally show up in books as a subplot or as one of several themes, most notably in Wilkie Collins' *The Moonstone*, Charles Dickens' *Bleak House*, and in several books by the French author Emile Gaboriau. But in none of these was the mystery the main plot or the detective one of the main characters (Haycraft 39). One exception is Anna Katharine Green's *The Leavenworth Case*, published in America in 1878, which focused on a police inspector and appears to have had no antecedents (Haycraft 84).

The popularity of the mystery genre rose abruptly in 1890 with the publication of Sir Arthur Conan Doyle's second Sherlock Holmes story in an American periodical (Haycraft 49).[1] Holmes quickly became a favorite on both sides of the Atlantic. Readers loved the cleverness displayed by Holmes and the brilliant story-telling of Doyle. Sherlock Holmes stories continued to be printed until 1927 (Haycraft 51). As could be expected, the success of the Sherlock Holmes stories encouraged many imitators. The early years of the twentieth century saw the proliferation of countless literary detectives. Some were professors, others were scientists, and one was even blind. But none of them differed much from the Holmes prototype.

Despite the profusion of authors, certain elements dominated the genre. The most important was simply that the story had to deal with a murder solved using deductive reasoning and logic (supernatural powers and mere intuition were not allowed) (Haycraft 4). A second tenet was that all pertinent information needed to solve the mystery had to be made known to the reader. A third requirement was that the murderer had to be a principal character, and a fourth element was that the solution could not be revealed before the denouement (Haycraft 54).

After the conclusion of the World War I, the mystery genre entered its Golden Age, which lasted through World War II. During this time, Agatha Christie, Daphne du Maurier, and Helen MacInnes emerged as mystery writers, each bringing fresh ideas and new conventions to the genre.

---

[1] The first Sherlock Holmes' story, entitled "A Study in Scarlet," was published in 1887 in a British periodical but to little popular approval (Haycraft 49).

In 1920 Agatha Christie, certainly the best known and most popular author of the genre,[2] published her first novel *The Mysterious Affair at Styles*. Her fame grew steadily in the ensuing years and reached new heights with the publication of *The Murder of Roger Ackroyd* in 1926 because of its innovative ending in which the narrator is revealed as the murderer (Symons 98). From that point on, Christie became a major force in crime fiction and added many new elements to the genre.

Christie's most significant contribution was the elevation of the mystery novel from lower society to upper-middle class society, transforming it into a "thriller of manners" (Shaw and Vanacker 17). In earlier mystery stories, there was a sharp distinction between the detective and the villain. The detective was respectable, intelligent, financially secure, and enjoyed a high social standing—Sherlock Holmes being the perfect example. The villain, on the other hand, was usually a reprehensible social outcast that no one would have any trouble hating. But in Christie's works, contrast is nonexistent. She deals almost exclusively with the upper echelons of society where the detective, the murderer, the murdered, and the suspects are all quite well-to-do. When the "poor" enter the narrative, they are never of the jobless, destitute kind, but rather those struggling on a fixed inheritance (Symons 96). The only members of the lower society that readers come in contact with are the servants whose roles are relatively minor. Christie frequently used the servants as suspects, but departed from many writers by avoiding the all-too-trite explanation that "the butler did it." In fact, the murder is never committed by a servant, but by somebody of the upper-middle class (Shaw and Vanacker 20). It made Christie's crimes much more disturbing because the murderer could no longer be stereotyped as a Jack-the-Ripper type criminal; the "murderer [became] one of us" (Shaw and Vanacker 20).

In this upper-class milieu, Christie conveys the attitudes of the rich and how they can lead to murder. The wealthy feel superior to servants, they do not like foreigners (the countless times Christie's detective Hercule Poirot is viewed as suspicious because he is not English is ample proof), and class distinctions are firmly in place and not to be tampered with (York and McAllister 74–76). Genealogy and family reputation are also of major importance (Maida and Spornick 6). These so-called virtues become vices since most of Christie's murders are committed to gain property, money, or a title (Maida and Spornack 19). Many murders occur in socially embarrassing situations. In *A Murder Is Announced* it occurs at a cocktail party; an uneasy reception provides the setting in *The Mirror Crack'd*; and the misappropriation of church funds serves as the backdrop for the *Murder at the Vicarage* (Shaw and Vanacker 18). Large country homes often serve as the setting for crimes (Maida and Spornick 14), as in *Funerals Are Fatal, The Mysterious Affair at Styles, And Then There Were None* (also known as *Ten Little Indians*), *The*

---

[2] As of 1998, Agatha Christie had sold more books than any other fiction writer in the world (including Shakespeare) and stands second only to the Bible. Her 78 novels have sold more than two billion copies and have been translated into 44 languages (Guinness 216).

Murder of Roger Ackroyd and *The Body in the Library*. Again, this was a major departure from the back street crimes Holmes and others were used to solving.

Christie went so far to incorporate murder into normal society that she even used innocent nursery rhymes in her stories. The most obvious and clever use is in *And Then There Were None* (1940). Ten murders occur at a country house on an island, each one corresponding to how the an Indian was killed in a rhyme. Perusing her titles reveals many more, such as *A Pocket Full of Rye, Five Little Pigs, Hickory Dickory Dock* (alternate title substitutes *Death* for *Dock*), *Three Blind Mice*, and *One, Two, Buckle My Shoe*. Even the elementary *A.B.C. Murders* can be included here. Using these children's rhymes, Christie reinforced the idea that murder can be committed by people among us for the most unlikely motives and that something seemingly innocent can be evil.

One of Christie's unique contributions was the creation of Miss Jane Marple. Marple's uniqueness did not lie in the fact that she was female, for women sleuths had existed since *The Leavenworth Case,* but rather in her age, person, and methodology. She was tall and thin, had white hair, was in her mid-sixties, and had never married. She stood in complete contrast to the Sherlock Holmes prototype. She enjoyed knitting, gardening, and gossiping. But Christie challenged the stereotype of older women and demonstrated that Marple was capable and intelligent. Marple's senior status became an asset in crime-solving since few characters ever suspected her of being a detective. In *A Murder Is Announced* (1950), Marple shows up to have tea with a suspect to get some information. She makes small chat, nonchalantly extracting what she needs to know. Her duplicity became a trademark (Hart 140). Christie even broadened the gap between the traditional detective by placing Marple in St. Mary Mead, a fictional village in the English countryside. Again, it would seem quite improbable that an older woman could solve crimes, especially one that lived in the country. But Miss Marple observed and studied human nature, which she said "is much the same everywhere, and, of course, one has opportunities of observing it at close quarters in a small village" (Christie, *Tuesday* 67). She liked to "class people, quite definitely, just as though they were birds or flowers, group so-and-so, genus that, species this. Sometimes, of course, one makes mistakes, but less and less as time goes on (Christie, *Murder at the Vicarage* 192). She maintained that what is true for people in St. Mary Mead would be true for those anywhere else in the world (Hart 136).

Christie also developed some clever and innovative murder techniques. The most ingenious were her group murders. The *Murder on the Orient Express* (1934) presented quite a puzzle for Poirot. The victim had been repeatedly stabbed, and yet no two wounds were alike. At the end it is discovered that each passenger literally took a stab at him. The mass murder in *And Then There Were None* mentioned above is another example of ingenuity. The real murderer, a judge who knows of the evil deeds of all the guests, even stages his own death to continue killing the others. For murder weapons, Christie used poisons, guns, and knives, but she also came up with a myriad of other objects to accomplish the nasty deeds. In particular, items like ice-picks, golf clubs, paperweights, a statue of Venus, and even a ukelele string were used in her novels (Riley 54). She also popularized items of women's apparel as weapons, including things such as the then-new nylons, a silk scarf, and even a raincoat belt (Riley 53).

Christie's popularity certainly attracted other writers to the mystery genre. Daphne du Maurier began publishing in the early 1930's with her first major success being *Jamaica Inn* (1937), a historical mystery. After *Jamaica Inn*, she again turned to the genre to write what would become her most famous book: the haunting *Rebecca* (1939), which Howard Haycraft called "one of the finest mystery stories of all time" (xxv).[3] Though not exclusively a mystery writer, du Maurier made some significant contributions to the genre.

Du Maurier introduced the marriage relationship as a major theme into the mystery genre. Marriage and romance had been largely ignored in most detective fiction because, as Dorothy Sayers quipped, heroes shouldn't be "fooling about after young women when they ought to be putting their minds to job of detection" and that "the less love in a detective story, the better" (qtd. in Symons 14). Hence, most sleuths, like Holmes, Miss Marple, and Hercule Poirot, were single and not involved in courting. Marriage and love had existed in earlier novels—Christie, for instance, never let a single man or woman get away without getting married (Maida and Spornick 23) —but these were mostly minor details. Du Maurier, in contrast, made them central, and even essential, to the main plot. But she always departed from the "happily ever after" scenario; in fact none of her novels ends with "the sound of wedding bells," though this is a common beginning (Light 29). Du Maurier looks almost exclusively at life *during* marriage. In *Rebecca*, the plot revolves around the mysterious dead Rebecca and her husband Maxim's supposed admiration of her, and with the new wife, who is the narrator (and who is, cleverly, never named) trying to figure out what is going on.[4] Du Maurier used a similar situation in the plot of *My Cousin Rachel* (1952), but this time the mysterious woman is still alive and the husband is dead. Ambrose Ashley, a confirmed old bachelor, suddenly marries Rachel while recovering from illness in Italy. He then dies. His nephew, Philip, tries to find out if Rachel murdered Ambrose to keep him from inheriting his uncle's estate. Philip then falls in love with Rachel and tries to marry her. The issue of marriage was not a sideline issue; if marriage had not been included the story could not exist.

---

[3] *Rebecca* is one of the few mystery novels to ever receive recognition as great literature. As early as 1950, Random House was including it in their Modern Library series as one of "the World's Best Books" right along with Dickens and the Bronte sisters (check any Modern Library booklist from this period usually found at the end of the editions). Many critics today still consider *Rebecca* a masterpiece (Williams 10).

[4] In almost every discussion of *Rebecca* there is inevitably some reference to it as a "Gothic Romance." Du Maurier insisted that "*Rebecca* isn't romantic . . . . It is a study in jealousy and murder, not romantic at all" (qtd. in Shallcross 83). I agree with du Maurier and have left this controversy out of my analysis.

Children also enter into du Maurier's plots. In the chilling short story "No Motive" (193?), an expectant mother unexpectedly commits suicide and her husband is unable to find an explanation for his wife's actions. A detective discovers that she had had a child out of wedlock. The experience had been so traumatic for the woman that she had blocked it from her mind until the child, unknowingly, shows up at her door as a salesman bringing it all back. The effects of children on murder were used in the disturbing *Don't Look Now* (1971), which presents a couple whose child has recently died and how they deal with that loss amidst psychological confusion and murder. *Rebecca* also involves a child to a lesser extent: Rebecca informs her husband that she is pregnant with another man's child in an effort to provoke him to murder her. Du Maurier made the family central to her stories instead of merely treating them as backdrops for crime. None of these stories would work without the inclusion of familial relationships.

Du Maurier popularized the use of a well-kept secret to heighten her mysteries. *Jamaica Inn* skillfully produces a tale of fear and hidden secrets. A young woman comes to stay with her uncle who, it turns out, has much to hide. She finally figures out that smuggling and murder are the reasons why the Jamaica Inn has been so prosperous. In *Rebecca*, the secret revolves around why Rebecca despised her husband and why she provoked her own murder. In the end, we find out that she had terminal cancer and wanted to die, but still wanted to punish her husband with guilt. Du Maurier pushes a secret to its limit in *My Cousin Rachel*. She ends the novel with a mystery. The reader never finds out if Rachel killed Ambrose or if she was just a victim of circumstance. There appears to be "No Motive" in the story of that name and the reader does not find out until the end what exactly happened. *Don't Look Now* does much the same by not revealing the secret of the husband's hallucinations until after he is murdered.

Du Maurier also influenced the genre by popularizing the use of mystery novels as great screenplays. Her prestige in this domain is evident since she is the only mystery author to have had three of her books turned into major motion pictures by Alfred Hitchcock.[5] Mystery novels had been used prior to the adaptation of du Maurier's work in the late 1930's, as in the cases of the Charlie Chan and Dick Tracy serials, but they were rather low-budget, matinee features for kids with trite plots and meager artistic merit. The use of du Maurier's work marked the beginning of an era when mystery novels were turned into quality motion pictures. Du Maurier's popularity made her an obvious choice for the cinema. *Rebecca*, for example, was one of the most popular books of the 1930's, second only to Margaret Mitchell's *Gone with the Wind* in the number of copies sold (Humphries 59). Before moving from England to Hollywood, Hitchcock had done a film adaptation of du Maurier's *Jamaica Inn* (1939). The film was financially successful, which was probably Hitchcock's motivating factor in wanting to film another du Maurier work. *Rebecca* became one of Hitchcock's most acclaimed works, financially and artistically, and went on to win the Academy Award

---

[5] Hitchcock never did a Christie or a MacInnes book, though both would have seemed perfectly suitable for his style.

for Best Picture in 1940, one of the few mysteries to have ever won this prestigious award.

Over twenty years later, Hitchcock returned to du Maurier's material for his film *The Birds,* released in 1963. Du Maurier had set the story, like most of her works, in her native Cornwall. A farmer and his family are the witnesses of nature gone awry as our fine-feathered friends begin taking over the countryside. In speaking of the film, Hitchcock stated that "it could be the most terrifying motion picture I have ever made" (qtd. in Humphries 152). The success of these du Maurier/Hitchcock collaborations sparked interest in mystery novel movies.[6] Christie, who had long been ignored by Hollywood (Haycraft 130), finally got some of her works turned into films. *And Then There Were None* was released in 1945 and *Witness for the Prosecution* was released in 1957. Helen MacInnes also had successful film versions done of her *Assignment in Brittany* and *Above Suspicion,* both released in 1943.

Unlike Christie and du Maurier, whose popularity took a few years to catch on, Helen MacInnes had immediate success with the publication of her first book *Above Suspicion* in 1941. MacInnes's name became synonymous with the spy thriller. Almost all of her novels involve international espionage and intrigue. She added many new elements to suspense literature including evocative descriptions of locales, the innocent getting involved, and using World War II and politics in her novels.

One of the most distinctive characteristics of a MacInnes novel is her adeptness in capturing the atmosphere of locales: France in *Assignment in Brittany* (1943), Austria in *The Salzburg Connection* (1968), or Italy in *The Venetian Affair* (1963). Her novels are not only entertaining, but they also become educational as geography lessons and travelogues. MacInnes works strictly with real places and often includes a map to better inform the reader.[7] This was novel because most suspense and crime fiction had used predominantly fictional settings. Christie and du Maurier, for example, created such places as Miss Marple's village of St. Mary Mead or the country house, Manderley, in *Rebecca* as settings for their stories. These places do not exist. The use of real places makes MacInnes's novels much more realistic as well as making the incidents that occur in them much more believable.

MacInnes is also skillful with her evocative descriptions. They are not long, usually consisting of a paragraph or two with tidbits thrown in here

---

6 Film versions were made of du Maurier's *My Cousin Rachel* (1952) and *Don't Look Now* (1973), as well as some of her non-mystery novels like *Frenchman's Creek* (1943) and *Hungry Hill* (1945) (Shallcross 183). Though all were respectable productions, none were as well-received or critically acclaimed as the Hitchcock productions.

7 In her novels published during World War II that dealt with underground movements against the Nazis, MacInnes gave fictional names to real places, such as the village St. Deodat in *Assignment in Brittany* in "order to not endanger anyone." She explained that "the Germans . . . were very thorough in working over every scrap of fact about the resistance . . . . I tried to give them no such scraps" (MacInnes, *Assignment Suspense* viii).

and there for embellishment. The details and adjectives are rich, precise, and splendidly capture ambiance. MacInnes has often been praised for having "a poet's eye for landscape" (Steinbrunner 267), a skill evident in her description of the Greek island Mykonos in *The Double Image* (1965):

> They came to Mykonos in a blaze of pink and vermilion sky, with feathered sweeps of cirrus clouds so high that they had already shaded into gray, leaving the last golden glow to the threatening mass of cumulus on the north horizon. The island was a spreading slope of hard rock molded into small hills barely green, its contours carved so near the bone that the occasional farm scattered over the rising land must have had its richest harvest in stones. Down below was a curve of bay, with the little town at one side—flat-roofed houses of brilliant white, their square outlines broken by blue- or red-domed churches, clustering in a tight mass at the water's edge—and there the long jetty formed a breakwater to harbor small craft, fishing boats, masted caiques. Across the bay, at the other tip of its crescent, there was a mooring quay in the shelter of a rocky headland for a few yachts. (187)

If readers had never been to these places, they would certainly feel like they had traveled there after reading a MacInnes book. If they had traveled to such destinations, they would easily recognize the places she describes.

Set against her realistic backgrounds, MacInnes popularized the motif of the innocent getting involved in espionage. In most crime novels, the detective actively seeks participation in solving a crime. Doyle's Sherlock Holmes or Christie's Hercule Poirot never turned down an opportunity to solve a crime, for example. MacInnes took the opposite approach, evident in her first novel *Above Suspicion* (1941). Richard and Frances Myles lead a quiet life in Oxford. He is a professor, and the couple vacation each year on the Continent. One day they are approached by a good friend who works for the government who asks them to travel to Germany to see if an underground information system has been infiltrated by Nazis. The couple has good cover as travelers because they are "above suspicion." In her later novels, MacInnes goes to the extreme, making participation of the innocent involuntary. Her characters simply find themselves in bad situations. In *North From Rome* (1958) Bill Lammiter, a writer visiting Rome, is enjoying a view from his hotel window late one evening when he witnesses an abduction. His scream saves the girl, who later meets him to express her thanks. During that meeting she implores him to help her since she is mixed up in international crime and he reluctantly agrees. In *The Double Image,* John Craig, a doctoral student, runs into his former professor who has just testified in Nazi war-crime trials. The professor is murdered and John saw the murderer, making him a target for death. Another example is found in *While Still We Live* (1944) in which a young British girl traveling in Poland is thought to be a spy by the Nazis. MacInnes's motif of innocent characters getting involved in crime was much like Christie's use of upper society: they both brought murder and corruption much closer to home.

A third area MacInnes redefined was her inclusion of war and politics in her mystery novels. In the cases of Christie and du Maurier, for example, politics were nonexistent. The mystery genre was escapist in nature and any reference to current events would have ruined the effect. We must remember that these authors were writing during the turbulent years leading up to and through World War II. Readers did not want to be reminded of the horrors to which they were witnesses. MacInnes changed that. Instead of avoiding the war, she skillfully used it to create realistic espionage stories. *Above Suspicion* and *While Still We Live* have already been mentioned as novels with war themes. *Assignment in Brittany* (1943) is probably MacInnes's best work in popular and critical circles. The story deals with a spy helping the French Resistance during the war by infiltrating the Nazi operations in a small town in Brittany. After the war, MacInnes emphasized the tensions between the Eastern communist countries and the Western democracies, as in *The Double Image* where a historian becomes involved in neo-Nazi influences. Another example is *Decision at Delphi* (1960), which presents the communist influences in Greece. MacInnes avoids being didactic or making overt political commentary (Horwitz 1168). She simply shows the conflicts between the political powers. Again, MacInnes' inclusion of politics gave the genre a realistic dimension that had not existed previously because of the largely fictional nature of mysteries.

MacInnes's innovations, like those of Christie and du Maurier, have become major trends in the genre. Just as Poe and Doyle influenced mystery writers in the nineteenth and early twentieth centuries, Christie's, du Maurier's, and MacInnes's works have had lasting effects for more than half a century. Christie's Miss Marple, for example, obviously provides the prototype for Angela Lansbury's Jessica Fletcher on the popular *Murder She Wrote* television series. Her influence can also be seen in the novels of Dick Francis, whose horse-jockey detective moves around in upper circles of society. Mary Higgins Clark and P. D. James have followed in du Maurier's footsteps by making familial relationships central to their plots. The trend started by Hitchcock of making quality motion pictures of mystery novels that began with successful adaptations of du Maurier's work continues today with the fine film versions of Tom Clancy and John Grisham books. MacInnes's novels have also influenced the works of Grisham, as well as the work of Robert Ludlum and John Le Carré, all of whom use real locales as settings and deal with political intrigues in their narratives. Although the motifs of Christie, du Maurier, and MacInnes have been used by other authors, their popularity has not diminished, as evidenced by the fact that many of their works are still in print. It appears that their status as classic mystery writers will live on and that their clever inclusions to the genre will continue to entertain future generations.

Works Cited

Christie, Agatha. *Murder at the Vicarage.* 1930. New York: Dell, 1966.

————. *The Tuesday Club Murders.* 1933. New York: Dell, 1969.

Guinness Book of World Records 1999. Ed. Rhondo Carrier. Guinness Ltd., 1998.

Hart, Anne. *The Life and Times of Miss Jane Marple.* New York: Dodd, Mead, 1985.

Haycraft, Howard. *Murder for Pleasure: the Life and Times of the Detective Story.* London: D. Appleton-Century, 1941.

Horwitz, Barbara. "Helen MacInnes." *Critical Survey of Mystery and Detective Fiction.* Ed. Frank M. Magill. 4 vols. Englewood Cliffs, NJ: Salem, 1988. 1167–1171.

Humphries, Patrick. *The Films of Alfred Hitchcock.* Greenwich, CT: Brompton, 1994.

Light, Alison. "Rebecca." *Sight and Sound* 6 (1996): 29–31.

MacInnes, Helen. Introduction. *Assignment Suspense: A Three-Novel Omnibus by Helen MacInnes.* New York: Harcourt, Brace, 1961. vii–ix.

——. *The Double Image.* 1965. New York: Fawcett, 1970.

Maida, Patricia, and Nicholas Spornick. *Murder She Wrote: A Study of Agatha Christie's Detective Fiction.* Bowling Green, OH: Bowling Green State UP, 1982.

Riley, Dick. "The Cruder Methods." *The Bedside, Bathtub, and Armchair Companion to Agatha Christie.* Eds. Dick Riley and Pam McAllister. New York: Ungar, 1979. 52–54.

Shallcross, Martyn. *The Private World of Daphne du Maurier.* New York: St. Martin's, 1991.

Shaw, Marion, and Sabine Vanacker. *Reflecting on Miss Marple.* London; New York: Routledge, 1991.

Steinbrunner, Chris, and Otto Penzler, eds. *Encyclopedia of Mystery and Detection.* New York: McGraw-Hill, 1976.

Symons, Julian. *Bloody Murder: From the Detective Story to the Crime Novel: A History.* New York: Viking, 1985.

York, Susan, and Pam McAllister. "Crime, Class, and Country in Christie's Mysteries." *The Bedside, Bathtub, and Armchair Companion to Agatha Christie.* Eds. Dick Riley and Pam McAllister. New York: Ungar, 1979. 73–77.

Williams, Tony. "Respecting Daphne du Maurier's *Rebecca*." *Notes on Contemporary Literature* 26 (1996): 10–12.

EVALUATION SHEET: DRAFT OF RESEARCH PAPER

Please circle only **one** answer for each question				Points
Is the draft complete? (Look for outline, abstract, introduction, body of paper, conclusion, works cited, appendix if necessary.)	Yes	About Half	No	of
Purpose: Is there a clear sense of purpose in the introduction?	Yes	Somewhat	No	
Do the details presented in the paper adequately support the purpose?	Yes	Somewhat	No	of
Does the organization (logical flow of ideas) enhance the understanding of the purpose?	Yes	Somewhat	No	
Audience: Is this report suitable for (does it meet the needs of) the specified audience?	Yes	Somewhat	No	of
Scope: Has the author focused properly for this assignment? Is the focus indicated clearly?	Yes	Somewhat	No	of
Format: Given the format of this draft, do you think the final product (paper) will be attractively arranged?	Yes	Don't Know	No	of
Mechanics: Does the draft read smoothly (i.e., are there adequate transitions, appropriate sentence structure, etc.)?	Yes	Some Problems	No	of
Is the draft free of spelling, punctuation, or grammar errors?	Yes	Some	No	
Documentation: Does the author seem to be using an approved system?	Yes	Sometimes	No	
Does the author correctly cite sources in the text?	Yes	Sometimes	No	of
Is the bibliography (works cited) set up correctly?	Yes	Sometimes	No	
Does the paper seem to be the author's "own" or does it seem more a compilation (summary) of someone else's ideas?	Own	Compilation		of
Total Points				of

_____

Signature of Evaluator

_____

Signature of Author of Report

INSTRUCTOR'S GRADING SHEET: RESEARCH PAPER

Name _____ Date _____

	POINTS
PURPOSE, CONTENT, SCOPE, AND DOCUMENTATION	**POINTS**
Information organized well according to ideas ❑ *Introduction* predicts what will follow (**purpose** and **direction** of report clearly stated) ❑ *Body* of the paper carries out that prediction ❑ *Conclusions* are based on the information presented ❑ *Content* flows in a logical order	
Concrete details support the major points and purpose	
Content provides *analysis/synthesis* of ideas (not just summary)	
Information *focused* appropriately for the requirements of the paper (scope)	
Documentation system (MLA unless instructor granted permission otherwise) ❑ a *variety* of pertinent source materials ❑ all sources *properly cited in the text* ❑ quotations and paraphrases properly introduced or integrated *(IQ)* into the text ❑ the sources *correctly documented* in the Works Cited	
AUDIENCE	
Report meets the needs of the intended audience; report has the following qualities ❑ has clear, coherent, mature, interesting *style* ❑ *delivers* on its "promise" to inform or persuade ❑ *explains/defines* technical terms (if used) where necessary ❑ *avoids any underlying assumptions* that could confuse reader or bias the data ❑ considers other specific needs (e.g., gender, age, educational level) where applicable	
FORMAT AND GRAPHICS	
Format (enhances the meaning and visual impact of the paper) ❑ *Layout* attractive, professional ❑ The/a prescribed format observed ❑ Graphics included OR ❑ Needed but not included OR ❑ Not applicable ❑ Graphics *positioned* well, of *good quality*, and *labeled* properly OR ❑ Not applicable ❑ Graphics help the reader understand the concepts better OR ❑ Not applicable ❑ Includes ❑ cover page, ❑ outline, and ❑ informative abstract OR ❑ Not required	
MECHANICS	
Report is free of mechanical errors (e.g., grammar, punctuation, spelling)	
SCHEDULE	
Report came in on schedule	
COMMENTS	**POINTS GIVEN OF 100**
	TOTAL POINTS

APPENDIX

Internet Resources for Writers

If you seek help in learning how to craft a paragraph, punctuate a series, or make your pronouns agree with their antecedents, help is as near as a computer with Internet access. Below is a list of sites organized by the type of assistance they offer.

General Writing Guides

Purdue OWL (Online Writing Lab) offers information sheets on writing, from inventing ideas to punctuation. Includes links to other online resources.

> http://owl.english.purdue.edu/handouts/index2.html

University of Victoria Writer's Guide offers an index to help on all aspects of writing.

> http://web.uvic.ca/wguide/Pages/MasterToc.html

University of Toronto's site for writing help, including links to other sites.

> http://www.library.utoronto.ca/www/utel/complang.html

POWA (Paradigm Online Writing Assistant) has discussions of different types of essays (thesis/support, argumentative, exploratory) and documenting sources.

> http://www.powa.org/

The English Browser, an encyclopedic list of online links, including a Reference Shelf with writing helps and dictionaries. A good starting point for general-purpose browsing.

> http://cobalt.lang.osaka-u.ac.jp/~krkvls/newsstand.html

Guide for Writing Argumentative Essays

> http://www.eslplanet.com/teachertools/argueweb/frntpage.htm

Brigham Young University's Reading Writing Center has a series of hand-outs on the writing process, grammar, punctuation, and other topics.

http://english.byu.edu/writingcenter

Grammar, Punctuation, and Mechanics Help

Grammar Slammer

http://englishplus.com/grammar/

On-line English Grammar

http://www.edufind.com/english/grammar/index.cfm

Darling's Guide to Grammar

http://webster.commnet.edu/HP/pages/darling/grammar.htm

PMS: Punctuation Made Simple

http://chuma.cas.usf.edu/~olson/pms

HyperGrammar

http://www.uottawa.ca/academic/arts/writcent/hypergrammar/intro.html

Style

Guide to Grammar and Style, by Jack Lynch, gives witty and concise explanations.

http://andromeda.rutgers.edu/~jlynch/Writing/

Bartleby's provides a link to Strunk and White's *Elements of Style*

http://www.cc.columbia.edu:80/acis/bartleby/strunk/

Sentence Craft gives an index for instruction and quizzes on writing better sentences.

http://www.writing.ucsb.edu/faculty/behrens/tc.htm

Research Paper Helps

A Guide for Writing Research Papers. This guide, prepared by the Capital Community–Technical College in Hartford, Connecticut, offers instruction on note taking, outlines, plagiarism, and most other aspects of research paper writing. It teaches the MLA (Modern Language Association) style of documentation.

http://webster.commnet.edu/mla/index.shtml

Words and Quotations

Hypertext Webster's Dictionary

http://smac.ucsd.edu/cgi-bin/http_webster

Roget's Thesaurus

http://humanities.uchicago.edu/forms_unrest/ROGET.html

Online Dictionaries will allow you to search several dictionaries

http://www.yourdictionary.com

Bartlett's Quotations (1901 edition, so it doesn't have the more recent sound bites)

http://www.bartleby.com/index.html

Works Cited

Bell, Arthur H. *Tools for Technical and Professional Communication*. Lincolnwood, IL: NTC Publishing Group, 1995.

Brehm, Sharon S. and Saul M. Kassin. *Social Psychology*. Boston: Houghton Mifflin, 1990.

Brodkey, Linda. *Academic Writing as Social Practice*. Philadelphia: Temple UP, 1987.

Bruffee, Kenneth. "Collaborative Learning and the 'Conversation of Mankind.'" *College English* 46 (1984): 635–52.

Burnett, Rebecca. "Substantive Conflict in a Cooperative Context: A Way to Improve the Collaborative Planning of Workplace Documents." *Technical Communication* Fourth Quarter, 1991: 532–39.

Burstein, Poundie. "Lyricism, Structure, and Gender in Schubert's G Major String Quartet." *Musical Quarterly* 81 (1997): 51–63.

DeFotis, William. "Mahler's Symphony No. 9: An Analytical Sketch in the Form of a Conductor's Guide." *Musical Quarterly* 80 (1996): 276–301.

Dysthe, Olga. "The Multivoiced Classroom: Interactions of Writing and Classroom Discourse." *Written Communication* 13 (July 1996): 385–425.

Ede, Lisa and Andrea Lunsford. *Singular Texts/Plural Authors: Perspectives on Collaborative Writing*. Carbondale: Southern Illinois UP, 1990.

Frye, Northrop. *Anatomy of Criticism: Four Essays*. Princeton, NJ: Princeton UP, 1971.

Garth, John. San Francisco *Argonaut* Aug. 1, 1952.

Hansen, Amy. "Teaching Techniques." *ATTW Bulletin* 6 (1996): 4–6.

Harris, Jeanette, and Donald H. Cunningham. *The Simon & Schuster Guide to Writing*. Brief 2nd ed. Upper Saddle River, NJ: Prentice-Hall, 1997.

Houp, Kenneth W., Thomas E. Pearsall, and Elizabeth Tebeaux. *Reporting Technical Information*. 8th ed. Boston: Allyn and Bacon, 1995.

Hult, Christine A. *Researching and Writing in the Humanities and Arts*. Boston: Allyn and Bacon, 1996.

Kennedy, Joyce Lain. *Electronic Revolution*. New York: Wiley, 1995.

Langer, Suzanne. "The Cultural Importance of Art." *Philosophical Sketches*. Baltimore: Johns Hopkins UP, 1962.

Morgan, Meg. "Patterns of Composing: Connections between Classroom and Workplace Collaborations." *Technical Communication* Fourth Quarter, 1991: 540–45.

Rosen, Leonard J. *Discovery and Commitment: A Guide for College Writers*. Boston: Allyn and Bacon, 1995

Scott, J. Blake. "Sophistic Ethics in the Technical Writing Classroom: Teaching *Nomos*, Deliberation, and Action." *Technical Communication Quarterly* 4 (Spring, 1995): 187–199.

Sharpe, R. A. "What is the Object of Musical Analysis?" *Music Review* 54 (1993): 63–72.

Weiss, Timothy. "Bruffee, the Bakhtin Circle, and the Concept of Collaboration." *Collaborative Writing in Industry: Investigations in Theory and Practice*. Ed. Mary M. Lay and William M. Karis. Amityville, NY: Baywood, 1991. 31–48.

Wells, Randall A. *Stretch: Explore, Explain, Persuade*. Upper Saddle River, NJ: Prentice Hall, 1998.